RENOVATION
OF THE HEART

RENOVATION OF THE HEART

PUTTING ON THE CHARACTER OF CHRIST

DALLAS WILLARD

Inter-Varsity Press

INTER-VARSITY PRESS
38 De Montfort Street, Leicester LE1 7GP, England
Email: ivp@uccf.org.uk
Website: www.ivpbooks.com

First published 2002

British Library Cataloguing in Publication Data
A catalogue record for this book is available from the British Library.
ISBN 0–85111–282–X

Set in Monotype Garamond 11/13pt
Typeset in Great Britain by Servis Filmsetting Ltd, Manchester
Printed and bound in Great Britain

Inter-Varsity Press is the publishing division of the Universities and Colleges Christian Fellowship (formerly the Inter-Varsity Fellowship), a student movement linking Christian Unions in universities and colleges throughout Great Britain, and a member movement of the International Fellowship of Evangelical Students. For more information about local and national activities write to UCCF, 38 De Montfort Street, Leicester LE1 7GP, email us at email@uccf.org.uk, or visit the UCCF website at www.uccf.org.uk.

CONTENTS

To
L. Duane Willard
Who was big when I was small
And always made a place for me.

Renovation of the Heart as here published differs substantially from the book with the same title published in North America by NavPress. The book was thoroughly rewritten for the UK edition by Paul Cavill, to whom I am very grateful.

PRELUDE

Whoever drinks the water I give him will never thirst. Indeed, the water I give him will become in him a spring of water welling up to eternal life. (John 4:13)

When we read the writings of the New Testament, when we focus our minds and hearts on one of the Gospels, for example, or on letters such as Ephesians or 1 Peter, we get the overwhelming impression that we are looking into another world and another life.

It is a divine world and a divine life. It is life in the kingdom of heaven. Yet it is a world and a life that ordinary people have entered and are entering even now. It is a world that seems open to us and beckons us to enter. We feel its call.

Consider Jesus' own words, that those who give themselves to him will receive *living water*, the Spirit of God himself, to keep them from ever again being thirsty, and becoming a spring *welling up to eternal life*. Indeed, the *living water* will become *rivers of living water* flowing out from the believer's life to a thirsty world (John 7:38).

Or think of Paul's prayer that believers *would have power, together with all the saints, to grasp how wide and long and high and deep is the love of Christ, and to know this love that surpasses knowledge – that you may be filled to the measure of all the fullness of God* (Eph 3:17–19).

Or look at Peter's words about how those who love and trust Jesus rejoice with *an inexpressible and glorious joy* (1 Pet 1:8), with genuine mutual love pouring from their hearts (1:22), ridding themselves of *all deceit, hypocrisy, envy, and slander of every kind* (2:1), silencing scoffers at the way of Christ by simply doing what is right (2:15), and casting all their anxieties upon God because he cares for them (5:7).

The picture is clear, and no-one open to it can mistake what it means. But while all is clear and desirable, we must admit that, in the past as well as today, Christians generally only find their way into this divine life slowly and with great difficulty, if at all. I believe one reason why so many people fail to find their way into this full life is that it is so unlike what they know from their own experience. The New Testament picture of life in Christ often discourages them or makes them feel hopeless, even though they are faithful church attenders, and really do have Jesus Christ as their hope.

Why is this? Surely the life God holds out to us in Jesus was not meant to be a puzzle? We are left with the explanation that, for all our good intentions and strenuous methods, we have got something wrong in our approach to that life. We do not fully understand the wisdom of Jesus and the Bible about our human life, and we have not fully grasped the message of God's grace. It isn't really true that where there's a will there's a way, though of course will is crucial. There is also a need for understanding exactly what needs to be done, and how it can be done, by what means and in what manner.

Spiritual formation in Christ is an orderly process. Although God can triumph in disorder, that is not his choice. And instead of focussing upon what God can do, we must accept the ways he has chosen to work with us. These are clearly laid out in the Bible, and especially in the words and person of Jesus.

He invites us to leave our burdensome ways, especially the 'religious' ones, and take upon us the yoke of training with him. This is a way of gentleness and lowliness, a way of rest to our souls. It is a way of inner transformation which proves that pulling his load and carrying his burden with him is easy and light (Matt 11:28–30). The difficulty of entering fully into the divine world and its life is due to our failure to understand that the way in is the way of inner transformation, and our failure to take the small steps that quietly and certainly lead to it.

This is a hopeful, vital insight. For the individual it means that the hindrances to our putting off the old person and putting on the new one can be overcome. And that process will enable us to walk increasingly in the wholeness, holiness and power of the kingdom of heaven. No-one need live in personal and spiritual defeat. A life of victory over sin and circumstances is available to us all.

For Christian groups and their leaders, it means that there is a straightforward way for Christians to fulfil Jesus' call to be radically different. Our fellowships can be places where heaven and earth meet, where the cross and resurrection can save the lost, and where the saved can be led into the fulness of Christ. No special facilities, programmes, talents or techniques are required. It doesn't even demand a budget! Just faithfulness to the process of spiritual formation in Christlikeness revealed in the Scriptures and in the lives of his people through the ages.

Above all else, guard your heart,
for it is the wellspring of life.
(Prov 4:23)

CHAPTER I

SPIRITUAL FORMATION: THE ISSUES

We live from our heart. The part of us that drives and organizes our life is not the physical. You have a spirit within you and it has been formed. It has taken on a specific character. I have a spirit and it has been formed. The spirit within us takes on whatever character it has from the experiences we have lived through and the choices we have made. That is what it means for it to be 'formed'.

How we live in the world now and in the future is, almost totally, a result of what we have become in the depths of our being – in our spirit, will or heart. That is where we understand our world and interpret reality. From there we make our choices, act and react, try to change the world. We live from our depths – and we understand little of what is there.

We find it comfortable to imagine that most of what we experience in life is imposed from outside. This saves us from having to take responsibility for the way things are in the world. But to a large degree what happens in the world derives from the collective choices that human beings have made. War and famine are not inevitable: they result from a long series of choices that people have made. Individual disasters, too, very largely follow upon human choices, our own or those of others.

But the situations in which we find ourselves are rarely as important as our response to them. And this response comes from our spirit. A carefully cultivated heart can, assisted by the grace of God, transform the most painful of situations. It can make us less inclined to stand like helpless children saying, 'Why me?'

We all face questions about life and its purpose. What makes our lives go as they do? What could make them go as they ought? If we have no adequate answers to questions like this, we are left rudderless in the flood of events around us, and at the mercy of whatever ideas and forces come to bear upon us. And that, basically, is the human situation. Thoughtful people through the ages have tried to answer these questions, and they have found that what matters most in life is not external but what we are on the inside. Things good and bad will happen to us, but what our life amounts to is largely, if not entirely, a matter of what we become within. This is the domain of spiritual formation and transformation.

The fact is that spiritual formation of one kind or another happens to everyone. It is the process by which the human spirit or will is given a definite 'form' or character. The most despicable as well as the most admirable people have had a spiritual formation. Terrorists as well as saints are the outcome of spiritual formation. Their spirits or hearts have been shaped and formed. We all become who we are in the depths of our being, gain a specific type of character, by a process of spiritual formation. The shaping and reshaping of the inner life is an issue that has been around as long as humanity itself, and the earliest records of human thought bear eloquent witness to the human struggle to deal with it.[1]

The depths within

Oscar Wilde once remarked that by the age of forty everyone has the face they deserve. This is a profound, if painful, truth. But it also applies to what is within: to the heart, and the soul, and not to the face only. Otherwise it would not much matter.

Within are our thoughts, feelings, motivations – and their deeper sources, whatever those may be. The life we live out in our moments, hours, days and years wells up from hidden depths. What is in our heart matters more than anything else for who we become and what becomes of us. 'You're here in my arms,' the old song says, 'but where is your heart?' That is what really matters, not just for individual relationships, but for life as a whole.

Some of our thoughts, feelings, intentions and plans lie on the conscious surface of the world within us. These are the ones we are aware of. They may be fairly obvious to others as well as to ourselves. But these surface aspects are also a good indication of the general nature of the unconscious spiritual depth within, of what sorts of things make it up. But the thoughts, feelings and intentions we are aware of are only a small part of those in our depths.

What we really think, how we really feel and what we really would do in various situations may be totally unknown to ourselves or even to those familiar with us. The hidden dimension of each human life is not visible to others, nor is it fully graspable even by ourselves. We usually know very little about the things that move in our own soul, the deepest level of our life. What is within is astonishingly complex and subtle – even devious. It has a life of its own. The psalmist cries out for God's help in dealing with himself! *Renew in me a right spirit.* My heart, what is within, has been formed and I am at its mercy. Only God can save me.

The greatest need you and I have, the greatest need of humanity in general, is renovation of our heart. That spiritual place within us from which outlook, choices and actions come has been formed by a world denying God. It must be transformed. Indeed, the only hope for humanity lies in the fact that, just as our spirit has been formed, so also it can be transformed. Disagreements in this area mainly have to do with what in our spirit needs to be changed, and how that change can be brought about.

Science, art and spirituality

We have already spoken of the hidden world of the self as our spiritual nature. The language of the 'spirit' and 'spirituality' has become increasingly common today, and it cannot be avoided. Type 'spirituality' into an Internet search engine and you will see what I mean. But it is often unclear in meaning, and it can lead to confusion. 'Spiritual' is not automatically good. We must be very careful with this language. Nevertheless, in the sense of 'spiritual' which means only 'non-physical', the inner world of the human self is indeed spiritual.

Interestingly, for all our advances in scientific knowledge, science tells us virtually nothing about the inner life of the human being. The sciences can indicate some fascinating and important correlations between our inner life and the physical and social world running alongside it. But the subject matter of the sciences is the physical, measurable, perceptible world: roughly, the world of the five senses. In its nature the physical is a totally different type of reality from the spiritual, which remains hidden in a way the physical world does not. Science misses the heart, because when science tries to go beyond the measurable, it ceases to be science.

Paradoxically, the spiritual side of us, though it is not perceptible by the senses, and though we can never fully grasp it, is never entirely out of our mind. It always stands in the margin of our consciousness if not at the centre. It is what is celebrated (or degraded) in the arts and humanities, and in most popular writing in magazines and the like. The emphasis is continually upon what people think and feel, on what they might or should do and why, and on what kind of people they are. Human beings gossip about little else, and now much of what is called news is mostly gossip.

But that only emphasizes how we are constantly aware of the spiritual side of life. We know immediately that it is what really matters. We pay more attention to it, in ourselves and others, than to almost anything else. The spiritual simply is our life, no matter what grand theories we may hold.

This irrepressible interest explains why, in recent decades and in many ways, the spiritual has repeatedly thrust itself to the forefront of our awareness. From the cultural and artistic revolts of the Sixties to the environmentalisms and countless 'spiritualities' of the Nineties, from pop-culture New Age to the postmodernisms of the academy, there has been a swelling protest that the merely physical cannot sustain our life: *Man does not live on bread alone.*

Spirituality is often understood today as entirely a human matter. The 'spiritual' is thought to be a human attribute which, when brought into play, will transform our life into something divine. Or at least it will deliver us from the chaos and brokenness of human existence, from life-destroying addictions such as alcoholism, work, drugs or violence. We are engulfed by books, programmes and seminars which rest upon this assumption. Thus, for example, one now hears spirituality described as 'the process of becoming a positive and creative person'. Or perhaps as 'our relationship to whatever is most important in our life'. These are words taken from contemporary writings, and they represent deep currents of human thought and culture.[2] I have no intention of deriding anything helpful and good, and I am thankful for whatever truly helps human beings in their desperation. The constant love of God is extended to everyone, even in places that God himself would not prefer. But whether or not a spirituality adequate to human need, producing genuine renovation of the heart, can be a product of mere human abilities is a vital question. To be mistaken about this will have the most serious consequences.

Man does not live on bread alone. Those are, of course, words from Jesus. And his way is truly the way of the heart or spirit. If we want to live fully, we must live with him at that interior level. And he gives this life as a gift. The spiritual renovation, the spirituality which comes from Jesus is nothing less than an invasion of natural human reality by a supernatural life from God. We can live by nourishing ourselves constantly on his presence, here and now, beyond his death and ours. But contrary to what many believe today, life in this full sense is not sustained simply by dabbling in the 'spiritual'. It is not an alternative lifestyle option, something to add on to an already busy schedule.

Human nature, sin and evil

'Lifestyle options' are in fact one outcome of a particular view of human nature today. You will hear many people say that there is no such thing as human nature, or that human beings do not have a *definable* nature. Some say that a human being is purely physical, just an animal, just a brain, and must act on instinct. Or that human beings are, as such, good, and if they go wrong it is the fault of their parents or society. Or that human beings are not fundamentally male or female, straight or gay, but that these classifications are socially constructed, with no reality apart from the judgments of social groups or cultures.

If I do not have a nature, I can choose who or what I am moment by moment. Choice is the great good of today in the developed world. I do not have to do or be anything I don't want to do or be. Integrity of character is unnecessary; indeed it is a restriction on my freedom. But this view of human nature is too forcefully propagated by people with vested interests entirely to escape suspicion. It defies common sense. It runs counter to the wisdom of centuries, in which integrity of character has been held to be the most valuable attribute of a human being. Moreover, it fails desperately to deal with the reality of sin and evil.

Sin as a condition of human life is not available as a principle of explanation for the realities we see around us. For example, why around half of marriages fail, or why we have massive problems with addiction, and with the moral failures of public leaders. Those who are supposed to know are lost in speculation about causes, while the real source of our failures lies in choice and the factors at work in it. Choice is where sin surfaces and dwells. It is also a key to spiritual transformation.

The social and psychological sciences stand helpless before the terrible things done by human beings, but the warped character of the human will is something we cannot admit into serious conversation. The only solution we know to human problems today is education. And indeed education is a good thing. But what kind of education? And can we really think that if people only knew what is the right thing to do, they would do it? Education as it is now practised cannot deal with the realities of the human self. Education as an institution has adopted values, attitudes and practices that make any rigorous understanding of the human self and life impossible.

Few are ready to deal with the realities within themselves or in others. And those few are not exactly welcomed by others if they are ready to do so. As Vance Havner used to say, Jesus was not crucified for saying, 'behold the lilies of the field, how they toil not, neither do they spin', but for saying ,'behold the Pharisees, how they steal'.

Some years ago there was a high-level conference in Aspen, Colorado, on the topic of evil. The outcome was that one or two participants out of a large group thought that there was such a thing as evil. But most were either non-committal on the point, or certain that it did not exist at all. From their comments it was clear that they simply could not conceptualize the evil to be seen flourishing abundantly around them. They had no intellectual resources to account for it. One of the most glaring evidences of the bankruptcy of contemporary ethical thinking is that it cannot deal with evil. A recent proposal to found a field of 'Evil Studies' within academia will not be enthusiastically received.[3]

When the floodtides of evil break across the television screen or wash the pages of the newspapers, people roll their eyes helplessly and say, 'Why?' They never say, 'Why?' when something good happens. They simply cannot deal with the actual content of the human heart, mind, body, social context and soul. In 'intellectual' circles evil, like sin, is a non-category. It is impolite and politically incorrect to speak seriously of it, and to suggest it might have a remedy.

The Bible's diagnosis

The Bible, from beginning to end, is starkly clear. The prophet Jeremiah, for example, says *the heart is deceitful above all things and is beyond cure. Who can understand it?* (Jer 17:9). Jesus spoke to the people most admired as religious in his day in language that may seem harsh to us. *Now then, you Pharisees clean the outside of the cup and dish, but inside you are full of greed and wickedness. You foolish people! Did not the one who made the outside make the inside also?* (Luke 11:39). He proceeded to point out how they loved public approval (11:43), and how in doing so they were like graves, all neat and prettied up on the outside, but full of disgusting rottenness inside (11:44; cp. Matt 23:27–28). They were unable to believe in Jesus because they wanted to be honoured by each other (John 5:44).

Of course these leaders had greater responsibilities and opportunities than ordinary people. But they were no more sinful. The condition addressed in them is the human condition, not the Pharisaical condition. The Pharisee only makes the true human condition more obvious by all his religiosity. Paul traces the human condition to its root in his letter to the Romans:

> *As it is written: 'There is no-one righteous, not even one; there is no-one who understands, no-one who seeks God. All have turned away, they have together become worthless; there is no-one who does good, not even one.' 'Their throats are open graves; their tongues practice deceit.' 'The poison of vipers is on their lips.' 'Their mouths are full of cursing and bitterness.' 'Their feet are swift to shed blood; ruin and misery mark their ways, and the way of peace they do not know.' 'There is no fear of God before their eyes.'*(Rom 3:10–18)

The very last statement from this collection of Old Testament passages goes to the core of the matter: *There is no fear of God before their eyes.*

This is exactly what the book of Proverbs tells us. Fear of God *is the beginning of wisdom* (Prov 9:10). Although it is not the totality of wisdom, to be sure, it is the indispensable beginning, I believe, and the principal part. You begin to get smart when you acknowledge God for who he is, and fear being on the wrong side of him. Intelligent people recognize that their well-being lies in being in harmony with God and what God is doing. God is not mean, but he is dangerous. Someone who does not worry about God, does not 'fear' God, simply is not intelligent.

Knowledge of the Holy One is understanding, this verse (Prov 9:10) concludes. 'Knowledge' in biblical language never refers just to what we today call 'head knowledge', but always to experiential involvement with what is known – to engagement with it. Thus, when Jesus defines the eternal life that he gives to his people as *that they may know you, the only true God, and Jesus Christ whom you have sent* (John 17:3), he is speaking of the grace of constant, close interaction with God that Jesus brings into the lives of those who seek and find him. This again is a deeper and fuller understanding of Proverbs 3:5–8:

> *Trust in the Lord with all your heart and lean not on your own understanding; in all your ways acknowledge him, and he will make your paths straight. Do not be wise in your own eyes; fear the Lord and shun evil. This will bring health to your body and nourishment to your bones.*

Not-God

When the Bible talks of the deceitfulness of the human heart, we have to recognize that we are the ones spoken of. When Jesus addressed the Pharisees, he was talking to 'good' people, but spoke of the filth inside them. The people Paul writes about are everybody, us included. This is a blow to our self-esteem because, realistically, I'm not okay and you're not okay. We're all in serious trouble. That must be our starting point. Self-esteem in such a situation will only breed self-deception and frustration. Reality will assert itself, regardless of what we or others may say to 'pump ourselves up' and to conceal and deny who we are. Denial is the primary device that humans use to deal with their own wrongness. It was the first thing out of the mouths of Adam and Eve after they sinned, and it continues. The Bible's diagnosis, fully based on empirical evidence, throws itself against the massive weight of institutionalized denial built into our customary way of life.

In Romans chapter 1, Paul describes the progressive departure from God that leads to life as we know and see it all around us. Human beings have always known there is a God and have had some degree of understanding of who he is and what he is like (Rom 1:19–20). Actually, they still do. But they were not pleased that he should have the place in the universe that he does have merely because he is who he is. And this is the key to understanding our present condition. The first of the Ten Commandments deals with this inclination away from God (Exod 20:2–3). As Augustine saw clearly, God being God offends human pride. If God is running the universe and has first claim on our lives, guess who isn't running the universe and does not get to have things as they please?

Philip Yancey writes:

> The historian of Alcoholics Anonymous titled his work *Not-God* because, he said, that stands as the most important hurdle an addicted person must surmount: to acknowledge, deep in the soul, not being God. No mastery of manipulation and control, at which alcoholics excel, can overcome the root problem; rather, the alcoholic must recognize individual helplessness and fall back in the arms of the Higher Power. 'First of all, we had to quit playing God,' concluded the founders of AA; and then allow God himself to 'play

God' in the addict's life, which involves daily, even moment-by-moment, surrender.[4]

But our natural tendency is to make ourselves god in practice. And then the great force of denial comes into play. It is this that accounts for our perpetual blindness to the obvious. Denial of reality is a capacity inseparable from the human will, and it has its greatest power when it operates without being recognized as such. Of course 'denial' includes not only rejection of what is the case, but also affirmation of what is not the case. In a world apart from God, the power of denial is absolutely essential if life is to proceed. The will or spirit cannot, psychologically cannot, sustain itself for any length of time against what it clearly acknowledges to be the case. Therefore it must deny and evade the truth and delude itself. Paul's inspired insight into the root of human evil, *there is no fear of God before their eyes*, must never be forgotten by anyone who wishes to understand spiritual formation.

Now when the light of fundamental truth and reality is put out in the heart and the soul, the intellect tries to devise a 'truth' that will be compatible with the basic falsehood that not God but man is god; and the affections, feelings, emotions, even sensations, soon follow along on the path to chaos. *Their thinking became futile*, Paul says, *and their foolish hearts were darkened. Although they claimed to be wise, they became fools.* The mind is now uprooted from reality. It is committed to the truth of a falsehood. 'Garbage in, garbage out' is a true account of this process.

Paul continues with his description of the process of corruption. People pretended God was an animal of some kind (1:23), and worshipping this god allowed them to worship instinct and pleasure, *created things rather than the Creator* (1:25). The human body becomes the primary focus for the person who does not live honestly and interactively with God. And since bodily enjoyment is what is most desired, God abandons them to their pursuit of every pleasurable sensation they can wring out of the body – primarily sexual, for that usually gives the greatest 'kick', and degenerating into perversion and violence. 'Free love', as it is euphemistically called, along with various forms of perversion, are simply an extension of body worship (1:26–27). This is the spiritual root of obsession with sex and violence in decadent societies, whether our own or those of other times and places. Paul observes to the Ephesians:

> *you must no longer live as the Gentiles do, in the futility of their thinking. They are darkened in their understanding and separated from the life of God because of the ignorance that is in them due to the hardening of their hearts. Having lost all sensitivity, they have given themselves over to sensuality so as to indulge in every kind of impurity, with a continual lust for more.* (Eph 4:17–19)

This is a natural progression in the flight from God. The drive to self-gratification leads to a life without boundaries, where nothing is forbidden, if one can get away with it. 'Why?' is replaced with 'Why not?' And it turns out that sensuality cannot be satisfied. It is not self-limiting. Sensual indulgence deadens feeling. What is left is the relentless drive, the desperate need simply to feel, to feel something. And because this is what people want – total licence – God abandons them to a mind which simply does not work. *Since they did not think it worth while to retain knowledge of God, he gave them over to a depraved mind, to do what ought not to be done* (Rom 1:28). And the outcome is a humanity

> *filled with every kind of wickedness, evil, greed and depravity. They are full of envy, murder, strife, deceit and malice. They are gossips, slanderers, God-haters, insolent, arrogant and boastful; they invent ways of doing evil; they disobey their parents; they are senseless, faithless, heartless, ruthless. Although they know God's righteous decree that those who do such things deserve death, they not only continue to do these very things but also approve of those who practise them.* (Rom 1:29–32)

A thoughtful and observant person will probably recognize in this description the usual course of human affairs. Paul was not hopeful that things would get better as human history moved along. He was not a believer in 'progress' as usually understood. In what seems to have been his last letter, perhaps the very last thing he wrote, he warns Timothy:

> *There will be terrible times in the last days. People will be lovers of themselves, lovers of money, boastful, proud, abusive, disobedient to their parents, ungrateful,*

unholy, without love, unforgiving, slanderous, without self-control, brutal, not lovers of the good, treacherous, rash, conceited, lovers of pleasure rather than lovers of God – having a form of godliness but denying its power. (2 Tim 3:1–5)

This certainly looks like now, when such behaviour if not approved outright, is excused or justified by psychological, legal and moral theories.

This has been, in fact, the end stage of every successful human society that has arisen. Invariably, such a society begins to believe it is responsible for its success and prosperity and begins to worship itself and rebel against the understandings and practices that made it successful in the first place. *Jeshurun grew fat and kicked,* says the Bible of one successful tribe (Deut 32:15).

Underneath it all is the radical evil of the human heart, the human heart which makes me god in place of God.

Being lost

What Paul is describing in his letters is 'lost' people. Considerable confusion on what it means to be lost has resulted from trying to think of it in terms of its outcome. Theologically, that outcome is hell – a most uncomfortable notion. But the condition of lostness is not the same as the outcome to which it leads. We're not lost because we are going to wind up in the wrong place. We are going to wind up in the wrong place because we are lost. To be lost means to be out of place. Think of what it means when the keys to your house or car are lost. They are useless to you, no matter how much you need them. Gehenna, the term often used in the New Testament of the place of the lost, may usefully be thought of as the cosmic dump for the irretrievably useless. And when we are lost to God, we are not where we are supposed to be in his world, and hence are not caught up into his life. We cannot *participate in the divine nature and escape the corruption in the world caused by evil desires* (2 Pet 1:4) We are our own god, and our god can't help us.

When we are lost to God, we are also lost to ourselves: we do not know where we are or how to get where we want to go. We may know we are lost or we may not. Many a driver is lost long before he knows he is. Many are lost before God but do not know it. They sincerely believe that they know where they are, where they are going and how to get there; but in fact they do not, and they often find out too late.

The lost in Christian terms are precisely those who mistake themselves for God. They falsely identify, and cannot recognize, what is closest to them, namely themselves. Then, as we have noted, they really do think they are in charge of life – though, admittedly, to manage it successfully they may have to bow outwardly to this or that person or power. But they are in charge, and they have no confidence in the one who really is God.

Their god, as Paul elsewhere says, is their *stomach* or *belly* as the older versions more graphically put it (Phil 3:19). They are willing slaves of their feelings or appetites (Rom 16:18). They 'want what they want when they want it', as the song says, and that is the ultimate fact about them. If they do not get it they become angry and depressed, and are a danger to themselves and others.

Edith Schaeffer, in one of her penetrating discussions of abortion, points out:

> The philosophy of living with an underlying motive of doing everything for one's own personal peace and comfort rapidly colors everything that might formerly have come under the headings of 'right' and 'wrong'. This new way of thinking adds entirely new shades, often in blurring brushstrokes of paint that wipe out the existence of standards or cast them into a shadow that pushes them out of sight. If one's peace, comfort, way of life, convenience, reputation, opportunities, job, happiness, or even ease is threatened, 'Just abort it.' Abort what? Abort another life that is not yet born. Yes, but also abort the afflictions connected with having a handicapped child, and abort the burdens connected with caring for the old or invalid. Added swiftly are the now supposedly thinkable attitudes of aborting a child's early security in his or her rights to have two parents and a family life; aborting a wife's need for having her husband be someone to trust and lean upon; aborting the husband's need for having a companion and friend as well as a feminine mate; aborting any responsibility to carry through a job started.[5]

Self-idolatry rearranges the entire spiritual and moral landscape. It sees the whole universe in relation to itself. If it is not abortion that is at the centre, it will be something else; but the fundamental pride of putting oneself at the centre of the universe is the hinge upon which the entire world of the lost turns.

John Calvin said that 'the surest source of destruction to men is to obey themselves'.[6] Yet self-obedience seems the only reasonable path to nearly everyone: 'So blindly do we all rush in the direction of self-love, that every one thinks he has a good reason for exalting himself and despising all others in comparison.'[7] What an exquisite eye for detail Calvin had! Dietrich Bonhoeffer says the same: 'Whereas the primal relationship of man to man is a giving one, in the state of sin it is purely demanding. Every man exists in a state of complete voluntary isolation; each man lives his own life, instead of all living the same God-life.'[8] Everyone is a god to themself.

Thus no-one chooses in the abstract to go to hell, or even to be the kind of person who belongs there. But their orientation toward self leads them to become the kind of person for whom away-from-God is the only place for which they are suited. It is a place which they would, in the end, choose for themselves, rather than humble themselves before God and accept who he is. Whether or not God's will is infinitely flexible, the human will is not. There are limits beyond which it cannot bend back, cannot turn or repent. A well-known minister of another generation used to ask rhetorically, 'You say you will accept God when you want to?' And then he would add, 'How do you know you will be able to want to when you think you will?'

The ultimately lost person is the person who cannot want God, who cannot want God to be God. There are countless multitudes of such people. The reason they do not find God is that they do not want him, or, at least, do not want him to be God. And of course wanting God to be God is very different from wanting God to help me. The fundamental fact about the lost is that they have become people so locked into their own self-worship and denial of God that they cannot want God.

Insulting our pride

Is it insulting to suggest that someone is or may be lost? There are so many fine looking people all about us! Well, is it insulting to say, in appropriate circumstances, that someone has a physical disease that may be fatal, say cancer or diabetes, when you know it to be true? Perhaps treatment depends upon coming to know it. No doubt in our hyper-sensitive, egotistical age that could be insulting to some people. But that merely illustrates the delusional human condition. If I am god, people shouldn't say such things to me.

Lostness is a real condition of the self. You either have it or not, just as you either have or do not have a physical disease that can kill you. If you have that condition of lostness, you may not know it. Indeed, it is most likely you will not know it, since it is inherently a condition of self-blindness. You need treatment nevertheless, if you are not to be lost forever; and being informed of your condition and what to do about it can help you find relief. Should I say nothing to you merely because you might find it offensive? I must think more highly of you than that. The reality of evil in the human heart is not something to be ignored or treated lightly.

We should be very sure that the lost person is not one who has missed a few more or less important theological points and will fail theological examination at the end of life. Hell is not a slip in the wrong direction. One does not miss heaven by a hair, but by constant effort to avoid and escape God. *Outer darkness*, as Jesus calls it, is for those who, everything said, want it, whose entire orientation has slowly and firmly set itself against God and therefore against how the universe actually is. It is for those who are disastrously in error about their own life and their place before God and in the world. The lost must be willing to hear of and recognize their own ruin before they can find how to enter a different path, the path of eternal life that leads into spiritual formation in Christlikeness.

Spiritual formation is not something that may, or may not, be added on to the gift of eternal life as an option. Rather, it is the path that the eternal kind of life should naturally take. It is not a project of 'life enhancement', where the life in question is the usual life of normal human beings – that is, life apart from God. It is, rather, the process of developing a different kind of life, the life of God himself, sustained by God as a new reality in those who have confidence that Jesus is the Son of God, those who *by believing . . . have life in his name* (John 20:31). Those caught up in Christ's life, in what he is doing, by the inward gift of new birth, are *a new creation* (2 Cor

5:17). The 'old stuff' no longer matters. Here in this new creation is the radical goodness that alone can thoroughly renovate the heart.

The necessity of remorse

To prosecutors and judges in our court system, as well as to people in ordinary situations of life, it still matters greatly whether a wrong-doer shows signs of remorse or seems to be truly sorry for what they have done. This is because genuine remorse tells us something about the individual. The person who can harm others and feel no remorse is, indeed, a different kind of person from the one who is sorry. There is little hope for genuine change in one who is without remorse, without the anguish of regret.

Much of what is called Christian profession today involves little remorse or sorrow over what we have been or even for what we have done. There is little awareness of having been lost, or of a radical evil in our hearts, bodies and souls, which we must get away from and from which only God can deliver us. To manifest such awareness today would be regarded as being psychologically sick. It is common today to hear Christians talk of their 'brokenness'. But when you listen closely it is clear that they are talking about their wounds, the things they have suffered, not of the evil that is in them. Few today have discovered that they have been disastrously wrong and that they cannot change or escape the consequences of it on their own. There is little of Isaiah's sense of unworthiness before God: *Woe is me! I am ruined! For I am a man of unclean lips, and I live among a people of unclean lips* (Is 6:5).

Yet, without this realization of our utter ruin, and without the genuine redirecting of our lives which that bitter realization gives rise to, no clear path to inner transformation can be found. It is psychologically and spiritually impossible. We will steadfastly remain on the throne of our universe, so far as we are concerned, perhaps trying to 'use a little God' here and there. The failure of the church to grasp this reality is all too evident today. And this has to be faced before we can seriously consider the process of spiritual reformation in Christlikeness that is the purpose of this book.

Matters for thought and discussion

1. Can it be true that 'spiritual' does not automatically mean something good?
2. Compare spiritual formation as a merely human project with distinctively Christian spiritual formation.
3. What are some of the issues that have driven the recent widespread interest in spiritual formation, both in wider society and among Christians?
4. Do you accept the idea that human beings apart from God are lost? How would you describe that? What does it mean in practical, day-to-day terms?
5. Do you see how lostness is the result of the spiritual formation people receive in the natural course of life?
6. What is your sense of how evil functions (or does not function) among 'informed' people today as a legitimate category of explanation of events around us?
7. Where can you see evidence of lostness in our wider world and in the church visible?
8. How is pride (being god) at the basis of human ruin?
9. Why does sensuality come to play such a major role in human ruin?
10. Apply Paul's discussion of moral corruption in the last days to the world we now live in. Use a daily newspaper or magazine to do this.

CHAPTER 2

SPIRITUAL FORMATION
AND THE CHURCH

We need to be changed and Jesus is vital. About two thousand years ago Jesus gathered a little group of friends and trainees on the Galilean hillsides and sent them out to make apprentices from all ethnic groups. He didn't just send them out to teach some new ideas. His objective was eventually to bring all humanity under the direction of his wisdom, goodness and power, as part of God's eternal plan for the universe. In thus sending out his trainees he started a perpetual world revolution: one that is still in process and will continue until God's will is done on earth as it is in heaven. As this revolution culminates, all the forces of evil will be defeated and the goodness of God will be known, accepted and joyously conformed to in every aspect of human life.[1] He has chosen to accomplish this with, and in part through, his apprentices.

The revolution of Jesus is in the first place a revolution of the human heart. It did not and does not proceed by means of social institutions and laws, the outer forms of our existence. Rather, his is a revolution of character, which changes people from the inside through personal relationships with God in Christ and with others. It is a revolution that changes ideas, beliefs, feelings, habits of choice, bodily actions, as well as social relations. It penetrates to the depths of the soul. External social arrangements may be useful in this revolution, but they are not the end, nor are they a fundamental part of the means.

T. S. Eliot once described human endeavour as that of finding a system of order so perfect that we will not have to be good. Jesus tells us, by contrast, that any number of systems – not all, to be sure – will work well if we are genuinely good. And we are then free to seek the better and the best. This impotence of man-made systems is a main reason why Jesus did not send his apprentices out to start governments or even churches as we know them. The reason why they were 'apprentices' is that they were to establish beachheads of his person, word and power in the midst of a failing humanity. Their mission was to bring the presence of the kingdom and its king into every corner of human life by simply living in the kingdom with him.

Churches, local assemblies of apprentices of Jesus, naturally resulted. Churches are not the kingdom of God, but are primary and inevitable expressions, outposts of the kingdom. They were societies of Jesus, springing up in Jerusalem, in Judea, in Samaria and to the furthest points on earth (Acts 1:8), as the reality of Christ was brought to bear on ordinary human life. Bringing Christ to bear is an ongoing process, not yet finished today.

Genuine transformation of the whole person into the goodness and power seen in Jesus remains the necessary goal of human life. But it lies beyond the reach of programmes of inner transformation that draw merely on the human spirit. The reality of all this is currently veiled from view by the very low level of spiritual life generally seen in Christianity. That low level explains why there are at present so many psychologies and spiritualities contesting the field, often led by ex-Christians who have abandoned recognized forms of Christianity as hopeless or even harmful. In its current public form, Christianity has not been imparting effectual answers to the vital questions of human existence. At least not to many self-identifying Christians, and obviously not to non-Christians. We need to face the fact that the church seems not to be modelling the transformation of human existence that was at the heart of Jesus' mission, and ask why.

Something is rotten in the church

The failures of prominent Christian leaders might make us think genuine spiritual formation in Christlikeness to be impossible for real human beings. How is it, exactly, that a man or woman can serve Christ for years and then morally disintegrate? And the failures that become known are few compared to the ones that remain relatively unknown and are even accepted among Christians.

Recently I learned that one of the most prominent leaders in an important segment of Christian life 'blew up', became uncontrollably angry, when someone questioned him about the quality of his work. This was embarrassing, but it is accepted behaviour; and, in this case, it was the person who was questioning the leader that was chastised. But what are we to say about the spiritual formation of that leader? Has something been omitted? Or is this really the best we can do? The same questions arise with reference to lay figures in areas of life such as politics, business, entertainment or education, who show the same failures of character while openly identifying themselves as Christians. It is unpleasant to dwell on such cases, but they must be faced squarely.

Of course the effects of such failures depend on the circumstances and on how widely the failure becomes known. In another case a pastor became enraged at something that was done during a Sunday morning service. Immediately after the service he found the person responsible and gave him a merciless tongue-lashing. With his lapel microphone still on! His diatribe was broadcast over the entire church building – in all the Sunday school rooms and the car park. Soon afterwards he moved to another church. But what about the spiritual formation of this leader? Is that the best we can do? And is he not still really like that in his new position?

The sad thing when leaders fail is not just what they do, but the heart and life and whole person that is revealed when they do it. What is sad is who they have been all along, what their inner life has been like, and no doubt also how they have suffered, during all the years before they did it or were found out. What kind of person have they been, and what, really, has been their relation to God?

Here is another story about a church, and one that would gener-ally be regarded as successful or prosperous. The church in question was established out of conflict in another church. It called its first pastor, and things seemed to be going well until that pastor committed adultery and 'cooked the books'. The congregation dismissed him, and a second pastor was appointed. He was very popular and the church grew, but he resigned after four years from stress, or a nervous breakdown, depending on who you believed.

A third pastor came and was quite popular. Again, the church grew, but after a while he started giving himself salary rises which the congregation did not knowingly approve. After ten years he left, started another church within ten miles of his former church, and took three hundred members with him.

A fourth pastor was called. Everything seemed fine. Then he had a sexual affair, which he eventually disclosed to his staff team, expecting them to cover it up. In the midst of much lying and discord among the staff the church seemed to go on as before. Of course the people in the community came to know about the affair anyway. A year or so later the pastor received a call from a larger church a long way away. He took the position, leaving behind a congregation and staff full of strife and anger. A long period followed in which almost every meeting was filled with tension, and in which people retreated into various camps, hardly speaking to each other. This all happened in one congregation over a period of thirty-six years.

This is a story about a church. And if we can't do what is right there, where can we? The story shows how sin, in a form everyone plainly recognizes as such, undermines the efforts of Christ's own people to be his people. That is its power. Although the degree and details differ, the story of this church, in spite of some very fine exceptions, is all too common. Leading Christian magazines now feature regular sections where the sad story is told month by month.

A major part of the response by Christians to manifest sin was, in this case, to cover it up. This is not uncommon. No doubt it was 'for the sake of the ministry', as people say. The 'confessions' of the various pastors were often half-truths or less, and were clearly formalities which would, supposedly, allow the pastors and staff members to 'get on with God's business'. The exit of the last pastor left the staff bitterly divided over issues of loyalty to the ex-pastor and whether or not the truth of what had happened should be publicly admitted. The words of James ring true: *where you have envy and selfish ambition, there you find disorder and every evil practice* (Jas 3:16).

In a period of a few weeks, some years back, three nationally known pastors in the Southern California area were publicly exposed for sexual sins. But sex is far from being the only problem. The presence of vanity, egotism, hostility, fear, indifference and downright meanness can be counted on among professing Christians. Their opposites cannot be counted on or simply assumed, in the 'standard' Christian group; and the rare individuals who exemplify genuine purity and humility, unselfishness, freedom from rage and depression, and so on, will stand out like a sore thumb. They will be a constant hindrance in group processes and will be personally disturbed by those processes, for they will not be living on the same terms as the others. Many Christians have never been in an intimate fellowship where the corrupted condition of the human soul did not in fact prevail. They have never been in a fellowship in which they could assume that everyone would do what everyone knew to be right. And many people in our culture have, on the basis of their experiences, simply given up on the church, many of them in the name of God and righteousness.

Righteously mean Christians

Christians take very seriously all kinds of things that may not be that significant, and all too often are distracted from what ought to be their focus. Warren Wiersbe tells how he was approached by an older gentleman at a church were he was to speak. The man expressed awareness that Warren sometimes quoted a certain popular paraphrase version of the Bible. Warren replied, 'When I write, I quote whatever translation best says what I want to teach at that point in the book, it doesn't mean I approve of everything in it.' To this the man replied, almost shouting, 'Well, I'm not going to sit and listen to a man who has no convictions about the Word of God,' and he 'turned and stormed out of the church in anger, disobeying the very Bible he thought he was defending'.[2]

A Christian college President recently devoted his periodic mailout to the question 'Why are Christians so mean to one another so often?' He quotes numerous well-known Christian leaders on this theme, and says for himself:

> As a leader of a Christian organization, I feel the brunt of just this kind of
> meanness within the Christian community, a mean-spirited suspicion and
> judgment that mirrors the broader culture. Every Christian leader I know
> feels it . . . It is difficult to be Christian in a secular world . . . But, you know,
> it is sometimes more difficult to be a leader in Christian circles. There too
> you can be vilified for just the slightest move that is displeasing to someone.

And he continues on with the details.

This is one of the most common points of commiseration among
our leaders. The leader of one denomination recently said to me,
'When I am finished with this job I am going to write a book on the
topic Why Are Christians So Mean?'

Well, there is actually an answer to that question. And we must
face this issue and deal with it effectively or Satan will sustain his
stranglehold on spiritual transformation in local congregations.
Christians are routinely taught by example and word that it is more
important to be right (always in terms of their tradition) than it is to
be Christlike. There are now 33,800 different Christian denominations, and they are all 'right'.[3] In fact, being right licenses you to be
mean, and, indeed, requires you to be mean – righteously mean, of
course. You must be hard on people who are wrong, and especially if
they are in positions of Christian leadership. They deserve nothing
better. This is a part of what I have elsewhere called the practice of
'condemnation engineering'.[4]

A fundamental mistake of the conservative side of the church
today is that it takes as its basic goal to get as many people as possible
ready to die and go to heaven. It aims to get people into heaven rather than to get heaven into people. This of course requires that people
who are going to be in heaven must be right on what is basic. You
can't really quarrel with that. But it turns out that to be right on
'what is basic' is to be right in terms of the particular church tradition in question, not in terms of Christlikeness.

Now the project thus understood and practised is self-defeating. It
defeats itself because it creates groups of people who may be ready to
die, but clearly are not ready to live. They rarely can get along with
one another, much less those outside. Often their most intimate relationships are tangles of reciprocal coldness and resentment. They
have found ways of being 'Christian' without being Christlike.

As a result they actually fall far short of getting as many people as possible ready to die, because the lives of the converted testify against the reality of *the life that is truly life* (1 Tim 6:19). Charles Finney used to say that the Christian minister is frequently in the position of a lawyer who states to the court the case he intends to prove (that would be the biblical picture of life from God), and then calls his witnesses (professing Christians), who contradict in their testimony (their life) every point he said he would prove. When we are calculating results we need to keep in mind the multitudes of people surrounded by churches who will not be in heaven because they have never, to their knowledge, seen the reality of Christ in a living human being. The way to get as many people into heaven as you can is to get heaven into as many people as you can: that is, to follow the path of genuine spiritual transformation or full-throttle discipleship of Jesus Christ.

The central cause of our current situation

What characterizes most of our congregations, whether big or small, is simple distraction. The failures of many kinds that show up within them and around them are not the fundamental problem of church life today. They are much more a result than a cause.

One of the most helpful statements I have read in recent years for understanding contemporary church life is by Leith Anderson. He notes:

> While the New Testament speaks often about churches, it is surprisingly silent about many matters that we associate with church structure and life. There is no mention of architecture, pulpits, lengths of typical sermons, rules for having a Sunday school. Little is said about style of music, order of worship, or times of church gatherings. There were no Bibles, denominations, camps, pastors' conferences, or board meeting minutes. Those who strive to be New Testament churches must seek to live its principles and absolutes, not reproduce the details.[5]

Those details simply aren't given.

Now you might ask yourself why the New Testament says nothing about all those matters to which the usual congregation devotes most of its thought and effort today. And the answer is, because those matters are not primary, and will take care of themselves with little attention whenever what is primary is appropriately cared for. Pay attention to the 'principles and absolutes' of the New Testament church and everything else will fall into place – in large part because 'everything else' really doesn't matter much one way or the other. If we fail to put the focus on those principles and absolutes, on the other hand, we will wander off into a state of distraction. And that is where most of our local congregations actually are. They wind up majoring on minors and allowing the majors, from the New Testament point of view, to disappear.

Vessel and treasure

Of course we do not think we are distracted. The things we are investing our efforts in seem absolutely primary. These are usually things that make up being a good and proper Christian of whatever sort – Protestant, Catholic, Anglican, Baptist. But people have actually mistaken the vessel for the treasure.

Paul gives us a crucial distinction:

> God, who said, 'Let light shine out of darkness,' made his light shine in our hearts to give us the light of the knowledge of the glory of God in the face of Christ. But we have this treasure in jars of clay to show that this all-surpassing power is from God and not from us. (2 Cor 4:6–7)

The vessels ('jars') in Paul's context were Paul himself and his companions, in their bodily weakness. He goes on to say, *outwardly we are wasting away* (4:16). He was not troubled by this, for he concentrated on the *treasure*, God's power within. And he wanted the faith of his hearers to stand on *a demonstration of the Spirit's power*, so that their faith *might not rest on men's wisdom, but on God's power* (1 Cor 2:4–5). The weakness of the vessel, Paul's physical being, was accepted and recognized by him as the occasion for the triumph of the treasure, God's power.

But the same principle of vessel and treasure applies to church congregations, their traditions and denominations. Now it is worth noting that nearly everything that defines any given denomination is negative, that is, something we do not do that 'they' do. By far most of our groups were born in negation. Just think of the mass of people of many denominations who are called Protestants.

Our various groups become over time nearly 100% 'vessel'. That is, what they seem to regard as essential, and what they devote almost all their attention and effort to, has to do with human, historical contingencies. They are more to do with the way we are brought up than the way of Christ. We of course love those contingencies, and we love the dear ones who shared life with us. And because the contingencies are dear to us – often there is much good associated with their past – we mistake them for the treasure of the real presence of Christ in our midst, and spend most of our time concerned with the historical accidents of our group, even trying to urge them upon others as essential to salvation. Or at least as what is best for us and for them. No wonder we are distracted from the path of spiritual formation in Christ.

So, what kinds of clothes should people wear to meetings, and should they stand still when they sing, and what should they sing? Should there be prayer ministry, and should it be part of the service, after the service, or at a different service? Should we be 'seeker friendly'? Should we expect or permit miracles to happen in our services, or just sound teaching? How should the Lord's Supper be done? And baptism? Should we use a prayer book, and if so should it be the old one or a new one? How should we raise funds for the church, and how should they be spent? Who should spend them? What should our creed be, and should we have one? What about incense? Or what about those who wear unusual clothes to do the ministerial things? And so on and on.

I am not saying that such things are of no importance, though for some of them it is a close call. I am saying two things. One is that they are not the starting points, or the essential and foundational matters. And that is why the New Testament, as Leith Anderson points out, says nothing about them. And secondly, if we make them out to be essential or even very important, even if we do so only practically, in the sense of spending most of our time on them, then the local congregation will make little or no progress in terms of the spiritual formation of those in regular attendance. These 'vessel' matters do not bring anyone into Christlikeness, whichever side of them one stands on. That is a fact of life.

How to avoid the 'vessel' trap

But is there another way for local congregations to go? Can we avoid the 'vessel' trap? Certainly we can't avoid *having* vessels. And we must be careful with them, for that is a part of what it is to be human and finite. Even Jesus had his 'vessel'. It was a Jewish one, and became the first vessel trap the earliest congregations of disciples faced. The book of Acts and the New Testament letters are a record of how it was transcended. We, too, can avoid making the vessel the treasure. We can identify the treasure without reference to any vessel, though the treasure will always have a vessel. Jesus himself has shown the way, and the local congregation can follow that way.

Simply stated, the congregation that wishes to adopt 'the principles and absolutes' of the New Testament, with the natural outcome of being and producing *children of light*, has only to follow Jesus' parting instructions: *go and make disciples of all nations, baptizing them in the name of the Father and of the Son and of the Holy Spirit, and teaching them to obey everything I have commanded you* (Matt 28:19–20). These instructions are set between categorical statements about the resources for this undertaking: *All authority in heaven and on earth has been given to me*, and *surely I will be with you always* (28:18, 20).

These few words give the 'principles and absolutes' of the New Testament church, and history declares the result. As long as we do what these words say, we can do anything else that is helpful to this end. And the rest does not even have to be 'right' for God to bless us. No doubt it is always better it should be so, as long as we do not put our confidence in that rightness. Anyone who thinks God only blesses what is 'right' has had a very narrow experience, and probably does not really understand what God has done for them.

'Miserable sinner' Christianity

We must recognize another factor that distracts the church from focusing on spiritual formation in Christlikeness. This is the view, widely held, that the low level of spiritual living among professing Christians is to be regarded as only natural, only what is to be expected, lamentable as it may be. According to this view, human nature, flesh, life and its world, are all essentially worthless. Everybody is equally bad, and it is only circumstances, directed by God, that make us behave differently. Saints and sinners are equally vile in their hearts, this view would say.

This outlook, historically called 'dualism', has sometimes been referred to as 'miserable sinner' Christianity. It feeds on a number of misunderstandings. One is that the ungodly condition of the human heart and life described in the Bible is essential to human beings as such, and therefore remains natural until we pass from this life. This account of things often associates wickedness with the body, and holiness with getting rid of the body. Fortunately, a careful study of the biblical sources makes it clear that such a view of the body is false.[6]

Another misunderstanding is that, unless the 'miserable sinner' account were true, we might rise to a position where we could deal with God on the basis of merit. To avoid any appearance of self-righteousness you will sometimes hear the greatest of Christians saying things like: 'I'm just as wicked as anyone else.' Was not the apostle Paul saying, long after his conversion, that he was *the worst of sinners* (1 Tim 1:15)? But it is hardly imaginable that Paul, at the time he wrote these words, was still the same person inwardly as he was when he was persecuting Christ through his people, full of rage and self-importance. That man could not have written words like those in Philippians 3:7–14, or 4:4–9. And he could not have said, as Paul did to the Corinthians, *Follow my example, as I follow the example of Christ* (1 Cor 11:1), nor could he admonish Timothy to *flee the evil desires of youth, and pursue righteousness, faith, love and peace, along with those who call on the Lord out of a pure heart* (2 Tim 2:22).

But no doubt the later Paul who wrote these words was very sure that whatever spiritual formation in Christlikeness he had received might be overwhelmed. There remained in him a spark of evil that could be fanned into a flame if he was not watchful, or if God did not continue to direct and uphold him in every part of his being.

Paul knew he was running a race, as you and I are. That race will not be over until we pass into God's full life. No doubt he had in his lifetime seen many falter and fail, many who would not be able to say at the end, as he was, *I have fought the good fight, I have finished the race, I have kept the faith* (2 Tim 4:7). The image of the athlete was powerful in Paul's world and in his own mind. He knew that you had to keep yourself in spiritual shape and to finish the race and finish well. In 1 Corinthians 9 he discusses how he therefore conducts himself in his course of life, how he exercises and treats his body severely, making it his slave, *so that after I have preached to others, I myself will not be disqualified* (9:27).

The valid point in 'miserable sinner' Christianity is correctly expressed in these well-chosen words by St Augustine:

> If anyone supposes that with man, living, as he still does, in this mortal life, it may be possible for him to dispel and clear off every obscurity induced by corporeal and carnal fancies, and to attain to the serenest light of immutable truth, and to cleave constantly and unswervingly to this with a mind wholly estranged from the course of this present life, that man understands neither what he asks, nor who he is that is putting such a supposition . . . If ever the soul is helped to reach beyond the cloud by which all the earth is covered (cf. Ecclus. xxiv, 6), that is to say, beyond this carnal darkness with which the whole terrestrial life is covered, it is simply as if he were touched with a swift coruscation, only to sink back into his natural infirmity, the desire surviving by which he may again be raised to the heights, but his purity being insufficient to establish him there. The more, however, anyone can do this, the greater is he; while the less he can do so the less is he.[7]

In the spiritual life no-one can afford to rest on their laurels. It is a sure recipe for falling. Attainments are like the manna given to the Israelites in the desert, good only for the day (Exod 16:4; 16:20). Past attainments do not place us in a position of merit that permits us to let up in the hot pursuit of God for today, for now. Paul knew that, and knew that others missed it or forgot it to their great harm.

We deserve nothing before God, no matter how far we have advanced, and we are never out of danger. As long as we are *at home in the body* (2 Cor 5:6) we are still just recovering sinners. And in these respects, though only in these respects, we remain as wicked as anyone else.

But to distort this important truth into a claim that we can never really change, especially in our hearts, is to substitute a glaring and harmful falsehood for a liberating and life-blessing truth.

That distortion is sometimes an expression of genuine humility, but it can also be an excuse, something to get us off the hook, a way to enjoy remaining the same in our inner life. It is not easy really to want to be different.

We are never on our own

And then, finally, there is a misunderstanding closely related to the one just discussed. This is the idea that the only alternative to 'miserable sinner Christianity' is holding that human beings are somehow good apart from God, and therefore capable of saving themselves, even saving themselves by merit.

The fear of many is that if you do not hold human beings to be essentially rotten, you are thereby committed to the view that they are essentially good, and therefore righteous and meritorious. This is a field of battle fought over by Pelagius and Augustine many centuries ago and repeatedly revisited through Christian history. It involves many important issues, which cannot be fully dealt with here.

We must keep clear, however, that everyone must be active in the process of their salvation and transformation to Christlikeness. This is an inescapable fact. But the initiative in the process is always God's, and we would in fact be able to do nothing without his initiative. That initiative is not something we need to wait upon. The ball is in our court. God has invaded human history and Jesus Christ has died on our behalf, is risen, and is now in control of events on earth. The issue now concerns what we will do. The idea that we can do nothing is an unfortunate confusion, and those who adopt it never put it into practice it, thank goodness.

If through well-directed and unrelenting action we effectually receive the grace of God, we certainly will be changed toward inward Christlikeness. The transformation of the outer life, especially of our behaviour, will follow suit. *No good tree bears bad fruit, nor does a bad tree bear good fruit* (Luke 6:43). But this means that goodness comes from union with God, not apart from him.

The transformation of the inner being is as much or more a gift of grace as is our justification before God. Of course neither one is wholly passive. To be forever lost you need only do nothing. But with reference to both justification and transformation, 'boasting is excluded' by the law of grace through faith (Rom 3:27–31 and Eph 2:1–10). In fact we are most dependent on grace leading a holy life, not when we continue to sin and are repeatedly forgiven. The interpretation of grace as having only to do with guilt is utterly false to biblical teaching and renders spiritual life in Christ unintelligible.

What is to be done?

If what we have said about spiritual formation is true, what would we expect to find in those gatherings of apprentices of Jesus into churches? Of the actual churches around us, what would they do better to omit, and what do they need more of?

A reasonable response might be that these local congregations would be entirely devoted to the spiritual formation of those in attendance – to the 'renovation of the heart', as we have called it here. This seems to have been Paul's idea, and he, more than any other, was given the role of defining the church, this new thing on earth, the people of God. In it there was to be *no Greek or Jew, circumcised or uncircumcised, barbarian, Scythian, slave or free, but Christ is all, and is in all* (Col 3:11). Identification with Christ and entering the community of Christ obliterated all other identities, not by negation, but by its new and positive reality.

Thus we have Paul's magnificent statement to the Ephesians that Christ, in his triumphant capacity as risen Lord of all (4:10), has given people to the church: *some to be apostles, some to be prophets, some to be evangelists, and some to be pastors and teachers.* And these special functions are solely for the purpose of equipping *God's people for works of service, so that the body of Christ may be built up until we all reach unity in the faith and in the knowledge of the Son of God and become mature, attaining to the whole measure of the fullness of Christ* (4:12–13). As a result of this building up

> *we will no longer be infants, tossed back and forth by the waves, and blown here and there by every wind of teaching and by the cunning and craftiness of men in their deceitful scheming. Instead, speaking the truth in love, we will in all things grow up into him who is the Head, that is, Christ. From him the whole body,*

joined and held together by every supporting ligament, grows and builds itself up in love, as each part does its work (4:14–16).

Now this represents the church, the people of Christ through the ages, at its best. But what we see here is not an impossible dream, a hopeless idealization. It has been done and can be done now, if we turn our efforts under God in the right direction. And that direction would be one that makes spiritual formation in Christlikeness the exclusive primary goal of the local congregation. The first steps on the way are to be clear about where the mainspring of change is – the heart, and that spiritual formation in Christlikeness, real, radical change, is possible.

Matters for thought and discussion

1. Do the common failures of Christian leaders and lay people prove that transformation into Christlikeness is impossible?
2. Does 'righteous meanness' actually happen? If so, do you agree with the explanation given in this chapter of why it happens? How would you explain it?
3. Do you agree with the claim that distraction is the central cause of our current situation in our churches? Reflect on Leith Anderson's statement.
4. Does the distinction between the vessel and the treasure make sense to you? As applied to Paul? To you? To religious traditions, denominations and local groups of Christians?
5. What effects of attributing too much importance to the 'vessel' have you personally seen in Christian practices and endeavours?
6. As simply as possible, explain how we can avoid 'the vessel trap'. We can't avoid having a vessel, can we?
7. Is 'miserable sinner' Christianity an accurate portrayal of life in Christ? What is the valid point in the 'miserable sinner' version?
8. If we are active in the process of spiritual formation does that mean we are acting on our own? How do grace and effort interrelate in spiritual growth?

*On one occasion an expert in the law stood up to test Jesus.
'Teacher,' he asked, 'what must I do to inherit eternal life?'
'What is written in the Law?' he replied. 'How do you read it?'
He answered: '"Love the Lord your God with all your heart
and with all your soul and with all your strength and with all
your mind"; and, "Love your neigh-bour as yourself."'
'You have answered correctly,' Jesus replied.
'Do this and you will live.'*
(Luke 10:25–28)

CHAPTER 3

THE HEART IN THE SYSTEM OF HUMAN LIFE

Understanding is the basis of care. If you want to care for your spiritual core – your heart or will – you must understand it. If you want to form your heart in godliness, or assist others in that process, you must understand what the heart is and what it does, and especially its place in the overall system of human life.

Some years ago *Reader's Digest* ran, at intervals, helpful articles on the various parts of the body: the ear, the lungs, the foot, the stomach, and so forth. The aim was to put readers in a better position to care for their physical health. The titles were always similar: 'Hi, I'm Joe's Liver' (lung, foot, etc.). The properties and structure of the liver or other organ would then be described, and its role in the body explained. Then there would be some discussion of how to keep that particular body part in good condition and to assist it in its function. The aim of this chapter is to explain the nature of the heart and its function in the person as a whole.

The heart directs the life

The person with a well-kept heart is someone who is prepared for and capable of responding to the situations of life in ways that are good and right. This person will choose what is good and avoid what is evil, and the other components of their nature cooperate to that end. They need not be perfect, but what all people manage at least a few times, they manage in life as a whole.

The human heart, will or spirit is the executive centre of human life. The heart is where decisions and choices are made for the whole person. This does not mean that the whole person actually does only what the heart directs, any more than a whole organization actually does precisely what the Chief Executive Officer (CEO) directs. That would be ideal, perhaps (and again, perhaps not); but as any CEO knows, the system rarely goes as directed, and never perfectly so. Many factors are always at work in the decisions and actions that actually occur. The individual's life is often divided into incoherent fragments. *Like a city whose walls are broken down is a man who lacks self-control* (Prov 25:28). In a world deeply infected with evil and 'stuff' that just happens, the usual case is that the individual does not consistently do what his or her own heart says is good and right. When successful, spiritual reformation unites the divided heart and life of the individual, and such people can then bring remarkable harmony into the groups where they participate.

The six basic aspects of a human life

Now when we take a closer look at the whole person, we find that there are six basic aspects in our lives as individual human beings, six things inseparable from human life. These together make up human nature.

1. Thought (images, concepts, judgments, inferences).
2. Feeling (sensation, emotion).
3. Choice (will, decision, character).
4. The body (action, interaction with the physical world).
5. A social context (personal relations to others).
6. Our soul (the factor that integrates all of the above).

Simply put, everyone thinks (has a thought life), feels, chooses, has a body, a social context, and integrates all of them to a greater or lesser degree. There might be other ways of describing these things, but they are essential factors in a human being, and nothing essential to human life falls outside them. The ideal of the spiritual life in Christian understanding is where all of the essential parts of the human self are effectively organized around God, as they are restored and sustained by him. Spiritual formation in Christ is the process leading to that ideal. The human self is then fully integrated under God.

The salvation or deliverance of the believer in Christ is to do with the whole of life. David says, *I will praise the Lord, who counsels me; even at night my heart instructs me. I have set the Lord always before me. Because he is at my right hand, I will not be shaken. Therefore my heart is glad and my tongue rejoices; my body also will rest secure* (Ps 16:7–9). Note how many aspects of the self are explicitly involved in this passage: the mind, the will, the feelings, the soul and the body. A major part of understanding spiritual formation in the Christian traditions is to follow closely the way the biblical writings repeatedly and emphatically focus on the various essential dimensions of the human being and their role in life as a whole.

The human self is not mysterious!

The human self is not mysterious in any sense not equally applicable to everything else. Ultimately the existence of anything is mysterious in the sense that it rests on God alone. But here we are talking about operation rather than origin. To understand anything, of course, some intelligent attention and methodical inquiry is required: what is not mysterious may not be obvious. God has created all things in such a way that they are inherently intelligible.

The basic structure of reality is that things have parts, these parts have properties, which in turn make possible relationships between parts to form more complex things, which in turn have properties that make possible relationships between them, and so on. This applies to everything from an atom to the solar system, from a thought or a feeling to a whole person to a society. In this style of description, a human being is a complex system, consisting of parts with properties and functions. These make possible the relationships which persons have to the world and society and beyond all these, if they are fully alive, as spiritual beings, to the kingdom of God.

The six aspects of the human person, as we have listed them above, are things all human beings can and must do to some degree. We can feel, think, choose, act and be acted upon through our body. We have some kind of personal relations, and we integrate these aspects of our being with the others.

Each aspect or dimension of the person will be a source of weakness or strength to the whole person, depending upon the condition it is in, and the condition it is in will depend, finally, upon the heart. A person who is prepared and capable of responding to the situations of life in ways that are good and right is a person whose soul is in order, under the direction of a well-kept heart, under the direction of God.

A brief survey of the six human dimensions

The focus of the rest of this book is on how these aspects can be shaped and spiritually formed into Christlikeness. But, for the time being, we will survey briefly each of the aspects of the person we have listed, and how they interact.

Thought. Thought brings things before our minds in various ways, perception and imagination for instance, and enables us to consider these things and trace their interrelationships. Thought is that which enables our will or spirit to range far beyond the boundaries of our immediate environment. Through it our consciousness reaches into the past, present and future, by reasoning and scientific thinking, by imagination and art – and also by divine revelation, which comes to us mainly in the form of thought.

Feeling. Feeling inclines us towards or away from things that come before our minds in thought. It involves pleasure or pain, attraction or repulsion in relation to what is thought of. How we feel about food, motor cars, relationships, positions, and hundreds of other things illustrate this point. What we call 'indifference' is never a total absence of feeling, positive and negative, but simply an unusually low degree of feeling, usually negative. The connection between thought and feeling is so intimate that the mind is usually treated as consisting of thought and feeling together. Of course the mind thus understood is a quite complicated aspect of the person. The mind is what Satan, *the prince of this world,* seeks to control, and his particular achievement is found in obsession, madness or possession.

Will. We could also call the will the spirit or the heart. They are broadly part of the same aspect of the person. Volition or choice is the exercise of will, the capacity of the person to originate things and events, to do things that would otherwise not be done. Freedom and creativity are really two aspects of the same thing, which is power to do what is good or evil: that is, they are expressions of the human will. The power in question belongs to individuals alone. A free action has many conditions, but the conditions do not make the action. Our actions are the result of our inner consent to the conditions, as we respond to various situations. This response is our unique contribution to reality. It is ours, it is us, as nothing else is.

Without the inner consent there is no sin, for only that 'yes' is just us. The thought of sin is not sin, and is not even a temptation. Temptation is the thought plus the inclination to sin, possibly manifested by lingering over the thought or seeking it out, whether or not we do what we imagine. Sin itself is when we inwardly consent to the temptation.

Now we need to be very clear on this point: we have a capacity for volition, and the acts of will in which it is exercised form the spirit in us. In this narrow sense, the spirit is the central core of the non-physical part of us. Only God is purely spirit, pure creative will and character. Only he can truly say, *I am who I am* (Exod 3:14). He is unbodily, personal power. Human beings have only a small element of unbodily, personal power at the centre, but it is crucial to who they are and who they become. So for us, it is above all the spirit or will, that must be reached, cared for, and transformed in spiritual formation. The human will is primarily what must be given a godly nature, and this must then expand its governance over the entire personality.

Thus the will or spirit is the heart in the human system. That is why we have the biblical teaching that human good and evil are matters of the heart. It is the heart (Mark 7:21) and spirit (John 4:23) that God looks at (1 Sam 16:7; Is 66:2) in relating to humankind, and in allowing us to relate to him (2 Chr 15:4, 15; Jer 29:13; Heb 11:6).

Thought, feeling and volition are closely intertwined. To choose, one must have some object or concept before the mind, and some feeling for or against it. So much is obvious. What is not so obvious is that what one feels and thinks can and should be to a very large degree a matter of choice in the competent adult. We should be very careful about what we allow our minds to dwell upon or what we allow ourselves to feel. Unfortunately this fact is not widely understood. We speak of feelings as if they were imposed from the outside and irresistible. People nearly always act on their feelings, and the will is then left at the mercy of circumstances that evoke feelings. But we are in fact very active in inviting, allowing and handling our feelings. Choosing within limits what we feel is crucial to the practical methods of spiritual formation.

It is important to recognize that human life as a whole does not run by will alone. Far from it. Nevertheless, life must be organized by the will if it is to be organized at all. Life can only be pulled together from the inside. And of course life must be organized, and organized well, if our existence is to be tolerable. That is the function of the will or heart, to organize our life as a whole, and, indeed, to organize it around God.

Body. The body is the focal point of our presence in the physical world. We become the people we are as bodily beings. The body is where our will has its primary energy source or strength. The body is where we can even defy God, at least for a while. It is where we are reached by stimulus from the world beyond ourselves, and where we find and are found by others.[1]

Personal relations cannot be separated from the body; and, on the other hand, the body cannot be understood apart from human relations. It is essentially social. Our bodies are forever a part of our identity as persons. For example, I am and will forever be the son of Maymie Joyce Lindesmith and Albert Alexander Willard. My body came from God through them, and they provided the relationships, the social and spiritual context that, more than anything else, made me the person I am.

It is the body from which we live. We have already said that we do not live by will alone. Our choices, as they settle into character, are imprinted on or ingrained into our body in its social context, where they then occur more or less automatically, without our having to think about what we are doing. And that is, in general, a very good thing. Just think how tedious it would be if you had to think about what you were doing all the time, and you had consciously to decide every action involved in driving a car, for example. The very purpose of learning or training in some activity is to bring it under our direction without our having to think about it or make decisions regarding it. The body makes this possible; it has a life of its own.

This basically good feature of the body, its capacity to have a life of its own, is also a major problem for, and a primary area of, spiritual formation. For, trained in a world of wrongness and evil, the body comes to act wrongly automatically, before we think, which may thwart the true intention of our spirit or will by leaping ahead of it. It is not me doing evil, says Paul, *but it is sin living in me* (Rom 7:17) And *the sinful nature desires what is contrary to the Spirit, and the Spirit what is contrary to the sinful nature. They are in conflict with each other, so that you do not do what you want* (Gal 5:17).

But at the same time this amazing capacity of the body means that it can be transformed to become our ally in Christlikeness. Such a transformation of the body is one major part of the process of spiritual formation, as we shall see. The body is not, on the biblical view, essentially evil; but while it is infected with evil, it can be delivered. Spiritual formation is essentially a bodily process. It cannot succeed unless the body is transformed.

Social context. The self needs others. This is primarily a matter of being what we are. It is not just a moral matter, a matter of how we should relate to others, but a fundamental human need. The moral aspect of it grows out of the ontological.[2]

The most fundamental 'other' for the human being is God himself, since all are rooted in God, whether they want it or not. Our ties to one another cannot be isolated from our relationship to him, nor our relationship to him from our ties to one another. Our relations to others cannot be right unless we see those others in their relation to God. *If anyone says, 'I love God,' yet hates his brother, he is a liar*, John says unapologetically. *For anyone who does not love his brother, whom he has seen, cannot love God, whom he has not seen* (1 John 4:20). We only live as we should when we are in a right relation with God and others. Hence the two greatest commandments, quoted at the head of this chapter. Rejection is a sword-thrust to the soul that has injured many. It seeps into our souls and is a deadly enemy to spiritual formation in Christ. The power of our personal relations with others is what gives them their incalculable importance for the formation of our spirit and our entire life, for good or ill. And of course our body is the focus of these relations.

But being with others, our social dimension, is also inseparable from our inner thoughts, feelings, choices and actions. Our very relation to Christ, our Saviour, teacher and friend, is located in the social dimension. It is true that there is no salvation outside the church.

The soul. The soul is that dimension of the person which integrates all of the other dimensions so that they form one life. The biblical view and understanding is that *soul* is a term that refers to the whole person in its most profound aspect.

Because the soul encompasses and integrates the whole person it is frequently taken to *be* the person. We used to refer to people as 'souls', as in 'a parish of two thousand souls'. But of course the soul is not the person. It is, rather, the deepest part of the self in terms of overall operations; and, like the body, it has the capacity to operate without conscious supervision.

The soul is rather like a computer that quietly runs a business or manufacturing operation and only comes to our attention when it malfunctions or requires some adaptation to new tasks. It can be significantly reprogrammed, and this too is a major part of what goes into the spiritual formation of the person.

Because the soul is so fundamental, and to some degree independent of conscious direction, biblical language often addresses it in the second person. The psalmist asks, *Why are you downcast, O my soul? Why so disturbed within me? Put your hope in God, for I will yet praise him, my Saviour and my God* (Ps 42:5). The rich fool of Luke 12 says to his soul, *You have plenty of good things laid up for many years. Take life easy; eat, drink and be merry* (12:19).

But for all the soul's independence, the executive centre of the

person – that is, the heart or will – can redirect and reform it with
God's help. It mainly does this by redirecting the body in spiritual
disciplines and toward various other types of experiences under God.
The soul can be sustained intact and function as it is supposed to
only in the keeping of God. *For every living soul belongs to me*, says
the Lord (Ezek 18:4).

Influence on action

But now we turn to action. Our actions always arise out of the inter-
play of the factors in human life: spirit, mind, body, social context
and the soul. Action never comes from the movement of the will
alone. Often what we do is not an outcome of deliberate choice and
a mere act of will, but is more a matter of conceding to pressure on
the will from one or more aspects of the self.

The inadequacy of good intentions to ensure proper action is
marked by Jesus' words *the spirit is willing but the body is weak*. If the
six dimensions are properly aligned with God and what is good, and
therefore with each other, that conceding will be good, and our
actions will simply be the good fruit of the good tree. If they are not
so aligned, however, they will be the inevitable bad fruit of the bad
tree.

We must clearly understand that there is a rigorous consistency in
the human self and its actions. This is one of the things we are most
inclined to deceive ourselves about. If I do evil, I am the kind of person who does evil; if I do good, I am the kind of person who does
good (1 John 3:7–10). Actions are expressions of who we are. They
come out of our heart.

One of the most common rationalizations of sin or folly today is
'Oh, I just blew it.' While there is some point to such a remark, it is
not the one those who use it hope for. It does not exonerate them.
While it may be true that there are other circumstances in which I
would not have done the foolish or sinful thing I did, and while what
I did may not represent me fully, 'blowing it' does represent me fully.
I am the kind of person who 'blows it'. 'Blowing it' shows who I am
as a person. I am, through and through, the kind of person who
'blows it' – hardly a lovely and promising thing to be.

The will or spirit is often at the mercy of the forces playing upon it from other aspects of the self and beyond. The God-intended function of the will is to reach out to him in trust. By standing in the correct relation to God through our will, we can receive grace that will properly reorder the soul along with the other five components of the self.

In the life away from God, the order of dominance is:

- Body
- Soul
- Mind (thought and feeling)
- Spirit
- God

This is the order in idolatry of all kinds.

'There are two Gods,' Tolstoy once said:

> There is the God that people generally believe in – a God who has to serve them (sometimes in very refined ways, say by merely giving them peace of mind). This God does not exist. But the God whom people forget – the God whom we all have to serve – exists, and is the prime cause of our existence and of all that we perceive.[3]

In the life under God, by contrast, the order of dominance is:

- God
- Spirit
- Mind (thought and feeling)
- Soul
- Body

Here the body serves the soul, the soul the mind, the mind the spirit, and the spirit serves God. Life flows from God throughout the whole person, including the body and its social context.

The former order is characteristic of what Paul describes as *the mind of sinful man*, which *is death* (Rom 8:6). The latter expresses *the mind controlled by the Spirit*, which is *life and peace*.

Those who live according to the sinful nature have their minds set on what that nature desires; but those who live in accordance with the Spirit have their minds set on what the Spirit desires. The mind of sinful man is death, but the mind controlled by the Spirit is life and peace; the sinful mind is hostile to God. It does not submit to God's law, nor can it do so. (Rom 8:5–7)

When the proper ordering of the human system under God is complete – which no doubt will never fully occur in this life – then we have a person who loves God with all their heart, and with all their soul, and with all their strength and with all their mind; and their neighbour as themselves (Luke 10:27 and Mark 12:30–33). When we are like this, our whole life is an eternal one. Everything we do counts for eternity.

The spirit must first come alive to and through God, of course. Otherwise we remain dead to him in trespasses and sins (Eph 2:1). But once the spirit comes alive in God, the lengthy processes of subduing all aspects of the self under God can begin. This is the process of spiritual formation viewed in its entirety.

We therefore live in 'hot pursuit' of Jesus Christ. *My soul clings to you,* the psalmist cries (63:8). And Paul wrote, *I want to know Christ and the power of his resurrection and the fellowship of sharing in his sufferings, becoming like him in his death, and so, somehow, to attain to the resurrection from the dead* (Phil 3:10–11). What are we to say of anyone who thinks they have something more important to do than that? The work of spiritual formation in Christlikeness is the work of claiming the land of milk and honey in which we are, individually and collectively, to dwell with God.

The old hymn rings out:

> On Jordan's stormy banks I stand
> and cast a wistful eye
> To Canaan's fair and happy land,
> where my possessions lie.

But the real Jordan, the spiritual Jordan, is not physical death, as has often been supposed. We need not and must not wait until we die to live in the land of milk and honey; and if we will only move to that land now, the passage through physical death will be but a part of the endless life we have long since begun. That is exactly what Jesus meant when he said, *I tell you the truth, if anyone keeps my word, he will never see death* (John 8:51).

'Helter-Skelter'

The man who prosecuted the infamous Manson family for their murders later wrote a book titled *Helter-Skelter*. This phrase was taken from a song performed by a well-known rock music group. It characterizes the state of confusion in which Manson kept his followers, and himself as well. In a state of helter-skelter nothing makes sense, and everything makes as much sense as anything else. So, for example, when you cut someone's throat or stab them repeatedly and they die, you didn't really kill them and they didn't really die. That was Manson's teaching.

Aldous Huxley in one of his retrospective writings commented on how among the associates of his youth the endless talk of 'meaninglessness' – the meaninglessness of life and therefore of everything in it – was merely an excuse to permit them to do whatever they wanted. Their life was organized around their feelings and wayward thoughts, with their will in tow.

But resolute action for the good requires that things make sense. You wouldn't want someone caught up in helter-skelter to work on your lawnmower or computer. Life makes sense only if you understand its basic components and how they interrelate to form the whole. Evil, on the other hand, thrives on confusion. That is why *God is not a God of disorder* (1 Cor 14:33).

Frankly, our Christian world is often not too far from 'helter-skelter' with regard to its understanding of the make-up of the person, and therefore of the spiritual life and spiritual formation. We need to grasp the fullness of biblical teachings on these matters. We suffer far too much from the influence of a surrounding culture that thrives on confusion. This may seem like a harsh thing to say about our Christian world, and I am sorry to say it; but the issues here are too important to mince words.

Accordingly, much of what we do in Christian circles with very good intentions, hoping to see steady, significant growth in

Christlikeness, simply makes no sense and leads nowhere, so far as substantive spiritual formation is concerned.[4] This may seem a brutal thing to say! But we need to recognize it, or prove that it is not the case. In this chapter I hope we have taken significant first steps toward a clarity that can serve as a foundation for the effectual practice of Christian spiritual formation.

Matters for thought and discussion

1. What is the relation between caring for something and understanding its nature?
2. What is the heart and what is its role in human life?
3. What are the six basic dimensions of the human being? Does the list here leave anything out?
4. Relate the six dimensions to the Great Commandment (Luke 10:25–28) and to spiritual formation in Christ.
5. Explore the role feelings play in our current social and personal life. In media and popular arts. In church activities. Would you say you are (sometimes? never? always?) controlled by your feelings?
6. Do you agree or disagree with the explanation of temptation presented in this chapter?
7. How does choice or volition depend upon thought and feeling? Why can't we just change our will?
8. Actions reveal who we are. Do you agree or disagree?

You were washed, you were sanctified,
you were justified in the name of the Lord Jesus Christ
and by the Spirit of our God.
(1 Cor 6:11)

CHAPTER 4

SPIRITUAL TRANSFORMATION

One of the amazing things about human beings is that they are capable of restoration, and indeed of a restoration that makes them somehow more magnificent because they were previously lost. This is a strange but hopeful thought. A key to understanding this re-ordering or restoration is given by John Calvin:

> For as the surest source of destruction to men is to obey themselves, so the only haven of safety is to have no other will, no other wisdom, than to follow the Lord wherever he leads. Let this, then, be the first step, to abandon ourselves, and devote the whole energy of our minds to the service of God.

Here Calvin simply restates the basic point of view of Christ's people through the ages.[1] He goes on:

> By service, I mean not only that which consists in verbal obedience, but that by which the mind, divested of its own carnal feelings, implicitly obeys the call of the Spirit of God. This transformation (which Paul calls the renewing of the mind, Romans 12:2; Ephesians 4:23), though it is the first entrance of life, was unknown to all the philosophers. They give the government of man

to reason alone . . . But Christian philosophy bids her give place, and yield complete submission to the Holy Spirit, so that the man himself no longer lives, but Christ lives and reigns in him (Galatians 2:20).[2]

It is such an overall transformation of personality that Calvin captured under the heading 'self-denial', a term which he used to summarize the entire Christian life.[3] Self-denial is not to be thought of as a painful and strenuous act repeated from time to time against great internal resistance. It is, rather, an overall, settled condition of life in the kingdom of God, better described as 'death to self'. In this lies the key to the soul's restoration. Christian spiritual formation rests on this foundation of death to self, and cannot proceed except in so far as that foundation is firmly laid and sustained.

But what is this self-denial or death to self? At first it sounds like some dreadfully negative thing that aims to annihilate us. And, frankly, self-denial is every bit as brutal as it seems to most people on first approach. We must lose our life. The ruined life is not to be enhanced but replaced. Jesus says, *Whoever finds his life shall lose it, and whoever loses his life for my sake will find it* (Matt 10:39).

Losing our life to find it

When Jesus says we must lose our lives if we are to find them, he is teaching, on the negative side, that we must not make ourselves and our survival the ultimate point of reference in our world – we must not, in effect, treat ourselves as God. Paul shockingly says, *greed . . . is idolatry* (Col 3:5). This might seem somewhat exaggerated, but greed idolizes the self, it makes my desires paramount. I would take what I want if I could. Making my desires paramount is what Paul calls having a *sinful mind* or in older versions a 'mind of the flesh', which is a state of death (Rom 8:6). Such a mind *sows to the sinful nature*, invests only in the natural self, *and from that nature will reap destruction* (Gal 6:8).

In other words, when Jesus says that those who find their life shall lose it, he is pointing out that those who think they are in control of their life – 'I am the master of my fate: I am the captain of my soul,' as the poet Henley said – will find that they definitely are not in control: they are totally at the mercy of forces beyond their control. They are on a sure course to destruction.

If, however, we give up the project of being in control, of doing only what we want, of sowing to the sinful nature, then there is hope. If we lose our life in favour of God's life, for the sake of Jesus, then we will find our true self in life given back to us.

For the first time we will be able to do what we want to do. Of course we will be able to steal, lie and murder all we want – which will be not at all. But we will also be able to be joyfully truthful and transparent and helpful and sacrificially loving – and we will want to be. Our life will be caught up in God's life. We will want the good and be able to do it. The mind *controlled by the Spirit is life and peace* (Rom 8:6), because it *sows to please the Spirit [and] from the Spirit will reap eternal life* (Gal 6:8).

Taking up the cross

The same kind of paradox is present in Jesus' teaching about who can be his disciple or apprentice. This too is put in very shocking language: *If anyone comes to me and does not hate his father and mother, his wife and children, his brothers and sisters – yes, even his own life – he cannot be my disciple* (Luke 14:26). And then he uses an absolutely shocking image, one all too familiar to his hearers, but rather hard for us fully to appreciate today. It was that of a man carrying on his back the timber that would be used to kill him when he arrived at the place of execution: *anyone who does not carry his cross and follow me cannot be my disciple.* The cross was an instrument of death. The teaching here is the same as that in the statements about losing and finding our lives. It is one of comparative costs, as the following verses in Luke 14 show. Those who are not genuinely convinced that the only real bargain in life is surrendering themselves to Jesus, abandoning all that they love to him and for him, cannot learn the other lessons Jesus has to teach. They cannot proceed to spiritual transformation. It is not that he won't let us, but that we simply can't succeed. If I tell you that you cannot drive a car unless you can see, I am not saying I won't let you, but that you can't succeed even if you want to.

Counting the cost

One of the great dangers is that self-denial and death to self will be taken as but one more technique to be mastered by people who want to save their life. Self-denial then becomes an activity that may seem very sacrificial, but can leave the *sinful mind* in full control. A well-known Methodist evangelist, Sam Jones, used to say that a dancing foot and a praying knee do not grow on the same leg. But not dancing hardly proves that the life is abandoned to prayer or to God.

Practices of mortification can become exercises in self-righteousness. This dreary and deadly self-denial is all too commonly associated with religion. But the outward manifestation of self-denial mattered little to Jesus; indeed he mocked people who made themselves miserable in this way. What mattered to Jesus was a loving commitment to God's kingdom. This is where correctly counting the cost comes in.

The notion of 'counting the cost' of following Jesus often leads to an impression that it a terrible and painful thing. But counting the cost means weighing up both the losses and the gains of the course of action. And as we have seen, it is true what has been said, 'He is no fool who gives up what he cannot keep for the sake of what he cannot lose.' Ultimately we have to give up our lives. We all die. But if we give them up to Jesus, we can't lose them.

Counting the cost is illustrated in Jesus' 'parables of the kingdom'. *The kingdom of heaven is like a treasure hidden in a field. When a man found it, he hid it again, and then in his joy he went and sold all he had and bought that field* (Matt 13:44). Imagine that you discovered gold or oil in a certain property and no-one else knew about it. Can you see yourself feeling deprived for having to gather all your resources and 'sacrifice' them in order to buy that property? Hardly! Now you know what it is like to deny yourself, take up your cross and follow Jesus.

Some pain is involved, no doubt, because the old attachments are still there in our hearts and lives. They do not all disappear at once. But the new vision becomes an attachment, and takes on an ever greater reality as we progress in spiritual transformation; and that, in turn, pushes the old attachments out of our lives. Our desires change.

The 'self-denial' of Matthew 16:24 and elsewhere in the Gospels is always the surrender of a lesser, dying self for a greater eternal one. Jesus does not deny us personal fulfilment, but shows us the only true way to it. In him we find our life. He wants to keep us from selling our birthright as creatures in God's image, a birthright of genuine goodness, sufficiency and power for which we are fitted by nature, for a mere bowl of soup (Gen 25:31) – money, a little illicit sex, reputation, power and so forth. Taking Jesus as our master means that we trust his way is right. He did not choose the cross and death because they were good in themselves, *but for the joy set before him [he] endured the cross, scorning its shame* (Heb 12:2).

Perfect joy

The person who is dead to self and surrendered to Christ will know the joy of spiritual transformation.

In chapter 8 of *The Little Flowers of St Francis* of Assisi, Francis teaches his friend Leo about what perfect joy is. For their brotherhood to give a great example of holiness and edification in all lands would not be perfect joy, Francis says. Nor would a great ministry of healing and raising the dead. Nor would possession of all languages and all science, nor all understanding of prophecy and Scripture, and insight into the secrets of every soul. Nor would even the conversion of all unbelievers to faith in Christ!

By this point brother Leo is amazed, and begs Francis to tell him what would be perfect joy. The reply is that if, when they come to their quarters, dirty, wet and exhausted from hunger, they are rejected, repeatedly rebuffed, and finally driven away by force, then 'if we accept such injustice, such cruelty, and such contempt with patience, without being ruffled and without murmuring', and 'if we bear all these injuries with patience and joy, thinking of the sufferings of our Blessed Lord, which we would share out of love for him, write, O Brother Leo, that here, finally, is perfect joy'.

If we are dead to self we will not notice some things that others would, for example things like social slights, verbal put-downs and innuendoes, or physical discomforts. These rebuffs will not take control of us, not even to the point of disturbing our peace of mind. We will, as St Francis of Assisi said, 'wear the world like a loose garment, which touches us in a few places and there lightly'.

Does this mean that we will be without feeling? Does Christ commend the apathy of the Stoic, or the Buddhist elimination of desire? Far from it. The issue is not just feeling or desire, but right feeling or desire, or being controlled by feeling and desire. Apprentices of Jesus will be deeply disturbed about many things, and will passionately desire many things, but they will be largely indifferent to the fulfilment of their own desires as such. Merely getting their way has no significance for them, does not disturb them.

We know that in all things God works for the good of those who love him, who have been called according to his purpose (Rom 8:28). We do not have to look out for ourselves because God is in charge. We do not worry about outcomes that merely affect adversely our own desires and feelings. We are free to focus our efforts on the service of God and others and the furthering of good generally, and to be as passionate about such things as may be appropriate to such efforts.

It is probable, perhaps, that we will never be totally above sensitivity to self. Mere sensitivity to self is not itself wrong or sinful, so long as we do not welcome it or allow it to take over our lives. The advice of Thomas à Kempis is very good as an antidote to improper sensitivity:

> Choose ever rather to have less than more.
> Seek ever the lower place and to be under all.
> Desire ever to pray that the will of God
>   may be all and wholly done.
> So, such a one enters the land of peace and quiet.[4]

If this plan were followed, and were sufficiently accompanied by the movements of God's spirit within us, we might make substantial progress toward what John Wesley described as the 'Character of a Methodist':

> His one desire, is the one design of his life, namely, 'not to do his own will, but the will of Him that sent him'. His one intention at all times and in all things is, not to please himself, but Him whom his soul loveth. He has a

single eye. And because 'his eye is single, his whole body is full of light'. Indeed, where the loving eye of the soul is continually fixed upon God, there can be no darkness at all, 'but the whole is light; as when the bright shining of a candle doth enlighten the house'. God then reigns alone. All that is in the soul is holiness to the Lord. There is not a motion in his heart, but is according to His will. Every thought that arises points to Him, and is in obedience to the law of Christ.[5]

This may be a bit more than many people could imagine for this life, but it is clearly the direction in which we can and should be moving as apprentices of Jesus. What we surely can say is that if we are dead to self we will not be controlled in thought, feeling or action by self-exaltation or by the will to have our own way, but controlled by love of God and neighbour. We will still have some self-will, no doubt, and will never be totally beyond the possibility of falling under subjection to it. Only a proper discipline and grace will prevent this from actually happening. But we will no longer be locked in a struggle with them.

The centrality of giving

We have looked at being dead to self under the aspect of not being dominated by the *sinful nature* as Paul calls it. This might make it seem rather a negative thing. But being dead to self means being able to be positively and joyfully generous. Even from his strictly humanistic perspective, Erich Fromm acknowledges this:

> The most widespread misunderstanding is that which assumes that giving is 'giving up' something, being deprived of, sacrificing. People whose main orientation is a non-productive one feel giving as an impoverishment . . . the virtue of giving, to them, lies in the very act of acceptance of sacrifice . . . For the productive character giving has an entirely different meaning. Giving is the highest expression of potency. In the very act of giving I experience my strength, my wealth, my power. The experience of heightened vitality fills me with joy. I experience myself as overflowing, spending, alive, hence as joyous. Giving is more joyous than receiving, not because it is a deprivation, but because in the act of giving lies the expression of my aliveness.[6]

Giving is good; it is part of not making myself the absolute point of reference in my life. But there will be times when it is not easy, and does not immediately fill us with joy or 'heightened vitality'. We must then rely on God, who, in Paul's words, *loves a cheerful giver* and who *is able to make all grace abound* to us, so that we have all we need (2 Cor 9:7–8). Love of God, confidence in his greatness and goodness, and the regular experience of his care, frees us from the burden of looking out for ourselves, and allows us to give freely.

Experience-based confidence in God's loving care allows all six dimensions of the self progressively to come into harmony with each other, and enables us to be generous in every respect to those around us. Love of God enables us love our neighbour. And love of God and neighbour gradually pulls the whole person into proper alignment. Without this, even something as good as giving can be mere self-deification. It can be totally me-centred, and thus foster and perpetuate the sinful nature rather than being part of the heart's renovation.

Dead to self

Self-denial is a process that leads to being dead to self. At first we must self-consciously deny ourselves and look for God's grace in and around us to guide and strengthen us in our self-denial. We will also need a wise and constant use of disciplines for the spiritual life. This is because we have been formed in a world which rejects God. Our habits of thinking, feeling and willing are wrongly shaped.

But there will come a time in the experience of the apprentice of Jesus where it is appropriate to speak of our being dead to self. Faithful servants of God know the secret, and many have left their testimony. George Mueller of Bristol said:

> There was a day when I died: died to George Mueller, his opinions, prefer-
> ences, tastes and will; died to the world, its approval or censure; died to the
> approval or blame even of my brethren or friends, and since then, I have
> studied only to show myself 'approved unto God'.

Someone said of Mueller that he 'had the twenty-third Psalm written in his face'.[7]

One of the sources of difficulty here is confusion of our desire for what is good and right to prevail with our desire to have our own way. One often sees the effects of this confusion in controversies in families, in churches, or between religious and political groups. In such cases, very important values are often at stake, and people are passionately committed to one side or another. But more often than not the contempt for others and anger that emerge in the conflict are nothing but a manifestation of self-will. Families, churches, communities and nations become embroiled in deadly conflicts that could immediately be resolved but for the relentless power of self-will.

To accept, with confidence in God, that I do not have to have my way immediately releases me from the great pressure that anger, unforgiveness and the need to retaliate imposes upon my life. This removes the root and source of by far the greater part of human evil we have to deal with in our world.[8] This is why Paul directed the Christians in Thessalonica to *make sure that nobody pays back wrong for wrong, but always try to be kind to each other and to everyone else* (1 Thess 5:15). Jesus commanded, *do not resist an evil person. If someone strikes you on your right cheek, turn to him the other also* (Matt 5:39). And Peter says, *do not repay evil with evil or insult with insult, but with blessing, because to this you were called so that you may inherit a blessing* (1 Pet 3:9).

These remarkable instructions all presuppose that one has laid down the burden of having one's own way. We can't begin to understand them, much less follow them, without knowing in experience God's all-sufficient presence in our life. Stepping with Jesus into the path of self-denial immediately breaks the iron-clad grip of sin and opens the way to radical goodness. It accesses incredible, supernatural strength for life. Because we must actively walk this way and pursue this radical goodness, it is crucial that we now seek to understand the three main components in the process of spiritual transformation.

Transformation into Christlikeness is possible

First of all we must be clear that the transformation of Christian spiritual formation can actually happen, and can actually happen to us.

This is not obvious today. What we see as the usual Christian life could easily make us think that spiritual transformation is simply impossible. Although there is much talk about changing lives in Christian circles, the reality is rare, and certainly much less common than the talk.

But we can be transformed to increasingly take on the character of Christ. That transformation is not only possible, but has actually occurred to a significant degree in the lives of many human beings; and it is necessary if our life as a whole is to manifest God's goodness and power. But before turning to the details of transformation in the various dimensions of the human being, we need to understand the general pattern of effective personal transformation – not just Christian spiritual formation.

Imagine someone wants to speak a new language, say French or Arabic or Japanese. In order to succeed in this simple project of personal transformation, they must have some idea of what it would be like to speak the language in question, some understanding of why this would be a desirable or valuable thing for them. They also need to have some idea how they can learn to speak the language, and why the expenditure of time, energy and money is worthwhile. In an ideal case all of this would be clear.

Without this vision, the language will pretty surely not be learned. Often language learning fails in our schools because pupils cannot see the benefit if it. On the other hand, people learn English all over the world because they can see the benefits of it as part of career development: they can see clearly the ways in which their lives would be improved by knowing English.

More than vision is required, though. Projects of personal transformation rarely if ever succeed by accident, drift or imposition. Indeed, where these dominate very little of any human value transpires. Effective action has to involve intention. Decisive choice matters. Imagine a person wondering day after day if they are going to learn Arabic, or if they are going to get married – just waiting, to see whether it will happen. That would be laughable. But many people seem to live in this way. Learning a language requires intention. We must intend and take steps to realize the vision.

Intention must result in action. There are various means available for learning languages: signing up for language courses, listening to recordings, reading books, associating with native speakers of the language, spending time in the foreign country. And endless practice, of course.

This is how you learn a language. If the vision is clear, the intention strong, and the means adequate, the thoughtful and persistent person will make significant progress in this area of personal transformation.

A more serious illustration of this general pattern of personal transformation is provided by Alcoholics Anonymous. Here, of course, the significance of the transformation is far greater for the person involved than in the case of learning a language: it is often a matter of life or death. The vision is freedom from alcohol dependency, a serious intention is expressed to realize it, and means are applied to fulfil the intention. The familiar means of AA, the famous 'twelve steps' which include a conscious reliance on God, are highly effective in bringing about personal transformation.

V-I-M: the general pattern

The general pattern of personal transformation is clear enough. Even spiritual formation, which can only occur at the initiative and through the constant direction and upholding of God, follows this pattern. To represent this general pattern we will use the acronym V-I-M, as in the phrase 'vim and vigour'. The acronym not only helps us to remember the pattern; it also helpfully reminds us that while the initiative is God's, spiritual transformation engages our effort.

- Vision
- Intention
- Means

If we are to be spiritually formed in Christ, we must have the appropriate vision, intention and means.

Here, in a nutshell, is the explanation for the widespread failure to attain Christian maturity among both leaders and followers. Christians today do not usually have the V-I-M which would enable them to progress to the point where what Jesus himself did and taught would naturally flow from them. Rather, they have a constant inward battle with their desires, and they have the constant outward demands of the religious culture. Authentic inward transformation into Christlikeness is left out. It is not envisioned, intended nor achieved.

If we are concerned about our own spiritual formation, then a vision of God's kingdom is the place to start. It is where Jesus started. It was the gospel he preached. He came announcing, manifesting and teaching the kingdom of heaven. The kingdom of heaven is where what God wants is done.[9] Planet earth seems to be the only place where God permits his will not to be done. That is why we pray, *Your kingdom come, your will be done on earth as in heaven,* and look for the time when God's kingdom will be established on earth.

The vision which underlies spiritual transformation into Christlikeness, then, is a vision of life now and forever in God's will and presence. What we are aiming for in this vision is to live fully in the kingdom of God, and as fully as possible here and now, not just hereafter. This is a vision that is given to humanity by God by revelation. It is not a vision that we could imagine on our own, though thinkers and artists have sometimes captured aspects of it.[10] It is a revelation that has been given through God's covenant people, the Jews, and especially through Jesus himself.

This vision of life in God's kingdom makes it possible for us to intend to live it. We can actually decide to do it. Of course that means first of all trusting him and relying on him as who he claimed to be, the Christ, *the way, the truth and the life.* We express our intention of living in the kingdom concretely by intending to obey the teachings of Jesus. This is the form that trust in him takes, not merely believing things about him. No-one can actually trust Jesus without intending to obey him. Gandhi, who had looked closely at Christianity as practised in Britain, remarked that if only Christians lived according to their belief in the teachings of Jesus, everyone would become Christians. We know what he meant, but the dismaying truth is that Christians *were* living according to their belief in the teachings of Jesus. And they didn't believe them! Perhaps the hardest thing for sincere Christians to come to terms with is the level of their

real unbelief: the unformulated scepticism about Jesus that undermines their efforts at Christlikeness. The idea that you can trust
Christ and not intend to obey him is an illusion generated by an
essentially unbelieving Christian culture.

Intention involves decision

An intention is brought to completion only by a decision to fulfil the
intention. There are lots of people who say they intend to do things
which they don't do. To be fair, circumstances may sometimes prevent them from carrying out the intention. And even sincere
intentions can be thwarted by bad habits for a while. But if nothing
is done we conclude that they never actually decided to do what they
said they would do, and therefore that they did not really intend to
do it. They might have wished for whatever they promised to do to
happen, but they did not decide to do it. Their intention was never
really formed.

Procrastination is a common way in which intention is aborted,
but there are many other ways. And people often profess intentions
they do not mean to carry out. But if the genuine intention is there,
the deed reliably follows. If it is not there, the deed will most likely
not follow. The person whose word is their bond is a person with a
vision of integrity, of Christlikeness, and intention, with its inseparable decision, can only be sustained by vision.

Means

The vision of Christlikeness and the solid intention of obeying
Christ will naturally lead to seeking out and applying means for
achieving those ends. Here the means in question are the means for
spiritual transformation, replacing our fallen character with the character of Jesus. We do not have to search too hard for these means; we
have rich resources available to us in the example and teachings of
Jesus, in the Scriptures generally, and in his people.

I will not immediately be able to do what Jesus would do if my
inner being is filled with all the thoughts, feelings and habits that

characterize the world which denies God. But if I intend to obey Jesus Christ, I will intend and decide to become the kind of person who would obey and be like Jesus. The means to that end are not all directly under my control, for some are the actions of God toward me and in me. But some *are* directly under my control.

I can retrain my thinking by study and meditation on Christ himself and on the teachings of Scripture about God, his world and my life. I can also help my thinking and my feelings by reflecting on the bitter outcome of the normal human way in such situations. I can also consciously practise explicitly self-sacrificial actions. I can become a person for whom looking out for number one is not the basis of life. I can learn about the lives of 'saints', who have walked in real life the way of Jesus. I can earnestly and repeatedly pray that God will work in my inner being to change the things there so that I will be able to obey him. All these and other things can be done as means to fulfilling the vision of life in God that we intend and have chosen.

What we need to emphasize here is simply that the means of spiritual formation are available. In the spiritual life it is actually true that 'where there's a will there's a way'. This is true because God is involved and makes his help available to those who seek it. On the other hand, where there is no will there is no way. People who do not intend to be inwardly transformed will not be. God is not going to pick us up and throw us into transformed kingdom living.

So the problem of spiritual transformation among those who identify themselves as Christians today is not that it is impossible, or that effectual means are not available. The problem is that it is not intended. People do not see its value and decide to carry it through. They do not decide to do the things Jesus did and said. And this largely due to the fact that they have not been given a vision of life in God's kingdom. Life in Christ is not the vision and intention of their life. No wonder the example and teachings of Christ look, to many, more like fairy tales than sober reality.

In the rest of the book we will turn to some of the things that can be done with God's assistance in each of the dimensions of our life to renovate the human heart and progressively form the inner world of the person so that life in Christ can become a realistic vision and an everyday reality. Spiritual formation is, in practice, the way of rest for the weary and overloaded, an easy yoke and a light burden (Matt 11:28–30). It is the process of becoming a good tree that cannot bear bad fruit (Luke 6:43). And it is the path along which God's commandments are found not to be burdensome (1 John 5:3).

Matters for thought and discussion

1. What do you think of John Calvin's understanding of human ruin and deliverance?
2. What do you believe Jesus means when he speaks of the necessity of losing our soul or life and finding it again in him? Try to be as concrete and practical as possible in responding.
3. Why can I not be Jesus' apprentice (disciple) if I do not take my cross and follow him?
4. What does it mean to count the cost?
5. Does St Francis' teaching about 'perfect joy' apply to you? Imagine some ways it might apply, what might actually happen in your situation.
6. Why is giving so central to the restoration of the soul? How does giving depend on the reality of the kingdom?
7. Is being 'dead to self' a realistic goal of growth in Christ? Is it 'healthy'?
8. How would you describe one who is dead to self in real-life, practical terms?
9. How, concretely, can we 'intend to live in the kingdom of God now'?
10. How does *intention* relate to *decision*? Can 'knowing the right answers' substitute for intention and decision in the spiritual life?
11. What are the main *means* that you personally use for implementing your decision to live in the kingdom of God now? Are they adequate to the intention?

INTERLUDE

We have now worked our way through some difficult material that has required careful study and thought. We have distinguished and put into proper relationship aspects of human life and divine operation. But it is very important that we not lose sight of the simplicity of spiritual formation in Christ. Otherwise putting it into practice, by individuals or by leaders of groups, will falsely appear to be difficult or impossible. And the result might be that spiritual formation is not seriously undertaken, or is undertaken in such a way that it will fail.

Individuals sometimes hear of spiritual disciplines, for example, and rightly understand how important they could be for growth in Christlikeness. Perhaps they learn what an effective role the disciplines have played for Christians past or present. But they have no idea how such disciplines fit into the overall process of spiritual formation in Christ. Or, more particularly, they are unable to connect disciplines such as solitude, Scripture memorization, or fasting with the rest of their life.

Now the simplicity of spiritual formation lies in its intention. Its aim is to bring every element in our being, inside and out, into harmony with the will of God and the kingdom of God. This is the simple focus. We must keep it constantly before us and not be distracted by other things, no matter how good they may appear.

Of course we cannot realize this goal on our own. But we don't have to. God has made provision for achieving this aim. To grow in grace means to use God's grace more and more, until everything we do is assisted by grace. Then, whatever we do in word or deed will all be done in the name of the Lord Jesus (Col 3:17). The greatest saint is not one who needs least grace, but the one who uses God's grace most, who, indeed, is most in need of grace. He or she is saturated by grace in every aspect of their being.

In what follows we will look at some things that will be of practical use to us in dealing with each of the six essential aspects of human personality briefly described in chapter 3 above. While we will consider each aspect separately for the sake of clarity, we must all along remain aware that they are not separate in reality and are always interacting in real life.

There are no easy formulas – no definitive 'how-tos' – for growth into Christlikeness. Such growth depends on constant seeking. But there are many things we can do to place ourselves at the disposal of God, and God's promise to us is *you will seek me and find me when you seek me with all your heart* (Jer 29:13). And, as the prophet Azariah said, *the Lord is with you when you are with him. If you seek him, he will be found by you* (2 Chr 15:2). We can count on his goodness. The aim in what follows is to point out some steps by which the seeker can start or progress along the road of spiritual transformation with God.

I have set the Lord always before me.
Because he is at my right hand,
I will not be shaken.
(Ps 16:8)

Jesu, the very thought of Thee,
With sweetness fills my breast;
But sweeter far Thy face to see,
And in Thy presence rest.
(Bernard of Clairvaux, trans. E. Caswall)

CHAPTER 5

TRANSFORMING THE MIND: THE THOUGHT LIFE

The ultimate freedom we have as human beings is the power to select what we will let our minds dwell upon. We are not totally free in this respect. But we do have great freedom here, and even though *dead in trespasses and sins* we still have the ability to retain God in our knowledge, if only in an inadequate manner. And we will surely make progress toward him, for if we truly seek God, he will certainly reveal himself to us. He knows what is really in our hearts. This is the reason why we remain responsible before God even though we are spiritually dead.

What thoughts are

When we talk about our 'thought life', we are talking about all of the ways in which we are conscious of things. That includes our memories, perceptions and beliefs, as well as what we would ordinarily refer to when we say, 'I thought of you yesterday'. Our thoughts determine the orientation of the things we do, and shape the feelings that frame our responses to the world around us. Interestingly, it is easier for us to evoke and to some degree control our feelings by directing our thoughts, than it is for us to evoke thoughts by feeling a certain way. We cannot just choose our feelings. Our feelings are not directly under the control of our will, but they can be directed by our thoughts.

The vast world of the imagination is an important aspect of our thought life. Imagination is our ability to represent things to ourselves in our minds, things possible and impossible, good or bad, creative or destructive. It is part of our essential nature as beings created in the image of God. At a basic level, to plan ahead involves imagination, the ability to conceive and consider something which does not as yet exist. And more than that, what we are able to imagine will shape what we believe, choose, create or do in life.

We will consider the realm of thought under four main headings. These are *ideas*, *images*, *facts* and *thinking* itself.

Ideas

When we talk about ideas, we use the word in two different ways. On the one hand, we might say the invention of the wheel was a good idea. On the other, we talk of the ideas of Wittgenstein. We will be using the second of these senses here. Ideas in this sense are models of, or assumptions about, reality.

Ideas underlie what a society takes for granted. They are patterns of interpretation, historically developed and socially shared. They reflect a society's beliefs, but are much more than any formulated creed. They are habitual ways of thinking about and interpreting things. They are central to our worldview, so much so that we are not aware of them. But our worldview is a cultural construct, a system of ideas distinct to the culture. And we are formed by the patterns of behaviour, the teachings and understandings in which we grow up.

Sociologists and anthropologists have observed that the world of human beings comprises not only the physical reality – the land, sea, plant and animal life – but also a 'symbolic reality' which is superimposed upon the physical reality. Cultures attribute different values to things: cows and pigs, for example, can be eaten in some cultures, but not in others. One symbolic reality which can be shared across cultures is money, essentially attributing value to metal, paper or numbers. These are ideas created by societies over the course of time, ideas which change and develop as the societies themselves change.

A good place to look for the ideas that drive a society is advertising. Cars of all kinds transport people from A to B; chairs have the function of supporting people in a sitting posture; shampoo is useful for washing hair. But what sells these items is the way advertising exploits the ideas that people have when they buy them. Cars are wrapped around with ideas of personal freedom, enhanced sexuality and individuality; chairs represent ideas of style and leisure; shampoos offer cutting-edge scientific progress and enhanced personal attractiveness. Marketing trades on our ideas about ourselves. And the interesting thing about the greater proportion of the ideas used in advertising is that they defy experience. Realistically, sitting in a new car in a traffic jam has the same lack of freedom, sexual appeal and individuality as the same situation in an old car.

This neatly shows how ideas function. They can be manipulated to persuade us to buy things. But at a much deeper level, ideas govern our lives in a way that is difficult to analyse because we take ideas as reality. We take for granted elements of morality, notions of progress, rights, freedom, justice, the reliability of science and mathematics. And in fact we regard people who do not share these ideas as mad or bad, and treat them accordingly.

Spiritual formation must transform ideas

The apostle Paul warned the Ephesians that *our struggle is not against flesh and blood, but against the rulers, against the authorities, against the powers of this dark world and against the spiritual forces of evil in the heavenly realms* (Eph 6:12). These powers and forces are spiritual agencies that work with the idea-systems of evil. Ideas are their main tool for dominating humanity. Christian spiritual reformation is a matter of recognizing in ourselves the idea-systems of evil. The needed transformation is very largely a matter of replacing evil ideas with the ideas that Jesus embodied and taught, and with the culture of the kingdom of God. Paul tells Christians that God has *rescued us from the dominion of darkness and brought us into the kingdom of the Son he loves* (Col 1:13). So, he urges, *your attitude should be the same as that of Christ Jesus* (Phil 2:5). And he writes to the Romans, *Do not conform any longer to the pattern of this world, but be transformed by the renewing of your mind* (Rom 12:2). This is Christian spiritual formation.

Changing ideas, whether those of an individual or a group, is difficult and painful. Genuine conversion is a wrenching experience. It involves the breaking down of a worldview and the acceptance of a different set of ideas. It can cause deep damage to the most intimate of relationships, as Jesus warned (Luke 12:51–53). It can seem like madness or wickedness, precisely because it goes against what everybody takes for granted. And in many parts of the world Christians are persecuted today because they threaten the dominant idea-system of their culture. Jesus himself confronted and undermined an idea-system and was killed for it. But he proved himself greater than any local idea-system. Indeed, his ideas transcend specific cultures because they constitute a complete and consistent worldview. The idea-system of Jesus works anywhere, anytime. But it involves radical change.

Images

Closely associated with ideas are images. Images are usually concrete, and they frequently associate a perception with an emotion. They work by using ideas. The image of a small human being standing in front of, and defying, a column of tanks in Tiananmen Square is imprinted on the memories of many. The contrast of frail humanity and mechanized power is stark. But clearly this is an image that has an entirely different impact from that of a photograph of a child standing beside a tank at a local army base open day. For people in the West, it stands for indomitable humanity, the courage of a lone man against the power of an oppressive regime; democracy resists totalitarianism, the individual affirms life against anonymous, mechanized means of death. For people in the East, the image almost certainly has different overtones.

Jesus understood the significance of images and used them in his parables: for a Jewish audience, a wealthy man's son reduced to feeding pigs was an image not only of financial destitution but also of spiritual destitution. Jesus also used an image that brilliantly conveys both something of himself and his message: the cross. The cross represents the paradox of Jesus' sacrifice – the death that brings life, the triumph of God in the frailty of human flesh. For their own benefit, Jesus' followers need to keep the image of the cross vividly present in their minds.

Strongholds of evil

Ideas and images are part of the way we think and can be used for spiritual enrichment. But they can also be a stronghold of evil. They determine the meanings we assign to what we deal with, and can blind us to the spiritual significance of what lies before us. This is evident over and over again in biblical and in Christian history, and in human life generally. The power for evil of ideas and images cannot be overestimated.

Ideas and images are the primary focus of Satan's efforts to defeat God's purposes with and for humankind. When he undertook to draw Eve away from God, he did not hit her with a stick, but with ideas and images. It was with the idea that she was a free agent, able to make up her own mind about what was good for her. And it was with an image that the fruit was good to eat, and desirable for achieving wisdom. This is how temptation works. God appears to be depriving us of what we want. We associate what we want with what is good, and so we make up our own minds and disobey him. We put ourselves on the throne of the universe, and we decide what is 'good'.

A. W. Tozer did not exaggerate when he wrote:

That our idea of God correspond as nearly as possible to the true being of God is of immense importance to us. Compared with our actual thoughts about Him, our creedal statements are of little consequence. Our real idea of God may lie buried under the rubbish of conventional religious notions and may require an intelligent and vigorous search before it is finally unearthed and exposed for what it is. Only after an ordeal of painful self-probing are we likely to discover what we actually believe about God.

A right conception of God is basic not only to systematic theology but to practical Christian living as well. It is to worship what the foundation is to the temple; where it is inadequate or out of plumb the whole structure must sooner or later collapse. I believe there is scarcely an error in doctrine or a failure in applying Christian ethics that cannot be traced finally to imperfect and ignoble thoughts about God.[1]

A right conception of God is vital, but so is a right conception of ourselves. The modern world often values appearance over reality, and many people suffer from an image of themselves which is false. They feel they are not clever, not good-looking, not talented, not valuable and not lovable. They are then tempted either to despair – to live down to their image of themselves; or to succeed – to prove themselves and others wrong. Henri Nouwen notes:

> Success, popularity and power can indeed present a great temptation, but their seductive quality often comes from the way they are part of a much larger temptation of self-rejection. We have come to believe in the voices that call us worthless and unlovable, then success, popularity and power are easily perceived as attractive solutions . . . Self-rejection is the greatest enemy of the spiritual life because it contradicts the sacred voice that calls us the 'Beloved'. Being the Beloved constitutes the core truth of our existence.[2]

Taking this idea, this profound truth, to heart is an important step towards reorienting our lives. The gospel of Jesus is the only complete answer to the false and destructive ideas and images that control life without God. The process of spiritual formation in Christ is one of progressively replacing destructive ideas and images with the images and ideas of Jesus himself.

Two other factors in our thought life can be used by God to break the power of the toxic system of ideas and images that make us *dead to God.* After he has given us new life we can and must begin to take the initiative in progressively reshaping our thought life. He will accompany us every step of the way, but he will not allow us to be merely passive in our spiritual formation in Christ.

These other two factors are *facts* or *information*, and *thinking* itself.

Information

Paul asks, *How can they believe in the one of whom they have not heard?*
(Rom 10:14). Without correct information our ability to think has
nothing to work on. Indeed, without information we may be afraid
of thinking at all, or simply incapable of thinking straight.

Lack of information can result in all kinds of difficulties, from
unnecessary hardship to stark tragedy. People make avoidable mis-
takes by simply not knowing about resources at a public library or on
the Internet. Thousands of people died in the past because medicine
was practised without knowledge of the processes of infection and
with inadequate hygiene.

The first task of Jesus in his earthly ministry was to proclaim God:
to inform those around him of the availability of eternal life from God
through himself. He made it clear that by putting their confidence in
him, they could immediately enter into eternal life in the kingdom of
heaven. Then Jesus had to combat a lot of false information and bring
to light the truth about the Father (Matt 11:27; John 6:46). He
showed how God is love by using God's power to help people. And he
taught about what the kingdom of heaven is like (Matt 4:23; 9:35).
On the evening before his death, Jesus said to his Father in prayer, *I
have revealed you to those whom you gave me* (John 17:6). Jesus' ministry was one of making known the truth by every means possible.

Failure to know what God is really like and what he asks of us is
destructive. God says through Hosea, *my people are destroyed from
lack of knowledge* (Hos 4:6), and *a people without understanding will
come to ruin!* (4:14). This is the tragic condition of Western culture
today, which has rejected the information about God that God himself has made available.

Thinking

Thinking is the activity of searching out what is true, or cannot be
true, in the light of given facts or assumptions. It interprets and
assimilates the information we have and enables us to see things in
relation to other things. Thinking shows up false or misleading ideas
and images for what they are.

Here is Paul: *If God is for us, who can be against us? He who did not spare his own Son, but gave him up for us all – how will he not also, along with him, graciously give us all things?* (Rom 8:31–32). Paul is thinking, 'if God gave us Jesus, it is hardly imaginable that he will refuse us anything we need'.

Here is Martin Luther standing before his examiners at Worms:

> Unless I am convicted by Scripture and plain reason – I do not accept the authority of popes and councils, for they have contradicted each other – my conscience is captive to the Word of God. I cannot and will not recant anything, for to go against conscience is neither right nor safe. God help me. Amen.

The earliest printed version of his statement added the famous words 'Here I stand, I cannot do otherwise.'[3] Luther is staking his life on what God has revealed in Scripture: he has thought about it and cannot honestly turn from the conclusion that God has said what he means.

And so we must apply our thinking to the Word of God. We must thoughtfully take in God's Word, dwell upon it, ponder its meaning, explore its implications. We must learn the facts of the gospel and devote our powers of thinking to understanding them. Then we must put our understanding into practice, because Christian thinking is not just activity of the brain cells, but a way of life.[4] *We must pay more careful attention, therefore, to what we have heard, so that we do not drift away* (Heb 2:1): thinking and living go together.

The crucial role of good thinking today

Now this is tremendously important for us today. Perhaps we are in a time when it is more important than ever before. To serve God well we must think straight. Crooked thinking, intentional or not, always favours evil. And when the crooked thinking gets elevated into orthodoxy, whether religious or secular, it always costs lives.

Today we are apt to play down the importance of good thinking to strong faith. Some, disastrously, even regard thinking as opposed to faith. They do not realize that in so doing they are not honouring God, but simply yielding to the deeply anti-intellectual currents of Western egalitarianism. It is easy to forget that it is great thinkers who have given direction to the people of God in history: Athanasius and Augustine, Luther and Calvin.

Isaac Watts (born 1674), the composer of such well-known hymns as 'Joy to the world', 'When I survey the wondrous cross', 'Jesus shall reign where'er the sun', 'O God, our help in ages past', and many others, also taught logic and wrote a widely used textbook, *Logic: The Right Use of Reason in the Inquiry after Truth*. Watts's hymns owe much of their power to the depth of thought they contain. That is why we return to them constantly.

Of logic, Watts wrote:

> the great design of this noble science is to rescue our reasoning powers from their unhappy slavery and darkness; and thus, with all due submission and deference, it offers an humble assistance to divine revelation. Its chief business is to relieve the natural weakness of the mind by some better efforts of nature; it is to diffuse a light over the understanding in our inquiries after truth . . . [And] it renders its daily service to wisdom and virtue.[5]

In other words, thinking clearly is to take the information of Scripture into a mind directed and empowered by the Holy Spirit, and to pursue the truth with the resolute intention of living it out. The psalmist sets it out like this:

> *The law of the Lord is perfect, reviving the soul. The statutes of the Lord are trustworthy, making wise the simple. The precepts of the Lord are right, giving joy to the heart. The commands of the Lord are radiant, giving light to the eyes. The fear of the Lord is pure, enduring forever. The ordinances of the Lord are sure and altogether righteous.* (Ps 19:7–8)

As in this passage from the Psalms, thinking about God and his truth moves seamlessly into worship. Thinking is not a cold, dispassionate activity, but one that moves us to deep love of God, and this in turn brings us back to think about him. Thomas Watson wrote this long ago:

The first fruit of love is the musing of the mind upon God. He who is in love, his thoughts are ever upon the object. He who loves God is ravished and transported with the contemplation of God. *When I awake, I am still with thee* (Ps. 139:18). The thoughts are as travellers in the mind. David's thoughts kept heaven-road, 'I am still with Thee.' God is the treasure, and where the treasure is, there is the heart. By this we may test our love to God. What are our thoughts most upon? Can we say we are ravished with delight when we think on God? Have our thoughts got wings? Are they fled aloft? Do we contemplate Christ and glory? Oh, how far are they from being lovers of God, who scarcely ever think of God! *God is not in all his thoughts* (Ps. 10:4). A sinner crowds God out of his thoughts. He never thinks of God, unless with horror, as the prisoner thinks of the judge.[6]

In heaven myriads of myriads of angels worship God: *Worthy is the Lamb, who was slain, to receive power and wealth and wisdom and strength and honour and glory and praise!* (Rev 5:12–13). They see and know and are lost in wonder at the majesty of God. But how sadly far from that glorious vision is our own vision and understanding of God. A. W. Tozer continues the passage quoted earlier as follows:

> It is my opinion that the Christian conception of God current in these middle years of the twentieth century is so decadent as to be utterly beneath the dignity of the Most High God and actually to constitute for professed believers something amounting to a moral calamity.

Why a *moral* calamity? Because absolutely nothing can inform, guide and sustain radical and radiant goodness in people than this true vision of God and the worship based it. The closer we are to the reality of God, the more he will fill our thoughts and transform our lives.

Thinking about God can and should be a life of worship. And worship is the single most powerful force in completing and sustaining restoration in the whole person. It subdues every evil tendency. Worship is at once the overall characteristic of the renovated thought life and the safest place for a human being to be.

An old hymn contains these lines:

> In our astonished reverence we confess
> Thine uncreated loveliness.

'Astonished reverence' is a good description of worship, as is 'admiration to the point of wonder and delight', as Tozer put it. The first petition in the Lord's Prayer is *hallowed be Thy name*. It is first because it is the most important. When God is exalted and revered in the minds of people, and his very name is cherished with utmost respect, the world is in its proper order. And when we pray that prayer, our lives are in proper order.

The effect of putting God first in our thoughts will be the transformation of our entire life. Everything else that enters our mind, and our reaction to the unexpected things that we encounter, will be properly ordered. The conclusions we reach will be in harmony with the realities of a God-governed universe. When I do a job, I will do it with God's power; when I face an emergency, I will meet it knowing that God is in it with me; if I am praised or reproached, elated or frustrated, I can be sure that God is over all, and that *in all things God works for the good of those who love him, who have been called according to his purpose* (Rom 8:28).

Dangers

There are, however, several pitfalls in this area which should be noted and guarded against.

First is pride. When we have learned from Scripture and thought about what we have learned, it is all too easy for us to turn it into a formula. Pride in doctrine, practice and tradition can masquerade as focus on God: 'We do it this way because God has told us to, and it is obviously the right way to do it.'

Second is simple ignorance of fact. A repeated story is of someone who has set out to prove Christianity untrue, and has ended up convinced it is true. In nearly every case this is simply because they were forced to examine the facts and to think carefully about them. As C. S. Lewis's Screwtape points out, a young atheist can't be too careful about what he reads, and must steadfastly protect his ignorance!

But even Christians can wilfully preserve their ignorance about important matters, including possible objections to faith in Christ and the beliefs and practices of other Christians. If we are to use our minds rightly, we must live in an attitude of openness and willingness to learn. Before we come to conclusions about serious matters we need to look into the facts and carefully consider their implications. Pride in our tradition and ignorance of fact all too often lead to disagreement between Christians.

Third is allowing our desires to control our thinking. Not everything in Scripture or life is clear-cut. On the one hand we want to be right, and on the other we can't face the implications of some things we believe. So sometimes we would rather win an argument than understand someone else's point of view, and at other times we fail to admit the unpalatable facts. If we allow our desires to control our thinking we can become at one extreme self-righteous, and at the other extreme dishonest.

We have to acknowledge that desires come into play in questions of faith. Often a good starting point in evangelism is to ask someone who does not believe in God what kind of God they do not believe in. It often appears that they have a very clear idea of what kind of God they do not believe in, and almost as often why they do not *want to* believe in that kind of God. We could argue and prove to our satisfaction that God exists, but fail to deal honestly with the questions and desires and ideas the person has. And in the process we could also fail to deal honestly with why we want our beliefs to be true.

We should make it a rule never to try merely to prove that we are right, and never to gloss over the difficult facts in life, history and faith.

A final danger has to do with the images that we admit into our minds. We have already seen that the idea of freedom is one of the most powerful ideas of Western culture. People resent being limited or controlled or restricted in almost any way. This has all kinds of resonances for Christians, especially as Paul wrote, *it is for freedom that Christ has set us free* (Gal 5:1). But he continued, *stand firm, then, and do not let yourselves be burdened again by a yoke of slavery.* The fact is that practising some kinds of 'freedom' can lead to bondage: 'garbage in, garbage out' nowhere has greater force than in the spiritual life.

If God's *eyes are too pure to look on evil* (Hab 1:13), we had better think it might be wise for us to look away from quite a lot of what passes for entertainment. We are free, and our most basic freedom, our first and primary freedom, is to choose what we allow into our minds. Anyone who thinks that if I have a right to do or see something it is *good* for me to see or do it, simply has not thought clearly about the matter. Paul's wise counsel was that Christians should exercise the right to choose: *whatever is true, whatever is noble, whatever is right, whatever is pure, whatever is lovely, whatever is admirable – if anything is excellent or praiseworthy – think about such things* (Phil 4:8). Make no mistake, this is a fundamental and indispensable part of our spiritual formation in Christ.

Images, as we saw earlier, are powerful because they link taken-for-granted ideas with emotions. In other words, they work at a subconscious level. Yet we can still choose which images we dwell upon. We must take care that we are nourished constantly on good and godly ones, so that we *do not give the devil a foothold* (Eph 4:27) in our lives and thoughts.

A way forward

Now there are no easy formulas in the spiritual life. But a key in this thought aspect of life is the V-I-M pattern. This chapter has dealt almost exclusively with the VISION part of the pattern. The greatest need lies there, and without it nothing will happen.

The INTENTION to be formed is to have the great God and Father of our Lord Jesus Christ a constant presence in our mind, crowding out every false idea or destructive image. Our intention is to use divinely powerful weapons which *have divine power to demolish strongholds.* And so, ultimately, to *demolish arguments and every pretension that sets itself up against the knowledge of God, and we take captive every thought to make it obedient to Christ* (2 Cor 10:4–5). Paul makes it clear in this passage that this is something *we* have to do. God will not do it for us: but he has provided the means for us to do it.

Once you have the vision and intention there, the means can be found. There are disciplines which we can use to help transform our thought life.[7] Disciplines are activities which enable us to do what we otherwise could not. Disciplines are processes of training. Just now, I could not swim 500 metres non-stop; but if I went into training I could probably do it in a couple of weeks. Just because we want to, we cannot transform the ideas and images, or the information and thought patterns we currently have. But if we train ourselves, adopt certain disciplines, we will in due course and increasingly be able to do that.

The most obvious thing we can do is to memorize and turn over in our minds key portions of Scripture. This is the primary discipline for the thought life. And not just odd verses, but longer passages. We need to know them like the back of our hand. And if you think this is impossible for you, think again. You can remember all sorts of things, and you can remember Scripture too. As you do, your mind will be filled with light, and your life will be reoriented around God, because you are choosing to focus on him and are spending time and effort on this permanently worthwhile activity.

Similarly, we need to choose the images we will allow to stay in our minds. Christian art, ancient or modern, is little appreciated today for no good reason. Music, poetry, and pictures can channel our thoughts towards God. The music of Bach, the poetry of Watts or Herbert or the Wesleys, and the two millennia of Christian architecture, sculpture, painting and drawing – all these can stir us and calm us, challenge us and reassure us, take us to the depths and lift us to the heights. They nourish us emotionally and intellectually.

Of course we need to do all these things that focus our thoughts on God not only on our own, but also with others. Spiritual formation cannot, in the nature of the case, be entirely a private thing, because it is a matter of whole-life transformation. We need to seek out others who are pursuing the renovation of the heart. They might be members of our own family, or a nearby congregation of Christians. We must pray that God will lead us to others who can accompany us.

Some of these will be writers from the past, and others, those who have been written about. We can learn a great deal from those who have written truly about living the Christian life, and from those who have lived it faithfully. Some excellent collections of spiritual writings have been published in recent years, and friends and companions in the way of renovation can be found among these writers.[8] It is easy to imagine that only modern writing will be relevant to us, but a glance at writers from Augustine to Bonhoeffer will dispel that illusion. The challenges facing us may be different, and the style of these writers may sometimes be difficult, but we share the desire to honour Christ and these are people who can help.

There is much more to be said on the details of the MEANS of transforming our thought life. But if we focus on God through his Word and walk in the way of those who know by experience the transformation of the mind, we will share in that transformation.

The power of thought

The simple power of ideas, images, information and thought is so great that it is used and manipulated for all kinds of ends. Advertising associates ideas and positive emotions in powerful images to persuade us to buy things. Aversion therapy, by contrast, uses images in association with pain or negative emotion in order to train people not to commit crime. Some false religions harness the power of thought to give leaders control over adherents.

Just because mental processes can be abused, it does not mean that using mental processes is wrong in itself. Effective spiritual formation in Christ requires a realistic understanding and careful use of the power of thought. We should thoughtfully and prayerfully assess the means of spiritual formation available to us, and consider whether they meet the criteria, firstly of the highest standard of cooperation with the Holy Spirit's work of giving glory to Jesus in every way, and secondly of meeting our human need for spiritual formation. The biblical way of transformation is in clear contrast to other ways, even if these other ways use what sounds like biblical language. It is a sobering thought that many 'alternative' paths of human help and healing are popular today largely because people have not been able to see the reality of spiritual transformation in Christians.

Matters for thought and discussion

1. What are three thoughts that have occupied your mind this week? Why those thoughts, and not others? What have their effects on your life been?

2. What are the main ideas that rule our society today? Do you think they favour a godly life or hinder it?

3. What are the major ideas Jesus brought into human history and how do you see them affecting the contemporary world? Think broadly, and of parts of our world unaffected by Christian teaching.

4. Think about the distinction between ideas and images. Where do you see images most at work in our lives today?

5. What images of God seem most common and influential in our world? How about in your own thinking and devotional life? In that of your friends?

6. Reflect on the gospel as basic information about reality. Is that a good way to think of it? What are the alternatives to thinking of it in that way?

7. Should followers of Jesus Christ be known as thinkers? Is thinking actually a good thing for Christians to do? How might it help us? Is it dangerous?

8. What is worship? How are thought, worship and spiritual formation related?

9. What steps can we take to make sure that thought is rightly directed and used in the process of spiritual formation? How can images help that process?

*The kingdom of God is not a matter of eating
and drinking, but of righteousness, peace and joy
in the Holy Spirit.*
(Rom 14:17)

*Those who belong to Christ Jesus have crucified
the sinful nature with its passions and desires.*
(Gal 5:24)

CHAPTER 6

TRANSFORMING THE MIND: SENSATION AND EMOTION

Feelings are a blessing and a problem. We cannot live without them and we can hardly live with them. Spiritual formation must deal with them if it is to be real and lasting.

Feelings encompass a range of things that are felt: sensations, desires and emotions. We feel warm, hungry, an itch or afraid. Feelings include dizziness and thirst, sleepiness and weariness, sexual interest and desire, pain and pleasure, loneliness and homesickness, anger and jealousy, comfort and satisfaction, a sense of power and accomplishment, curiosity and intellectual gratification, compassion for others and the enjoyment of beauty, a sense of honour, and delight in God. There is no complete list of human feelings. A familiar range of feelings frame our day-to-day existence, and we know these feelings are important to our lives and to how we act and relate to one another.

Our first inquiry as we greet people is likely to be 'How are you?' Feelings clamour for attention. They need no justification, no argument, they are just there. Feelings are natural and powerful, and we shudder if we encounter someone who apparently lacks them. Feelings are a point of contact with someone or something else, a 'touch' that communicates something to us. We do not always understand what is communicated, and why we feel what we feel, but we know we have been touched. The power of feelings can be simply overwhelming.

Feeling is natural and essential to life. We know, for example, that feelings move us, and that often we enjoy being so moved. Feelings give us a sense of being alive. Without feelings we would have no interest in things, no inclination to action. 'Losing interest in life' means having to carry on by mere willpower or by passively waiting for things to happen. That is a condition to be dreaded. And it is one of the reasons why people become dependent upon substances which heighten feeling, or activities that give them feelings, even if the dependency harms them and those closest to them.

The attraction of feeling is so great that we project it on to other beings, imagined or real. In Tolkien's *The Lord of the Rings*, the immortal Elf Arwen gives up immortality for love of Aragorn. A more recent theme in art and literature is that of angels wishing to know what it is like to have a fleshly body and feel what humans feel. In the film *City of Angels*, Nicholas Cage's character makes the switch from angel to human. Asked if it was worth it, he replies, 'I would rather have had . . . one kiss of her lips, one touch of her hand, than an eternity without it.' The film closes with the angel-human frolicking in the surf at sunset and the landscape full of angels, now including Meg Ryan, watching with either envy or delight at his pleasure. When you reflect on what is involved, both the blindness and power associated with feelings becomes obvious. The theology or angelology is pretty weak, but the story clearly demonstrates the idolatry of feeling that is current today. There has been a shift from the obvious notion that feelings are natural and powerful, to the idea that they are therefore right and good, ultimately desirable and worth any sacrifice. They have become almost a moral absolute. Many people want to assert that *any* feeling is better than no feeling at all.

Deciding by how we feel

All of this has special relevance to contemporary life. We live in a world suspicious of the patterns, forms and disciplines of the past.

Time-worn rituals and moral authorities no longer govern our lives. Societal structures have been loosened and in some cases destroyed. Rights are more important than responsibilities, the individual is more important than the forms of relationship in a coherent society.

Fundamentally, what I want is more important than what others can expect or demand of me. Choice is my ability to assert my will, and it is the great desideratum of the modern world. It hardly matters that industrialization and mass production have made choice in many cases almost redundant – choice between products and lifestyles almost indistinguishable from each other. In this world, feeling exercises almost total mastery over the individual. This is because people constantly have to decide what they want, and feeling is all they have to go on. People are overwhelmed with decisions and can only make those decisions on the basis of feeling.

More than a century ago, Leo Tolstoy experienced some of the effects of the breakdown of the old social pattens in the circles of wealthy, upper-class Russians who made up his world. In that world, he relates, 'My life came to a standstill. I could breathe, eat, drink, and sleep, and I could not help doing these things; but there was no life, for there were no wishes the fulfilment of which I could consider reasonable.' He continues, 'Had a fairy come and offered to fulfil my desires, I should not have known what to ask.'[1] This is exactly the world of pointless activity portrayed in such staples of contemporary consciousness as television's *Cheers, Seinfeld, Friends* and *Will and Grace.*[2]

In the course of events, however, Tolstoy became involved in the life of the Russian peasants. He says:

> I saw that the whole life of these people was passed in heavy labor, and that they were content with life . . . And they all – endlessly different in their manners, minds, education, and position, as they were – all alike, in complete contrast to my ignorance, knew the meaning of life and death, labored quietly, endured deprivations and sufferings, and lived and died seeing therein not vanity but good. (p. 57)

The peasants whom Tolstoy admired were not yet swallowed up by the directionless choices of the modern world. They had solid traditions of faith and community that provided a meaningful form of life and death. The result was that they knew what was good to do without regard to their feelings. Good was not determined for them by how they felt or by what they thought was the best deal.[3]

The same was true for the homemaker and the wage-earner of our recent past. This is not to say that all was well with them or with Tolstoy's peasants. But individuals knew what to do with their time without thinking about it, and were rarely faced with having to do what they felt like doing. The overall order in which they lived usually gave them strength and inner freedom derived from their sense of place and direction, even in the midst of suffering and frustration.

Today, by contrast, people constantly have to decide what to do, and they are almost invariably governed by feelings. Often they cannot distinguish between their feelings and their will, and, in their confusion, they also quite commonly take feelings to be reasons. And since feelings are essentially the means of negotiating the choices, people in general lack self-control. Choice is between competing available alternatives rather than between having or not having, doing or not doing. Soaring debt is evidence of this fact.

Addiction

The modern sensibility, with its emphasis on 'spontaneity' and enjoying the 'rush' or the 'buzz' of feeling, can provide a way into addiction. Abandoning ourselves to feeling, allowing ourselves to be 'carried away', is exhilarating. It is actually sought by many, and on a regular basis. People want to feel, and to feel strongly.[4] Feeling is sought for its own sake; and as feeling fades, stronger feeling and greater stimulus is demanded. Feeling seems to offer an escape from the situation described by Thoreau, where 'the mass of men lead lives of quiet desperation'; but in fact the urgent demand for feeling and satisfaction is an aspect of that very 'quiet (or not so quiet) desperation'.

This simple point is what explains the powerful grip of addiction in the modern world, including various forms of sexual perversion, violence, alcohol or drug abuse, or self-aggrandizement. Addiction is a feeling phenomenon. Addicts are those who, in one way or another, have given in to feelings of one kind or another, and placed them in the position of ultimate value in their lives. They have inwardly conceded the final word to some feeling, emotion, sensation or desire. They may fear or even hate that feeling, but they can see no way out, and the feeling demands to be satisfied. Habit and chemical dependency can make a tragic mess of ordinary lives, but the less obviously tragic addictions are nearly as destructive.

Feelings and conditions

The relationship between feelings and conditions of life is complex. Love, for example, can be an intoxicating feeling, but it can also be a settled, sometimes teeth-gritted, determination to act in the best interests of the person loved. We tend today to associate 'love' with the feeling and not with the condition. Another example might be 'peace': we tend to associate it with the feeling of looking out over sunlit hills with nothing to trouble us, but peace can be a condition of life present and working when a person is under extreme pressure and making difficult and vital decisions.

Now there are some extremely serious dangers here. When we confuse the condition with the feeling we will very likely try to manage or produce the feelings and disregard or deny the conditions. That way lie such things as 'falling in love with love' and many other feeling-dependencies or addictions. The person who primarily wants the feeling of being 'in love' will be incapable of sustaining loving relationships. And the person who primarily wants the feeling of peace will be unable to do the things that make for peace, especially the hard things like doing what is right and confronting evil.

This illustrates the fact that feelings help to shape our view of the world. Feelings in themselves are not rational, and we don't decide that we are going to feel happy or sad. Conditions of life are much more the product of rationality: we do in fact choose whether or not to love others in a long-term, committed way, or indeed to love ourselves. But it is sometimes hard to draw the line between the feelings and the condition. Feelings spread through our lives and attitudes, they become hardened by habit, and they affect how we respond and can even determine the tendency and outcome of our life as a whole. In Shakespeare's *Twelfth Night* falling in love, while generally regarded as a good and wholesome thing, is spoken of as 'catching the plague'; and Malvolio, the main butt of the comedy, is 'sick of self-love'. On the one hand, the feeling of falling in love is like catching a disease – it is involuntary, and makes a person do strange things. On the other, the settled concern with himself that characterizes Malvolio is a sickness, a condition that leaves him untouched by the fun and happiness that the rest of the play generates.

The involuntary nature of feeling explains why it is so hard to reason with some people. Their very mind has been taken over by feelings and the mind is made to defend and serve those feelings. Thoughts are shaped and formed by the feelings, and feelings are generated by the thoughts. For example, a woman (it could just as well be a man) who has taken in the thought that she has been treated unfairly for years in her marriage and her job. She feels aggrieved. Rather than addressing the circumstances or just turning her mind away from this thought, she receives it and broods over it for years, developing a tremendous sense of injustice and outrage, which she also welcomes and cultivates with the aid of sympathetic friends. This bitterness gradually spreads over her whole personality, seeping deeply into her body and her soul. It becomes something you can see on her face and in her actions and hear oozing through the language she uses. It affects her capacity to see what is actually going on around her, to realize what she is actually doing, and to think thoroughly and consistently. She is in what Bob Mumford has called 'the prison of resentment', though she thinks she is free.

Beyond the individual level, poisonous emotions and sensations can take over entire social groups, blinding them and impelling them on terrible courses of action. This is nearly always the root cause of ethnic strife. Combined with a sense of rightness, strong feeling becomes impervious to reason. Thus to the onlooker, the participants seem to be deaf, blind and insane – which, in a sense, they are. They are imprisoned by resentment, fear, or anger, and simply cannot see the point of view of their opponents. Oliver Cromwell once famously wrote to the General Assembly of the Church of Scotland, 'I beseech you, in the bowels of Christ, think it possible you may be mistaken' (3 August 1650), but perhaps the point is that when we think we are right and when we feel resentment against an opponent, it is extremely difficult even to imagine we may be mistaken.

Feelings good and bad

Our obsession with feelings is directly contrary to the wisdom of the past. It is in fact another way of characterizing the lost, those who make themselves 'god' in this world. To such, the idea that they should not honour their feelings is an insult. Paul puts it succinctly: *their god is their stomach* (Phil 3:19). The Jewish philosopher Spinoza put it differently, referring to human reliance on feelings and the circumstances which produce them as 'human bondage'.[5]

The good Samaritan, in Jesus' parable (Luke 10:30–37), was distinguished from the priest and the Levite by the fact that, confronted by human need, he acted to help the man who had been attacked: *when he saw him, he took pity on him* (33). The Samaritan was moved by the plight of the man half-dead beside the road. Did the priest and the Levite have no feelings? Of course not. They had feelings, perhaps fear of a similar fate to that of the man lying there, perhaps a sense of urgency as they thought of the need to get to their destination, perhaps the awareness that the precious opportunity of serving in the Temple would be forfeited if they were to touch anything unclean, especially what looked like a corpse. Whatever they might have thought, their feelings motivated them to abandon the man. They acted in what was ultimately a selfish manner because they put their own desires before the obvious need of the man lying beside the road. Whereas the Samaritan acted as a *neighbour* to him. There are, then, feelings that produce good actions, and feelings that produce ultimately selfish and destructive actions.

Christians will instinctively identify with the Samaritan in his neighbourly action. But the Bible warns that even towards our nearest and dearest we can sometimes have deeply destructive feelings. James pointedly asks, *What causes fights and quarrels among you? Don't they come from your desires that battle within you? You want something but don't get it. You kill and covet, but you cannot have what you want. You quarrel and fight* (Jas 4:1–2). And elsewhere he points out that *where you have envy and selfish ambition, there you find disorder and every evil practice* (Jas 3:16). It is sobering to remind ourselves that James was writing to church people.

The Old Testament book of Proverbs is full of wise sayings about the good and evil of feelings in human life. As we have already seen, *the fear of the Lord is the beginning of wisdom* (9:10). Then, *hatred stirs up dissension, but love covers over all wrongs* (10:12), and *a heart at peace gives life to the body, but envy rots the bones* (14:30). And again, *the cheerful heart has a continual feast* (15:15), and *a cheerful heart is good medicine, but a crushed spirit dries up the bones* (17:22). This is a book which makes very clear distinctions between feelings that are good and life enriching, and feelings that are destructive.

Mastery of feeling

How can we deal with feelings? This is a vital question for spiritual formation. We all have destructive feelings sometimes. The answer to these destructive feelings is not to deny that we have them or try to repress them. We should not, of course, dump them on others by acting them out. But the answer to our problem is not repression. The proper course of action is to replace destructive feelings with others that are good, or to subordinate them intelligently to a rational order so that they become constructive. It is part of divine and human wisdom to realize that feelings are central to our existence and to make sure they are good, strong, healthy feelings. We do not have to be subject to destructive feelings. Even harmful feelings are, for the most part, not bad in themselves, but are somehow not properly limited or subordinated. They are out of order. Feelings are, with a few exceptions, good servants, but disastrous masters. The process of spiritual formation in Christ will transform our feelings by grace.

Now one thing quickly becomes clear when you think about the power of feeling. No-one can succeed in mastering feelings in their life who tries simply to take them head-on and resist or redirect them by willpower in the moment of choice. To adopt that strategy is to misunderstand radically how life and the human will work, or, more likely, it is actually to have decided, deep down, to lose the battle and give in. This is one of the major areas of self-deception in the human heart. The very act of giving in can be among the most exhilarating feelings, though it can also be one of complete despair and defeat. Those who continue to be mastered by their feelings, whether it is anger, fear, resentment, sexual desire, appetite for food, wanting to look good, or whatever, are typically people who in their heart of hearts believe that their feelings must be satisfied. They have long chosen the strategy of selectively resisting their feelings instead of that of not having them, of changing or replacing them. They have no real basis on which to deal with their feelings.

By contrast, people who happily let God be God do have a basis on which to deal with their feelings. They have the resources to act against the demands of their feelings if necessary. They know and accept that their feelings, of whatever kind, do not have to be fulfilled. They spend little time grieving over this, because they know they are growing in character. And with respect to feelings that are injurious and destructive, their strategy is not one of resisting them in the moment of choice, but of living in such a way that they do not have such feelings. Those who let God be God get off the conveyer belt of emotion and desire when it first starts to move toward the buzz saw of sin. They do not wait until it is moving so fast they cannot get off. Their first aim is not to avoid sin, but to avoid temptation, the inclination to sin. They plan their path accordingly. So far as possible, they walk away from painful and destructive feelings.

Healthy feelings, properly ordered among themselves, are essential to a good life. So if we are to be formed in Christlikeness we must take good care of our feelings and not just let them happen. Feelings can be regulated by ordered, godly habits and self-control. Self-control is the steady capacity to direct yourself to accomplish what you have chosen or decided to do and be, even though you don't feel like it. Self-control means that you, with steady hand, do what you don't want to do (or what you want not to), when that is needed, and do not do what you want to do (what you feel like doing) when that is needed. A powerful feeling may blot out everything else, and will invariably do so in those who have not trained themselves to be critical of their own feelings. But feelings can be reasoned with, can be corrected by reality, in those who have the habit and are given the grace of listening to reason even when they are subject to violent feelings. The psalmist questions his feelings of dejection, *Why are you downcast, O my soul? Why so disturbed within me?* (Ps 42:11), and answers himself, *Put your hope in God, for I will yet praise him, my Saviour and my God.*

Beyond feelings

A first step is to desire sincerely feelings that lead away from sin. At this early stage, we need to want to turn away from the things that seem attractive to our sinful nature, to want to want what we do not now want! We have to feel a strong attraction to good feelings that we do not presently feel. So, for example, we do not merely want to not verbally assault people, or not to fall into fornication, but we really want to feel genuine love for others. This is part of what Paul means when he tells Christians to *put off your old self, which is being corrupted by its deceitful desires* (Eph 4:22), and *be made new in the attitude of your minds.*

If a strong and compelling vision of myself as one who is free from vanity or desire for wealth or for sexual indulgence can possess me, then I am in a position to change, and be made new in the attitude of my mind. I can have desires that I do not currently have, and not have desires that I now have. And means can be effectively sought to those ends. The V-I-M pattern of change will work here as elsewhere.

The vision

But achieving this new vision of myself will not be at a mere snap of the fingers. It will require genuine openness to radical change in myself, careful and creative instruction, and abundant supplies of divine grace. For most people all of this only comes to them after they hit rock-bottom and discover the total hopelessness of being who they are. Most people cannot imagine who they would be without the fears, angers, lusts, power ploys and woundedness with which they have lived so long. They identify with their habit-worn feelings.

When Jesus asked the man by the pool of Bethesda, waiting for the angel to stir the water, *Do you want to get well?*, he was not just passing the time of day (John 5:6). We are not told how old the man was, but he had been in his disabled condition for thirty-eight years. If he got well, he would have to deal with a career change of immense proportions. To all his relatives and acquaintances he would no long-er be the disabled man whom they took to the pool every day to wait for the angel. He would be . . . what? How would he even identify himself? How would he relate to others and they to him? How would he get on in life, and what would he do for work?

But really this man's problems were nothing compared to those faced by people undergoing the transformation of feelings, emotions, sensations and desires, from those learned at home, in school and in work, to those that characterize the inner being of Jesus Christ. People undergoing this transformation will no longer spend hours fantasizing about sensual indulgence or revenge, or try to dominate or injure others in attitude, word or deed. They will not repay evil for evil, push for push, blow for blow, taunt for taunt, hatred for hatred, contempt for contempt. They will not be always on the hunt to satisfy the *cravings of sinful man, the lust of his eyes and the boasting of what he has and does* (1 John 2:16). No wonder that they have no real idea of who they will be, and must content themselves with the mere identity 'apprentice of Jesus'. That is the starting point from which this new identity will emerge, and it is in fact powerful enough to bear the load.

Godly feelings

Now the realm of feelings may appear at first sight to be an area of total chaos. But this is not so. There is order among feelings, and it is a much simpler one than most people think. When we properly cultivate with divine assistance those few feelings that should be prominent in our lives, the remainder will fall into place.

What then are the feelings that will dominate in a life inwardly transformed to be like Christ's? They are the feelings associated with love, joy and peace. These are not in fact only feelings but conditions of the whole person that are accompanied by positive feelings.

Love, joy and peace are, we recall, the three basic dimensions of the fruit (singular) of the Holy Spirit. They inform one another and express themselves in the remainder of that one fruit, *patience, kindness, goodness, faithfulness, gentleness and self-control* (Gal 5:22–23).

Faith and hope are also very important in properly structuring the feeling dimension of the mind and self. But they play their role in that regard in subordination to love, joy and peace – that is, because of their relationship to them. The three primary dimensions of the fruit, love, joy and peace, are in fact not separable from the three things of 1 Corinthians 13:13 that endure for eternity, namely faith, hope and love. They are aspects of the same character. All are focused on goodness and what is good, and all are strength-giving and pleasant even in the midst of pain or suffering. That is not what we seek them for, or something we try to make of them. It is, simply, their natural attire.

Hope and faith

Hope is anticipation of good not yet here, or as yet unseen. It is inseparable from joy. Sometimes the good in question is deliverance from an evil which is present. *But*, as Paul writes, *if we hope for what we do not yet have, we wait for it patiently* (Rom 8:24–25) and we are *joyful in hope, patient in affliction, faithful in prayer* (12:12). That eager anticipation strengthens us to stay faithful to God and to stay on the path of what is right.

One of the remarkable changes brought by Jesus and his people into the ancient world was the elevation of hope into a primary virtue. Hope was not well regarded by the Graeco-Roman world. It was thought of as a desperate measure. And while, according to the myth of Pandora's box, it may be all we have left with which to endure the agonies of life, it must be grimly held in check, or it will give rise to vain expectations that only cause more misery. Christ, by contrast, brings solid hope for humanity.

Clearly, then, hope also is closely related to faith. Faith is confidence grounded in reality, not a wild, desperate leap in the dark. It is, as Hebrews 11:1 says in the Authorized Version, *the substance of things hoped for, the evidence of things not seen*, not as contemporary translations usually have it, subjective psychological states such as *being sure of* or *having a conviction of* something. Faith sees the reality of the unseen or invisible, and it includes a readiness to act as if the good anticipated in hope were already in hand because of the reality of God (cp. 2 Cor 4:17–18). Jeremy Taylor drives the point home with these words: 'He that believes dares trust God for the morrow, and is not more solicitous for the next year than he is for that which is past.'[6] No-one worries about what was going to happen last year.

Faith and hope the foundation

Romans 5:1–5 outlines an instructive and inspiring progression from an initial faith in God through Christ, with an accompanying initial hope, to a subsequent or higher-level hope that *does not disappoint us*. The apostle Paul writes this way because, in the progression of our experience, the Holy Spirit pours out into our own hearts the kind of love God has. This important passage needs to be studied in depth for an adequate understanding of spiritual formation in Christlikeness, especially as it concerns feelings.

Initial faith in Christ gives us *peace with God through our Lord Jesus Christ, through whom we have gained access . . . into this grace in which we now stand* (1–2). This is new birth into Christ's kingdom. It puts an end to the war between us and God that has gone on most of our life and surrounds us with God's grace. Now, because of Christ's death for us and his continuing grace, we know that God is good, and we are thrilled with the hope that God's goodness and greatness will serve as the basis of our own existence as well as of everything else. Thus *we rejoice in the hope of the glory of God* (2).

This opens the path for transformation of our character. We are also thrilled about our tribulations! We know that they will prove God's power and faithfulness in love to us, and to trust him in all things becomes the settled character of our life. So *we also rejoice in our sufferings, because we know that suffering produces perseverance; [and] perseverance, character* (3–4; cp. Jas 1:2–4).

But godly character now brings about a different quality of hope (4). Character is a matter of our entire personality and life, which has now been transformed by the process of perseverance under God. Hope therefore now pervades our life as a whole. And this new and pervasive hope, which is an outgrowth of our initial *hope of the glory of God* but now covers our entire life, *does not disappoint us, because God has poured out his love into our hearts by the Holy Spirit, whom he has given us* (5:5).

Thus, faith in Christ and the initial hope it inspires lead us to stand in the grace of God, and standing there leads, in turn, to a life full of love. We will want to see how this love relates to joy and peace, as well as to the rest of the fruit of the Spirit. But first we need to get a clearer picture of love itself, of the four movements required to complete its work in our life, of how, when completed, it *drives out fear* (1 John 4:18). Then we shall see the effect of all this on the feeling aspect of our life.

Love

And first, what exactly is love? It is will-to-good or benevolence. We love something or someone when we promote their good for their own sake. Love's contrary is malice, and its simple absence is indifference. Its normal accompaniment is delight, but a twisted soul may delight in evil and take no pleasure in good. Love is not the same thing as desire, for I may desire something without wishing it well, much less willing its good. This is the difference between lust, or mere desire, and love, as between a man and a woman. Desire and love are of course compatible when desire is ruled by love; but many people today do not even know the difference between them. Hence in our world love constantly falls prey to lust. That is part of the deep sickness of contemporary life.

By contrast, what characterizes the deepest essence of God, is love: that is, will-to-good. His creation of the world expresses his will-to-good, and he found his world *very good* (Gen 1:31). His love and goodwill toward humans is not an add-on to a nature that is indifferent; it is another expression of what he always and in every respect is. It is not hard for God to love; it is impossible for him not to love.

Our nature is not like that of its maker, though it was intended to be. Love is not natural in our world, though desire or lust certainly is *everything in the world – the cravings of sinful man, the lust of his eyes and the boasting of what he has and does*, the apostle says, *comes not from the Father but from the world* (1 John 2:16). Pride and boasting are the products of desire, not of love. They result from the assumption that our desires should be fulfilled, and that it is an injustice, an injury, if they are not.

Lust and pride all around us inevitably result in a world of fear. For they bring us into a world of little dictators, and the most likely thing is that people will be used and abused, even destroyed, by others, and not helped and cared for with love. Our families, which should be a refuge from such a world sadly often turn out to be where victimization is worst. The young are initiated into an adult world hardened in evil. Injury brings pain and loss, then fear and anger, which mingles with resentment and contempt and settles into attitudes of coldness and malice, with brutal feelings that drain the body of health and strength and shatter social well-being.

Four movements toward love

In such a world God intrudes, gently and in many ways, but especially in the person of Jesus Christ. He stands for love as no-one else has ever done, and pays the price for it. His crucifixion is the greatest mark of love on earth: *when we were still powerless, Christ died for the ungodly* (Rom 5:6). Nothing, whether inside or outside religion, even comes close to what God in Christ shows of love. This is the first movement of love in the process of redemption. *He first loved us* (1 John 4:19), and so, *love comes from God* (1 John 4:7). Therefore, *this is how we know what love is: Jesus Christ laid down his life for us* (1 John 3:16). All other loves are to be measured by this standard.

When we receive what is thus clearly given, the revelation of God's love in Christ, that in turn makes it possible for us to love. Love is awakened in us by him. We feel its call, first to love Jesus himself, and then God. Thus the first great commandment, to love God with all our being, can be fulfilled because of the beauty of God given in Christ. This is the second movement in the return to love: *we love because he first loved us.*

The second movement is inseparable from the third movement: our love of others who love God. *If we love one another, God lives in us and his love is made complete in us* (1 John 4:12). The first great commandment makes it possible to fulfil the second: love of neighbour as oneself. And loving others under God will assure that we are loved by others. For to the others in our community of love we are the others whom they love because they love and are loved by God. The fellowship of Christ's apprentices is a community of love (John 13:34–35). This is the fourth movement in the process of redeeming love.

Here, then, is a full account of the movements of love in our lives: we are loved by God who is love, and in turn we love him, and others through him, who in turn love us through him. Thus is love made perfect or complete. And *perfect love drives out fear* (1 John 4:18). That is, those who live in the fulfilment of God's redemptive love in human life will no longer experience the kind of fear we have been talking about. *Fear has to do with punishment,* John notes, and punishment is incompatible with living in the full cycle of love (1 John 4:18).

Now, as St Augustine saw long ago, the opposite of love is pride. Love eliminates pride because its will for the good of the other nullifies our arrogant presumption that we should get our way. We are concerned for the good of others and assured that our good is taken care of without self-will. Thus, pride and fear and their dreadful offspring no longer rule our life as love becomes complete in us.

Joy

Joy is natural in the presence of such love. Joy is a pervasive sense of well-being: of overall and ultimate well-being. Its is primarily a delight in an encompassing good. It is not the same as pleasure, though it is pleasant. It is deeper and broader than any pleasure. Pleasure and pain are always specific to some particular object or condition, such as eating something you really like (pleasure) or recalling some really foolish thing you did (pain). For joy all is well, even if we are in the midst of suffering or loss. Self-sacrificial love is always joyous, no matter the pain and loss it may involve, for we are always looking at the larger scene in which love rules. *All things,* no matter what, *work together for good to those who love God* and *have been called according to his purpose* (Rom 8:28).

Joy is a basic element of inner transformation into Christlikeness and of the outer life that flows from it. Thus when Jesus was explaining things to his closest friends on the night before his crucifixion he left his peace with them (John 14:27). Then, after explaining to them how he was the vine and they the branches, constantly drawing rich life from him, he said, *I have told you this so that my joy may be in you and that your joy may be complete* (15:11). This theme of being full of joy is repeated twice more in John's version of Jesus' final discourse and prayer (16:24; 17:13).

Having *complete joy* means that there is no room for any more of it. Complete joy is our first line of defence against weakness and failure. But even when they break through into our life, *the joy of the Lord is our strength* (Neh 8:10). Thus the tribulation that came upon the Thessalonians who received the word of Christ went hand in hand with *the joy given by the Holy Spirit* (1 Thess 1:6). The joy of Christ that fills us is a gift of God. *The kingdom of God is not a matter of eating and drinking, but of righteousness, peace and joy in the Holy Spirit* (Rom 14:17). That is, it is righteousness, love, peace and joy of a kind that can only be produced in us by the Holy Spirit.

But here again we must not be passive. We may allow joy to dissipate through looking backward at our sins and failures, or forward at what might happen to us, or inward at our struggles with work, responsibilities, temptations and deficiencies. But this means we have placed our hopes in the wrong thing, namely ourselves, and we do not have to do this. It is our option to look to the greatness and goodness of God and what he will do in our lives. Therefore Paul, in jail, remarks to the Philippians that he has *learned to be content whatever the circumstances* (4:11), and urges them to *rejoice in the Lord always. I will say it again: Rejoice!* (4:4). We will be empowered by the Spirit of God to do this if we choose it and fix our minds on the good that God is and will certainly bring to pass. *For you make me glad by your deeds, O Lord; I sing for joy at the works of your hands* (Ps 92:4).

Peace

Peace is the rest of will that results from assurance about how things will turn out. 'I am at peace about it,' we say, and this means I am no longer striving, inwardly or outwardly, for some outcome I want, or to avoid one that I dislike. I have released whatever is at issue, and am no longer allowing to affect my spirits.

Of course everyone is at peace about some things, but few have peace in general, and fewer still have peace that reaches their body and its automatic responses to such a depth that they do not live in a covert state of alarm. Most people carry heavy burdens of care, and these burdens are usually things that are most important in life: what will happen to their loved ones, their finances, health, death, their physical appearance or what others think of them, the future of society, their standing before God and their eternal destiny. To be at peace with God and others is a great attainment and depends on grace far beyond ourselves as well as on our own efforts.

Peace with God comes only from acceptance of his gift of life in his Son (Rom 5:1–2). We are then assured of the outcome of our life and are no longer trying to justify ourselves before God or others. We have accepted that we are not righteous, and cannot be so on our own. We have laid down the burden of justifying ourselves before God and are learning not to justify ourselves before people. This is a peace that grows within us.

From those around us we must simply assume grace and mercy, not that we will get what we deserve. We are beggars on our way through the world. Justice is not enough for our needs, and we couldn't stand it if we got it. When others do not extend the grace and mercy we need, we have to draw on the abundance of it in God. *Who is he that condemns?* we remind ourselves, *Christ Jesus, who died – more than that, who was raised to life – is at the right hand of God and is also interceding for us* (Rom 8:34). Assurance of this allows us to *seek peace and pursue it* (1 Pet 3:11), no matter who is involved, and to *live in peace with all* (Heb 12:14). That includes all our family members and co-workers!

Even in cases where, through no fault of our own, there must be a struggle between us and others, there does not have to be a struggle within. We may have to resist others, for some good reason, but even so, we do not have to make things come out right. We are not in control of outcomes. We do not have to hate those whose course of action we resist, or even get mad at them, and so we can always be at peace within as well as toward them.

Rest on the greatness of God

The secret to this peace is being abandoned to God. We have to return to this for a fuller treatment in the next chapter, on the will; but those who are heartily abandoned to God know that all shall be well because God is in charge of their life. Our peace is the greatness of God. Since he, who not only loves us, but is love, is so great, we live beyond harm in his hands; and there is nothing that can happen to us that will not turn out to our good. Nothing. That is what Romans 8:28 really means. Thus, Isaiah says, *You will keep in perfect peace him whose mind is steadfast, because he trusts in you* (Is 26:3).

It makes supreme sense, therefore, that we should accept Paul's instruction not to *be anxious about anything, but in everything, by prayer and petition, with thanksgiving, present your requests to God. And,* we are assured, *the peace of God, which transcends all understanding, will guard your hearts and your minds in Christ Jesus* (Phil 4:6). The poet Sidney Lanier put this into images from nature:

> As the marsh-hen secretly builds on the watery sod,
> Behold I will build me a nest on the greatness of God:
> I will fly in the greatness of God as the marsh-hen flies
> In the freedom that fills all the space 'twixt the marsh
>   and the skies:
> By so many roots as the marsh-grass sends in the sod
> I will heartily lay me a-hold on the greatness of God.

The greatness and love of God is our peace, and, at the same time, our love and joy. Job had many difficult questions in his troubled life. But when he beheld God, they simply did not matter and no longer seemed to need answering. He did not raise a single one of the questions he earlier had wanted to press upon God when he had the opportunity (Job 42:2–6). He was not bullied into silence by God, but really saw the all-sufficiency of God to his life and his soul. And this brought love, joy and peace to him at a stroke.

Love, joy and peace cannot be separated

Of course it is impossible to separate love, joy, peace, faith and hope from one another in practice. They lose their true nature when separated. Try imagining love without joy and peace, joy without love and peace, or peace without love and joy, or any combination of them without faith and hope. You will see that love, joy and so on, without the others, would not be themselves or have the same essential character. The 'love' that the world takes as the height of human attainment, without joy and peace is a tawdry sham, because they complement it and make it whole and link it to its source in God.

The positive movement into love, joy and peace, based on faith and hope in God, eliminates the destructive feelings, or at least eliminates them as governing factors in our life. We do not go at the change the other way around, trying first to root out the destructive feelings. That is the common mistake of worldly wisdom and of much 'religion' on such matters. But we know that life in Christ brings the fruit of the Spirit, and destructive feelings, and actions, will be replaced. Love, joy and peace fostered in fellowship with God simply crowd out fear, anger, unsatisfied desire, woundedness, rejection. There is no longer room for them. Well, perhaps there is for a while, but increasingly less so. Belonging to Christ does not immediately eliminate bad feelings, and we must not pretend that it does. But it does crucify them. *Those who belong to Christ Jesus have crucified the sinful nature with its passions and desires* (Gal 5:24).

Notice the past tense, *have crucified.* Belonging to Christ means that the merely fleshly passions and desires are on the way to death, and already have ceased leading a life of their own. Much less, then, will they lead our whole life as they used to. That is how it is with all negative and destructive feelings for those who have put Christ on the throne of their life.

Some things we can do

And so, practically speaking, the renovation of the heart in the area of feeling is a matter of opening ourselves to and carefully cultivating love, joy and peace: first by receiving them from God and from those already living in him, and then, as we grow, extending love, joy and peace to others and everything around us, in attitude, prayer and action. Following our V-I-M pattern, we must intend this, and decide that it shall be so in all we are and do. Of course our thought life, as already described, will be focused upon God. Then through grace we can translate this intention into the fine texture of daily life. Our walk with Jesus and the Father will teach us the means required to bring it about.

Here is some of the work to be done. For many of us, just coming honestly to terms with what our feelings really are will be a huge task. Paul says in Romans 12:9, *Love must be sincere.* To do only this will require serious effort and much grace. Ordinary life, and often church life too, is so permeated with insincere expressions of love that it is hard not to feel forced into hypocrisy in some situations. But we can learn to avoid it, and we will immediately begin to see what a huge difference that alone makes.

But there is much more to do. Very few people are without deep negative feelings toward others who are or have been closely related to them. Wounds carried steadily through the years have weighed us down and prevented spiritual growth in love, joy and peace. These wounds may have shaped our identity. We wouldn't know who we are without them. But they can be healed or dismissed, if we are ready to give them up to God and receive the healing ministry of his Word and Spirit. Similarly with hopelessness over not achieving things long sought or long lost.

In general, the task, once we have given ourselves to Christ, is to recognize the reality of our feelings and agree with the Lord to abandon those that are destructive and that lead us into doing or being what we know to be wrong. This he will help us with. We may need to write out what those feelings are in a 'letter to the Lord', or perhaps talk them over with a wise Christian friend who knows how to listen to us and God at the same time.

Perhaps individuals or our fellowship group can minister to us in prayer. Journalling about progress with feelings can also help. It can bring to light the ideas and images or past events on which our destructive feelings are based. These, too, will need to be replaced. Many things may play a part as we progress toward predominance of love, joy and peace in that aspect of our life and our self which is our feelings.

We can be very sure that this is God's intention for us. Thus Paul prayed for his friends in Ephesus that they would be *rooted and established in love,* and *would know this love that surpasses knowledge* so that they would *be filled to the measure of all the fulness of God* (Eph 3:17–19). And we have seen the intention of Jesus, that *my joy may be in you and that your joy may be complete* (John 15:11), and, *Peace I leave with you; my peace I give you. I do not give to you as the world gives. Do not let your hearts be troubled and do not be afraid* (John

14:27). And here is Paul's benediction to the Romans: *May the God of hope fill you with all joy and peace as you trust in him, so that you may overflow with hope by the power of the Holy Spirit* (Rom 15:13).

The seriousness of feelings

Understanding the role of feelings in life and in the process of spiritual formation is absolutely essential if that process is to succeed as it should. There are many ways we can go wrong with reference to feelings. They are extremely influential on all that we are and do. Feelings, more than any other aspect of our nature, are the trigger of sinful action. If you consider all of the Ten Commandments after the first two, for example, you will see that it is feelings out of control that lead to their violation. In his own magnificent treatment of the moral life Jesus makes a point of putting anger, contempt and lust in their place (Matt 5:21 and following). Until that is done, nothing else works.[7] We have noted how we go wrong in trying to manipulate feelings themselves, without regard to their underlying condition. This is often done with good intentions, but it is nearly always harmful, and especially so when we try to stir up feelings as a means of getting people to do what we think is good in the course of Christian ministry.

Feelings have a crucial role in life, but they must not be taken as a basis for action or character change. That role falls to insight, understanding and conviction of truth, which will always be appropriately accompanied by feeling. Feelings are not fundamental to moral decision-making, but can become so if we give them that role in response to the complexities of modern life. Many sincere Christians suffer in their walk with God because they made a commitment prompted by a feeling of need and not by conviction, or from insight into the truth of God and their own condition.

Partly because of this faulty basis of commitment, the area of feeling is, I suspect, the most likely place of defeat for those sincerely seeking to follow Christ today. Satan uses feelings to ensnare us, deceiving us into making them more important than they really are, as well as by inducing much false guilt about what we do and do not feel. Nowhere is this more obvious than in marriage and divorce as now practised. But at all stages of adult life feelings are among Satan's primary instruments. They are used to devastate the soul among Christians and non-Christians alike. This need not be the case. Appropriate spiritual formation in Christ will prevent it. We must understand how love, joy and peace can be our portion in every state of life, and can lead us into a radiant eternity with God.

Matters for thought and discussion

1. Think of the power of feeling over human life. How do you see this at work in daily life? For good? For evil? In yourself? In others?
2. What has been your experience with controlling feelings? Can it reliably be done? How does it work in others around you? Say with anger, lust or addiction?
3. Ask yourself, 'Who would I be if I had different feelings?' Is this question one that strikes you as hard to answer, and if so, why?
4. When you need to resist a feeling, on what basis do you do it? What are your available resources? Consider, for example, irritation at an interruption, or anger at another driver.
5. Did it make any sense to you that love, hatred, etc. are not just feelings, but conditions of the will, body, etc., that have feelings linked to them? Do you see any problems with trying to manage feelings directly without changing the underlying condition?
6. What is your experience with feelings spreading over different parts of your life?
7. What are some of the problems you see with basing decisions on feelings? Can we decide without feelings?
8. How can feelings be 'godly'? Which ones are or are not?
9. How are hope and faith related to love, joy and peace?
10. How does pride affect our other feelings, say love and peace?
11. How would you distinguish peace and joy? Can you really have one of them without the other one? Under what conditions?
12. How can peace, or joy, or love, or hope be cultivated? What are some specific ways you have found to be helpful? How does faith fit in?

If anyone chooses to do God's will, he will find out whether my teaching comes from God or whether I speak on my own.
(John 7:17)

Would you know who is the greatest saint in the world? It is not he who prays most or fasts most; it is not he who gives most alms or is most eminent for temperance, chastity, or justice; but it is he who is always thankful to God, who wills everything that God wills, who receives everything as an instance of God's goodness and has a heart always ready to praise God for it.
(William Law)

CHAPTER 7

TRANSFORMING WILL AND CHARACTER

By this point we are beginning to get a glimpse of what people reno-vated in Christlikeness look like. We know that such people will have a thought life centred on God in his goodness and greatness, and therefore on truth. Also, they will be dominated by the rich array of positive feelings that naturally accompany love, joy and peace, along with their foundational conditions of faith and hope.

But such conditions of thought and feeling cannot be produced and sustained without massive changes in other aspects of the human being, nor do those massive changes in the other aspects come about without corresponding transformations of thought and feeling. Each constituent of the human being we have distinguished is only one element in an interlocking whole. Those constituents can to some degree be distinguished and described in isolation from the others, but they cannot actually exist or develop except in union with the others.

This is true in a special manner with the will. We have already noted how the will is totally dependent in its functioning upon what goes on in the mind. It is not possible to choose, except in terms of thoughts and feelings. The will is directed by what our thoughts and feelings actually are at the time of willing. But now we need to develop further the idea that our thoughts and feelings also have a crucial dependence on our will, on our choices.

What we think is very much a matter of what we allow ourselves to think, and what we feel is very much a matter of what we allow ourselves to feel. Further, what we think is very much a matter of what we want to think, and what we feel is very much a matter of what we want to feel. In short, the condition of our mind is very much a matter of the direction in which our will is set.

There is a kind of interaction here, and it is very important for the purposes of spiritual formation that we understand it. Obviously the thoughts and feelings that the will depends on in any given moment of choice cannot be changed in that moment. But the will or heart can change the thoughts and feelings that are available to it in future choices. It is because of this that we are responsible for our character.

Our character is revealed by our habitual patterns of behaviour. This is why we ask for applicants' curriculum vitae and references when we appoint people to jobs. They do not just tell what someone has done, but they reveal what things the person is in the habit of doing, what sort of person we are dealing with, and therefore how they will very likely act in the future.

But character can be changed. And that, of course, is what spiritual formation in Christlikeness is about.

Domestic violence is a sad fact of life the world over. But most people who perpetrate violence against their loved ones are remorseful and hate themselves for what they do. Many times they tell themselves that they will never do it again. But resolution on this point is insufficient to prevent it happening again because a violent behaviour pattern is quickly established and very hard to change. It is in fact necessary to change the thoughts and feelings that make the pattern of behaviour and shape it into the character of a violent person. Ultimately, the most effective remedy for negative behaviour patterns comes from the impact on the human mind and will of repentance and faith in Christ, but even that is only the start of a deep change of character.

So what is a will or heart like that has been transformed into Christlikeness?

Jesus said of himself, *the one who sent me is with me; he has not left me alone, for I always do what pleases him* (John 8:29). And Paul had this to say: *I have been crucified with Christ and I no longer live, but Christ lives in me. The life I live in the body, I live by faith in the Son of God, who loved me and gave himself for me* (Gal 2:20). We might also recall John Calvin's words: 'The only haven of safety is to have no other will, no other wisdom, than to follow the Lord wherever he leads. Let this, then, be the first step, to abandon ourselves, and devote the whole energy of our minds to the service of God.'

So here we have the answer to our question: a will transformed into Christlikeness is single-minded and joyous in devotion to God and his will. That is the outcome of Christian spiritual formation with reference to the will, heart or spirit. And this becomes our character when it is the governing response of every aspect of our being.

But how far this is from the usual human will and character! Instead of being simple and transparent through a constant devotion to God, the usual human will is chaotically duplicitous and confused, the playing field of pride and fear, shrouded in layer upon layer of destructive habits.

The basic nature of the will

We recall that the will is the radical creativity which makes the individual unique and irreplaceable. In other words, it is what prevents a person from being a mere thing. Will is the ability to originate or refrain from originating something. It brings things into existence. Sticks and stones do not have that ability. So will is the core of who and what we are as individuals. It is that aspect of personality by virtue of which we have a likeness to God and are in his image. We are created to be creators.

'Our consents and non-consents', as William James said, 'are the measure of our worth . . . the one strictly underivative and original contribution which we make to the world.'[1] And our will is our capacity for 'consents' and 'non-consents'. It is the core of our non-physical being. It is our spirit, though it comes directly from God and is meant to be in his keeping through our trust in him. It is the power to select what we think on and how intently we will focus on it, and it is this from which our other decisions and actions then more or less directly flow. Functionally, the will is the executive centre of the human self. From it the whole self is directed and organized, and must be if it is to be directed or organized at all. That is why we recognize the will to be the same as the biblical heart or centre.

It is also clear, then, that will is not the same thing as character, but character develops from it, as specific choices become habitual and, to some extent, automatic. Character is revealed most of all in what we feel and do without thinking. But to a lesser extent it is revealed in what we repent of after thinking, and what we then do as a result of repenting. Thought, feeling and will give rise to character.

Why, then, doesn't God just force us to do the things he knows to be right? It is because that would deprive us of precisely what he intended in our creation: freely chosen character. The centrality of the will is what makes it precious and gives the person dignity.[2] The great worth of the person explains why Jesus died for the sake of individuals and was satisfied with the outcome (Is 53:11; Heb 12:2).

We treasure the will in ourselves and in others spontaneously, without having to learn it. Will has obvious, intrinsic value. The child, without learning to do so, values its capacity to act on its own, which it quickly identifies and stubbornly defends. The sense of things flowing from itself is unmistakable and joyous and irrepressible. And adults delight to see the child's will emerge – 'Look at what she did!' and 'Did you hear what he said?' This creativity and individuality is basic to health and well-being.

Choice, the exercise of will, is valued and carefully guarded throughout life. At the end of life we want to think we have made a difference. But such an outcome is not automatic. For the human will is not only precious; it is a problem. Everyone has the experience of willing in a way that runs counter to choices they have already made or that they should make. Human life is characterized by conflict within the will and between wills. But that statement hardly does justice to the facts. Civilization, we sometimes realize, is a thin veneer over savagely competing wills.

The desire for good implanted in the human will by its Creator is corrupted, and has turned against itself as a result of self-deification. The question 'What good can I do?' is replaced by 'How can I get my way?' Manipulation, deception and malice replace transparency, sincerity and goodwill, as exaltation of self replaces submission and service to God. In modern thought sincerity is merely self-deception.[3]

Nietzsche saw claims to truth, along with all ideas of authority, as the 'will to power'.

Whereas in other times a focused and coherent will was assumed to be necessary to human freedom, today the assumption is that freedom only comes with an incoherent and vagrant will. Truth is regarded as bondage, and integrity as a prison that prevents me from endlessly creating and recreating myself.

God chooses not to override our will and force us to take on a specific character. But that does not mean that we get what we want. We have choice, but we cannot choose the consequences of the choices we make. And one of the consequences of choosing what we want without regard to God's will is enslavement to our own self-conflicted will. On the path of self-will we eventually reach a state where we cannot choose what God wants and cannot want God. We can only want ourselves! 'I wake and feel the fell of dark', the poet Hopkins writes,

> The lost are like this, and their scourge to be
> As I am mine, their sweating selves.[4]

This is what it means to be lost.

God permits the wills of human beings to be set on what is evil, wrong or foolish. He even permits good and wise inclinations to be defeated by sin, social influences, mistaken ideas, overwhelming feelings, or disconnections and ruptures in the depths of the soul. The outcome is often a whole society baffled and torn by the chaos and evil it finds within itself. The liberal ideal of free choice results in conflict and intolerance.[5]

Duplicity, deceitfulness and darkness

Apart from God, the will is characterized by duplicity or fragmentation. It wills many things which cannot be reconciled with each other. Turned away from God, thought and feeling fall into chaos, and the will cannot but follow. There is no focus outside itself that can pull or push it right.

This conflict and complexity may go unacknowledged. Decisions we make seem very simple: we decide to go out, we decide to tell the truth (or not) in a difficult situation. But when we reflect more deeply, we realize that a choice or act of will is not simple at all. The understandings, feelings and purposes that enter into it may be extremely complicated. We often find it difficult to analyse why we acted as we did, why we reacted so strongly (or not), and why we chose the particular course of action that we did.

In a condition of alienation from God, the human will moves toward duplicity and deception. This is the result of pretending to feel and think one way while acting in another. Often the deception involved is self-deception. Our pride will constantly trap us between desire and fear. Rather than surrender our desire, we will do what we want, but conceal it because of fear of the consequences. And then perhaps we will also try to conceal our fear because of our pride. We will try to pretend that there is nothing the matter, when in reality we are seething, or frightened or sick. The result is a descending cycle of deception, and finally darkness. In this condition, we cannot understand ourselves and why we do what we do. As Jeremiah says, *the heart is deceitful above all things and beyond cure. Who can understand it?* (Jer 17:9). And the only answer to that question is, as the prophet says in the next verse: *I the Lord search the heart and examine the mind, to reward a man according to his conduct, according to what his deeds deserve.* To God the human heart is totally transparent.

But it is not only our own hearts and wills that are opaque to us. We live in a world where duplicity is institutionalized. How often we have to deal with someone whom we know at the moment to be simply working out how they are going to mislead us. Few of us could honestly say that we do not have to struggle to overcome deceit and darkness within ourselves and around us, even among those we love.

God hears the heart

The heart is what God observes and addresses in human beings. He cares little for outward show. He responds to the heart because it is, above all, who we are: who we are choosing and have chosen to be. What God wants of us can only come from the heart. He respects the centrality of our will and will not overrule it. He seeks godly character in us. He is sensitive to the slightest move of the heart toward him. This is the witness of the Bible. It doesn't matter whether you are religious or not, for *the same Lord is Lord of all and richly blesses all who call on him, for, 'Everyone who calls on the name of the Lord will be saved.'* (Rom 10:12–13).

Multitudes of people have come to a full knowledge of God because in a moment of complete hopelessness they prayed the 'atheist's prayer' or something like it: 'God, if there is a God, save my soul if I have a soul.' When that is the true cry of the heart, of the inmost spirit of the individual, who has no longer any hope other than God, God hears and responds without fail. And he responds with the gift of *life from above.*

In fact, God is constantly looking for people who will *worship him in spirit and in truth.* What does that mean? It means people who have free and whole-hearted respect for and commitment to God. People who never try to conceal anything from him, and always rely completely on him. God is seeking such people, whoever they may turn out to be, even a despised, sixth-hand woman of Samaria, so ashamed that, to avoid other people, she dared to go to the well for water only in the heat of noon (John 4:6). Nothing is hidden from God, so those who worship him must worship him in spirit and in truth (4:23–24).

No great sophistication or information about God is required to be reached by him. Edith Schaeffer tells of a man from the Lisu tribe far out in the hills of China. There was in him a great longing for a God he did not know. One day he found on a mountain path a page torn from a Lisu catechism. It read:

> Are there more gods than One?
> – No, there is only One God.
> Should we worship idols?
> – No . . .

And the rest was torn away.

He went home and destroyed his altars. Immediately his daughter became very ill and his neighbours abused him for making the demons angry. The man thought that if there was One True God perhaps he could reach that God with his voice. He knew nothing about prayer, but he climbed to the top of the highest peak in the vicinity, twelve or fourteen thousand feet high, and shouted out, 'O God, if You really are there and You are the One I am to worship, please make my little girl well again.'

It took a long time to climb back down, but upon arriving home he found the little girl completely well, with no time of recuperation needed. She had recovered at the time he had prayed. That man became an effective evangelist across the entire area. Edith Schaeffer comments, 'There will be so many stories to compare with [this man's] that I picture us taking thousands of years to find out about them all.'[6] This is because of the seeking God who constantly monitors our hearts.

The Bible promises that *the eyes of the Lord range throughout the earth to strengthen those whose hearts are fully committed to him* (2 Chr 16:9). And, *the eyes of the Lord are on the righteous and his ears are attentive to their cry* (Ps 34:15).

From surrender to drama

There are some quite distinct stages in the identification of our will with God's. First there is *surrender*. When we surrender our will to God we consent to his supremacy in all things. Perhaps we do so grudgingly. We recognize his supremacy intellectually, and we concede to it in practice, though we still may not like it, and may still resist it.

We may not be able to do his will, but we are willing to will it. In this condition there is still much grumbling and complaining about our life and about God. Andrew Murray comments that 'we find the Christian life so difficult because we seek for God's blessing while we live in our own will. We should be glad to live the Christian life according to our own liking.'[7]

Still, this is an important move forward. The centre of the self, the heart or spirit, is now willing for God to be God, even if it is with little hope or enthusiasm. Perhaps it is only willing to be made willing. But it is for lack of this minimal identification with God's will that many of people are unable to understand the truth of Jesus (John 7:17). Such people are not willing to do his will, and hence God does not open their minds to his truth, and they cannot do so on their own. They struggle in the darkness and they will probably reproach God for not giving them more light, even though they are unwilling to act on the light they have.

But if grace and wisdom prevail in the lives of those who surrender to God's will, they will move on to *abandonment.* Then they will no longer hold back any part of themselves from God's will. Surrender now covers all of life, not just intellectual assent to the truth about God and his commandments. God allows some things – the loss of a loved one, for example – but we no longer fret unduly over the bad things that happen to good people. While God does not cause these things to happen, we now accept them as within his good plan for those who love him (Rom 8:28). Irredeemable harm does not happen to those who willingly put their lives in God's hands. We cease to live on edge, wondering if God will do what we want. Pain will not turn into bitterness, nor disappointment into paralysis.

But there is still more. Beyond abandonment is *contentment* with the will of God: not only with his being who he is and ordaining what he has ordained in general, but with the particular lot that he has given to us. At this point gratitude and joy are the steady tenor of our life. We are now assured that God has done, and will always do, well by us. Dreary, foot-dragging surrender to God is well in the past. And from here, duplicity looks like utter foolishness in which no sane person would be involved. Grumbling and complaining are gone (Phil 2:14–15), not painstakingly resisted or eliminated, but simply unthought of.

But we are not done yet! Beyond contentment lies intelligent, energetic *participation* in accomplishing God's will in the world. We are no longer spectators, but are caught up in a vivid and eternal drama in which we play an essential part. We embrace our circumstances, no matter how tragic they seem, and act for good in them. *Those who receive God's abundant provision of grace and of the gift of righteousness [will] reign in life through the one man, Jesus Christ* (Rom 5:17). We will take action to accomplish the will of God in his power. Our own will is not the source of our strength: we hardly notice of it. But we are carried along by the power of the divine drama in which we live. Far from struggling to resist sin we are devoted to the realization of righteousness all around us. This is the real meaning of Christ *living* in us. The strongest human will is the one that is surrendered to God's will and acts with it.

This progression toward full identification of our will with God's will is one which, perhaps for most people, may not be fully realized in this life. But that does not really matter. We can enter into it now, as disciples of Jesus Christ, through the power *at work within us*. It may be that at present we cannot even imagine what it would be like for us. But we must never forget that he *is able to do immeasurably more than all we ask or imagine, according to his power that is at work within us* (Eph 3:20). Our part is to begin as best we can.

To will one thing

Now when we set out on the path of the surrendered will we find we have to grapple with our fallen character. This character will have been shaped by our habitual ways of thinking and feeling, our social world past and present, will have permeated our body and its responses, and even penetrated into the unconscious depths of our soul. The condition we find ourselves in can best be described as one of entanglement. The condition we must move to is that of single-minded focus upon doing the will of God in everything.

C. T. Studd once upset some of his missionary colleagues in the Congo by what he called his 'DCD Campaign'. 'DCD' stood for 'Don't Care a Damn' for anything but Christ. He made a skull and crossbones with DCD superimposed as a badge to wear on jackets and caps and to stick on buildings and equipment.

His intention was that he and his missionary team should care for nothing before Christ (not even their family and friends). Nothing should be allowed to detract from that or conflict with it. All lesser desires had to be done to death (hence the macabre badge!).[8] Some people were more concerned about language they thought was wrong than about hearts not set wholly on Christ.

In our fallen world very few people live with a focused will, even a will focused on evil. W. B. Yeats wrote that

> The best lack all conviction, while the worst
> Are full of passionate intensity.

But in fact even the worst rarely have much intensity about them. There are some evil people who are genuinely focused and can gain great power over others because good and evil people alike are, for the most part, simply drifting through life. In our culture today the direction of the self is usually left to feelings; and the will, if recognized at all, is either identified with feelings or else is regarded as helpless in the face of feelings. 'Reason is . . . the slave of the passions', as David Hume claimed in the eighteenth century. But Kierkegaard wrote, 'Purity of heart is to will one thing.'

Before we can rest in single-mindedness as the habitual orientation of all aspects of our being, a serious battle is necessary. The call of grace and wisdom is nonetheless to *throw off everything that hinders and the sin that so easily entangles, and . . . run with perseverance the race marked out for us,* with our eyes fixed on Jesus (Heb 12:1–2). *No-one serving as a soldier gets involved in civilian affairs,* Paul reminds Timothy, *he wants to please his commanding officer* (2 Tim 2:4). Martha was *worried and upset about many things,* as Jesus pointed out, but *only one thing* was necessary, and Mary had chosen the better part (Luke 10:41–42). And Paul's testimony was that he really did only one thing, which was to *press on towards the goal to win the prize for which God has called me heavenwards in Christ Jesus* (Phil 3:13–14).

Now the primary source of entanglement is our desires, or to be precise, not our just our desires themselves, but our enslavement to them. Temptation to sin always originates in desire (James 1:14–15). We set our hearts on too many things, some of which are wrong and some of which are in conflict with others. Habitual following of a desire leads to that desire having a stronger hold over us. It is easier to do what you have done than what you have not done; and it is very much easier to do what you have always done than what is contrary to what you have done before. You tend to keep on doing what you have done.

When the will is enslaved to a desire through habit, desire will in turn enslave the mind. To justify itself in satisfying the desire, the will enlists the intellect to provide rationalizations. Some early Christian cults justified their sinful behaviour by claiming that sin allowed God to exercise his grace more freely (Rom 6:1–2), but Paul points out that this argument is merely a rationalization of sin, and utterly illogical. Rationalization is an internal process, and the result can be behaviour that makes no sense to anyone else. People can be hypnotized by evil desires. One of the staples of television comedy is the character who tells one lie and has to resort to ever more bizarre explanations to avoid admitting the lie. In comedy it can be amusing, but in real life it is simply sad. Perhaps we should face the fact that these entanglements are the kinds of things that keep well-intended people from following Christ into the depths and heights of spiritual transformation.[9]

Getting free from entanglement

Our primary, practical aim in freeing ourselves from entanglement must be to overcome duplicity. And to overcome it we must become conscious of it and confront it, and take appropriate steps toward integrity. The point of reference in all of this is the explicit teachings of the Bible concerning the will of God. *Whoever has my commands and obeys them, is the one who loves me*, Jesus said (John 14:21). The person who intends to will what God wills has to begin with what God has said he wills. We do not need to know everything he has said, though that is not as difficult as it sounds (Rom 13:8–10): we can begin with what we know he has said. Let us firmly decide to do that. This will quickly lead us into the depths of spiritual transformation.

Who does not know, for example, that it is God's will we should be without guile and malice? Then let us decide never to mislead people and never to do or say things to cause pain or harm. Let us decide today, right now, that we will not do such things. You might think that this is a very small part of identifying with God's will. But in fact lying and malice are fundamental sins. They make possible and actual many other sins. If you removed them, evil in the individual and in society would be very largely eliminated. From family fights to international warfare, the world would be transformed beyond recognition.

Of course when we begin to implement our decision, we discover that it is no simple task. We discover what a grip duplicity and malice have on us. Our thoughts and feelings and our usual routines of action have an influence over our choices that is much more powerful and complex than we ever imagined while we simply went along with them. Spiritual formation cannot be a matter of just changing the will itself. That is central, of course, but it cannot be accomplished except by transformation of the other aspects of the self. We discover that mere intention or effort of will is not enough to bring about the change in us we have hoped for, which will free us from duplicity and malice. Still, we must hold to that intention and sincerely make the effort, and then we will find that help is available.

The role of spiritual disciplines

Spiritual disciplines such as solitude (being alone with God for long periods of time), fasting (learning freedom from food and how God directly nourishes us) and service (doing good for others with no thought of ourselves), help the duplicity and malice that is buried in our will and character to surface. Those disciplines make room for the Word and the Spirit to work in us, and they permit destructive feelings to be perceived and dealt with for what they are: our will and not God's will. Those feelings are normally cloaked in layer upon layer of habitual self-deception and rationalization. They will have enslaved the will, and it in turn will have coerced the mind to conceal or rationalize what is really going on. Your mind will really 'talk to you' when you begin to deny fulfilment to your desires, and you will find how subtle and shameless it is. I know this from experience.

For example our 'righteous judgments' on others may, as we practise solitude or service, be recognized as ways of putting them down. Our extreme busyness may be revealed as inability to trust God, or unwillingness to give others a chance to contribute. Or our readiness to give our opinions may turn out to be contempt for the thoughts and words of others, or simply a desire to shut them up.

Truly becoming someone who wills above all to have God's kind of goodness (Matt 6:33) is not something that will happen overnight. But with a clear intention and decision, with appropriate spiritual disciplines and with God's grace to correct us when we fail, it is not as far away as many might suppose. The duplicities, entanglements and evil intentions that infect our will can be eliminated as we *fix our eyes on Jesus, the author and perfecter of our faith, who for the joy set before him endured the cross, scorning its shame, and sat down at the right hand of the throne of God* (Heb 12:2).

Sweet will of God

Do we then lose ourselves? To succeed in identifying our will with God's will is not, as is often mistakenly thought, to have no will of our own. Far from it. To have no will is impossible. Rather, it is for the first time to have a will that is fully functional, not at war with itself, and capable of directing all of the parts of the self in harmony with one another under the direction of God. In this case, we do not hesitate to do what is right, and to do wrong we would have to work against ourselves. When through spiritual transformation we have in some measure come to know the well-kept heart in real life, we experience it as a gift of grace, no matter how hard we may have had to struggle in the process of growing into it. And it is a gift in which we find ourselves, just as Jesus taught: *Whoever finds his life will lose it, and whoever loses his life for my sake will find it* (Matt 10:39). For the first time we will not only have a harmonious will, but we also know who we are in the kingdom of God, and be able live that eternal life in day-to-day experience. The will of God is not foreign to our will. It is sweetness, life and strength to us.

> Sweet will of God,
> Oh, hold me closer,
> Till I am wholly lost in Thee.

Matters for thought and discussion

1. How can we be responsible for our character if in the moment of choice we are always dependent upon thoughts and feelings? How can we set about changing our own character?
2. What, in your own words, does it mean to have put on Christ, or to have put off the old person and put on the new (Col 3:9–10)?

3. What in our make-up constitutes our will?
4. How does 'getting my way' result in a will that is duplicitous and incapable of sincerity.
5. What is the condition of will in a person who is lost?
6. How do duplicity, deception and darkness descend upon those who want to be their own god?
7. What do you think of C. T. Studd's 'DCD Campaign'? Could you have one in your church?
8. Have you seen first hand the effects of the entanglements of desire on life?
9. Do you know anyone who cannot tell the difference between desire and will, and hence do not know how to oppose their own desires?
10. Does it make sense to you that spiritual disciplines could retrain the will and reform character?
11. What would it be like for you to be 'wholly lost in the will of God'?

Do you not know that your body is a temple of the Holy
Spirit, who is in you, whom you have received from God?
You are not your own; you were bought at a price.
Therefore honour God with your body.
(1 Cor 6:19–20)

Do not offer the parts of your body to sin, as instruments of
wickedness, but rather offer yourselves to God, as those who
have been brought from death to life; and offer the parts of
your body to him as instruments of righteousness.
(Rom 6:13)

CHAPTER 8

TRANSFORMING THE BODY

Spiritual transformation into Christlikeness is the process of forming the inner world of the person in such a way that it takes on the character of Jesus himself. The result is that the outer life of the individual increasingly becomes a natural expression of the reality of Jesus and of his teachings. Doing what he said and did increasingly becomes a part of who we are.

But for this to happen our body must increasingly be prepared to do good and to refrain from doing evil. The inclinations to wrongdoing must be eliminated. The body must come to serve us as a primary ally in Christlikeness.

For good or for evil, the body is crucial to the spiritual life. Some will find this a strange notion, but it remains a fact. We can see wherever we look that the human body is a major barrier to renovation of the heart in Christ, perhaps even the most significant barrier. This certainly is not God's intention for the body. It is not in the nature of the body as such: the body is not inherently evil. Nor is it even caused by the body. The body is a good thing; God made it for good. That is why the way of Jesus Christ is so specifically incarnational. The body must be cherished and properly cared for, not as a master, but as a servant of God.

But the body at some stage usually hinders people in doing what they know to be good and right. For many, the body governs life. There lies the problem. Even professing Christians, by and large, devote to their spiritual growth and well-being a tiny fraction of the time they devote to their body.

What is going on here? Can our body truly become our ally in becoming Christlike? It can and it must, but its essential role in spirituality is the thing most likely to be overlooked in understanding and practising growth in grace.

We saw earlier that being lost results from putting oneself at the centre of the universe in place of God. We further saw how this naturally leads to the worship of the body and to a life of sensuality. The body becomes the primary source of gratification and the chief instrument for getting what we want. That is a perversion of the role for the body that God intended; and it results in spiritual death, in alienation from God and the loss of all we will have invested our lives in (Gal 6:8).

In Paul's writings, this aspect of human life is called *the flesh*, or *the sinful nature*: it is the purely natural powers and pleasures of the human being, based in the body. Paul tells us,

> *Those who live according to the sinful nature have their minds set on what that nature desires; but those who live in accordance with the Spirit have their minds set on what the Spirit desires. The mind of sinful man is death, but the mind controlled by the Spirit is life and peace.* (Rom 8:5–6)

The mind focused on the sinful nature is naturally hostile toward God because God threatens the 'god' it takes itself to be. And it is unable to please God (Rom 8:7) because it is working against God. Spiritual transformation inescapably involves the body, and we must explore how.

My body becomes me

My body is the focus of my dominion and my responsibility. Through it I live in the world. It is only through my body that I have a place in time and space and history. My body gives me a family and a gender, talents and opportunities to use them. My parents and my date and place of birth are bodily realities that are foundational to who I am. Experiences come to me through my body. Through it I have a language and culture. My body is essential to my identity. It at least partly defines me and shapes who I am and what I am able to become.

Growing up has a great deal to do with taking control over my own body, but very quickly it becomes a matter of influencing other bodies, especially those of my parents. In due course, individuals generate a realm in which they are driven by desire and channelled by ideas, sensations and emotions that are mediated through the body. We learn many things that are good for ourselves as well as those around us. Most of these positive things, along with their accompanying ideas, sensations and emotions, become positioned in our body, and by habit they enable us to do what we do without any special thought or conscious direction. This permits us to handle the complexities of day-to-day existence.

But we soon run into realities that do not yield to our will. Often these are the realms of other individuals, organized around their desires and contrary to our own. So we begin to experience destructive emotions, especially fear, anger, envy, jealousy and resentment. These may in time develop into settled attitudes of hostility, contempt or indifference. Such attitudes make us ready to harm others, or to see them suffer, and these attitudes quickly settle into my body. They become more or less overt tendencies to act without thinking in ways that harm others or even ourselves. These attitudes are quite apparent to others, even if they are unwilling or unable to say it. Unchecked, they will rule our lives and will constantly inject poison into our personal relations.

Most of what we call character, whether good or bad, depends on what our bodies are ready and prepared to do in various situations. These responses enter our consciousness hardly at all. They are either fully automatic, triggered by events and circumstances, for example aggression or flight in response to danger; or they are semi-automatic, for example resisting or embracing temptation on the basis of what we feel. These responses and feelings reside or are expressed in fairly specific parts of our bodies. They can often be communicated unconsciously by our 'body language', and can be read with some accuracy by observant people around us. Our body language often determines how other people respond to us.

Incarnation and the body

All of this makes clear why, as we noted above, the way of Christ is so specifically incarnational, so bodily. Incarnation is not just an essential fact about Jesus: that *Christ came in the flesh*. Rather, he came in the flesh, with a real human body, so that he could bring redemption and deliverance to our bodies. Our bodies are an essential part of who we are, and no redemption that omits the body is full redemption. Those who deny that Christ has come in real flesh, John says, cannot be Christian (1 John 4:3).

Such a strong position is taken in the New Testament because redemption is in the first place for *the life I live in the body* (Gal 2:20). This bodily life is to be caught up into the eternal life of God. But of course *the life I live in the body* must become holy, must be lived *by faith in the Son of God*. Only this way can we *have confidence on the day of judgment, because in this world we are like him* (1 John 4:17). The redemption of the body will be completed later, but for now, *if the Spirit of him who raised Jesus from the dead is living in you, he who raised Christ from the dead will also give life to your mortal bodies through his Spirit, who lives in you* (Rom 8:11). We are to know now *the power of his resurrection* (Phil 3:10). Our body is not just a physical system, but is inhabited by the real presence of Christ.[1]

The profundity of Paul

Once we are clear about the centrality of the body to our identity and life, the profundity of Paul's teachings about the body will strongly impress us.[2] If we do not first understand this, however, his words will be incomprehensible. I'm afraid that's what they are to most people today. They cannot understand how Paul could mean what he says about the role of the body in the life of one who belongs to Christ.

For example, in Colossians chapter 3 he tells the *holy and faithful* people (Col 1:2) to whom he is writing, to *put to death . . . whatever belongs to [their] earthly nature* (Col 3:5). And among the things belonging to the earthly nature he lists *sexual immorality, impurity, lust, evil desires and greed, which is idolatry.*

The Authorized Version of the Bible translates Paul's Greek more literally as *mortify therefore your members which are upon the earth.* This recognizes that the earthly nature which he is talking about is made up of parts of our body and person, and that this affects our whole life. Those *members which are upon the earth* are those parts of life lived entirely in terms of the natural powers of the embodied self. You need no help from supernatural sources to engage in *sexual immorality,* to indulge in passions and desires for what is evil, or to have greed to possess what belongs to others. Just follow the inclinations now built into your bodily existence and they will all happen. Just let the demands of your 'members' guide your life. These are the parts of our lives which are *earthly,* in the sense that they do not come from heaven or God. Because of them we become *children of disobedience.* It is natural, part of our earthly nature, to be disobedient and rebellious. Our members are inherently at war with God and therefore subject to God's wrath (Col 3:6–7).

But it wold be a mistake to imagine that everything about the earthly nature is therefore unpleasant: often it is very nice. Think for a minute about what religious people often regard as important and respond positively to. When Paul explained to the Philippians what his qualifications were as religious man, he listed these: *circumcised on the eighth day, of the people of Israel, of the tribe of Benjamin, a Hebrew of Hebrews; in regard to the law, a Pharisee; as for zeal, persecuting the church; as for legalistic righteousness, faultless* (Phil 3:5–6). You can easily translate this into modern-day terms by listing the things which religious people are apt to present as good qualifications. But Paul actually regarded all this as loss, as rubbish, compared to the real treasure of the resurrection life of Christ living in him (3:3–11).

That is why he said to the Colossians, *put to death, therefore, whatever belongs to your earthly nature.* The word *therefore* refers back to the fact he had just cited in this passage, that Christ's people have received a different life, not an earthly one, but the life of Christ himself, raised up beyond natural death. *For you died,* he says, *and your life is now hidden with Christ in God* (Col 3:3). This is a theme developed at many other points in Paul's writings, but at greatest length in Romans chapters 5 to 8.

There Paul has been describing how sin, and therefore death, has governed human life. But as he comes toward the end of chapter 5, a new kind of reign emerges. Death had reigned because of sin, which came into the human world by one man, Adam. Yes, but *how much more will those who receive God's abundant provision of grace and of the gift of righteousness reign in life through the one man, Jesus Christ* (Rom 5:17). Sin indeed has flourished. But grace, life from above, has flourished and will flourish all the more, *so that, just as sin reigned in death, so also grace might reign through righteousness to bring eternal life through Jesus Christ our Lord* (Rom 5:21).

Now we must emphasize that the grace in question is not merely a judicial action, though it involves that. It is above all a presence and power in life, which provides an alternative to the merely natural forces accessible to the individual in and through their body without any specific divine intervention from God. So now Paul lays out the alternative open to those already born from above and therefore experiencing a life that is not of the flesh or the earth. They are given the option of walking in the new, different life that is already 'doing things' in them. *Just as Christ was raised from the dead by the glory of the Father*, Paul says, *so we too might walk in newness of life* (Rom 6:4 NRSV). *Walk* in it, as a steadily moving force, not just feel it in fits and starts!

But since we are now in the grip of grace it is up to us: Paul writes, *do not let sin reign in your mortal body so that you obey its evil desires* (6:12). And we do this by refusing to surrender our body parts to sin as instruments of wickedness. Instead, having been invaded by a life beyond death, and hence by one that is not of the body or flesh, *we offer the parts of [our] body to him as instruments of righteousness* (6:13). Because we are in the grip of grace, sin does not exercise control over us except in so far as we allow it. And, with divine assistance, we can break whatever control remains to it in every aspect of our life (6:14). So, just as once, while *dead in transgressions and sins* (Eph 2:1), we surrendered our body parts to be servants of impurity, and to lawlessness leading to more lawlessness, so now we *offer them in slavery to righteousness leading to holiness* (6:19).

Now these words of Paul refer precisely to the process and out-come of spiritual formation, of which we have spoken. *Now that you have been set free from sin and have become slaves to God, the benefit you reap leads to holiness, and the result is eternal life* (6:22), *the life that really is life* (1 Tim 6:19). The parts of our death-bound body are not mere physical things, but now carry in them a life that is not of them. *And if the Spirit of him who raised Jesus from the dead is living in you, he who raised Christ from the dead will also give life to your mortal bodies through his Spirit, who lives in you* (Rom 8:11).

The centrality of spiritual formation of the body

This discussion of the place of the body in our life, and of how the apostle Paul understood its transformation, will make very clear why spiritual formation requires the transformation of the body. The proper retraining and nurturing of the body is absolutely essential to Christlikeness. The body is not just a physical thing. As it matures it increasingly takes on the quality of its inner life. The body of a child, by contrast, has little 'interiority' to it, which is why the child can really hide nothing. The body as it matures increasingly reflects the source from which our life flows.

The outcome of spiritual formation is the transformation of the inner reality of the self in such a way that the deeds and words of Jesus become a natural expression of who we are. But it is the nature of the human being that the inner reality of the self settles into the body, and then works outwards. Formed in sin, our character and body are set against God and God's ways, and, as we look about us, we find them running pretty much on their own.

When our heart comes to new life in God, the old 'programmes' are still running, contrary to our new heart, and for the most part they are running in our body and its parts. Sin was *living in me*, that is *in the members of my body* (Rom 7:12–22). *Sinful passions* were *at work in our bodies*, even though there is no longer the consequence of *death* (Rom 7:5). That is because my identity before God has been shifted over to another life that is also now in me as God's gift. While *the spirit is willing but the flesh is weak* (Matt 26:41), I may find myself doing the thing I hate (Rom 7:15). But it really is no longer me doing it, but the sin still functioning as a living force in the members of my body (7:23).

This is only a transitional state for those who can say with David, *my soul clings to you* (Ps 63:8). The law or force of the spirit of life that is in Christ Jesus is now also a real presence in my body and it opens the way to liberation from the force of sin in my bodily parts (Rom 7:23). By not walking in terms of the flesh but in terms of the spirit we are increasingly able to do the things that Jesus did and taught (Rom 8:4). We move toward the place where both the spirit is willing and the flesh is strong for God because the spirit now drives it. We *offer the parts of [our] body in slavery . . . to righteousness leading to holiness* (Rom 6:19).

The greatest danger to our prospects for spiritual transformation at this point is that we fail to take all this talk about our bodily parts literally. It may help us to consider ordinary situations of temptation. We said earlier that temptation is a matter of being inclined to do what is wrong. But where do those inclinations primarily reside? The answer is, they primarily exist in the parts of our body.

Those inclinations are present in those parts, and can even be felt there by anyone who is attentive to their body, and who is informed, thoughtful, and willing to admit what they find. Others, too, can recognize the tendencies present in our bodily parts to our detriment. They can 'read' our hands, feet, shoulders, eyebrows, loins, tongue, overall posture, and they can play upon our tendencies to trap us, ensnare us, use us, destroy us. Those who purposely prey upon others constantly do this. They become experts at it.

The tendencies present in our bodily parts can move our body into action independently and contrary to our overall intentions, often quite genuinely held. Thus we act or speak before we think. The part of our character that inhabits our body carries us away.

Take the tongue, for example. James says that the tongue is a small part of the body (Jas 3:5). But *the tongue also is a fire, a world of evil among the parts of the body. It corrupts the whole person, sets the whole course of his life on fire, and is itself set on fire by hell* (Jas 3:6). James had no doubt observed the incredible power of the tongue to stir up the inclinations of the whole body and of all of its parts. In turn that stirs up the inclinations of others – one piece of gossip leads to many more. Have you noticed this? The tongue is perhaps the last bodily part to submit to goodness. No-one can tame it, James says. Physical violence is nearly always initiated by verbal violence.

It is only as we habitually subject the tongue to the grace of God as an instrument reserved for him, to do his will, that grace comes to inhabit it and govern it. And when that happens the effects spread throughout the body. *If anyone is never at fault in what he says*, writes James, *he is a perfect man, able to keep his whole body in check* (Jas 3:2). *The tongue of the righteous is choice silver* (Prov 10:20), and *the tongue that brings healing is a tree of life, but a deceitful tongue crushes the spirit* (Prov 15:4).

Other members of the body, though not as central to life as the tongue, have their own tendencies and associated feelings to act wrongly:

> There are six things the Lord hates, seven that are detestable to him: haughty eyes, a lying tongue, hands that shed innocent blood, a heart that devises wicked schemes, feet that are quick to rush into evil, a false witness who pours out lies and a man who stirs up dissension among brothers. (Prov 6:17–18)

The eyes, the stomach and the genitals, the fists and the face, the feet and the tongue, are constantly moving us away from God, if they have not been permeated by the real presence of Christ.

A person caught up in rage or lust or resentment – or religious self-righteousness, for that matter – is basically one whose body has taken over and is running their actions or even their life. Sometimes we say, 'I just lost my temper.' 'Temper' is the capacity to handle all kinds of situations and maintain one's balance. It is in fact close to character, so we talk of someone 'acting out of character' or someone who is 'not themselves today'. But what do you lose your temper *to*? Things happen around us, of course, and they may get blamed, rather like when a baby spanks the floor because the floor hurt it when it fell. But what we lose our temper to, what begins to govern our actions at that point, is our body and the inclinations to wrong that inhabit its parts as living forces. You can verify this by observing the bodily behaviour of the next person you see in a rage.

Christ delivers from body hatred

A burning sense of the powers of evil inhabiting specific parts of the body, is one of the reasons for body hatred. Throughout the ages and right across cultures, body hatred has been a dreadful feature of life, and all too often of 'spirituality'. Sincere people really do find evil in their body and wrongly blame the body for it.

This misguided attitude toward the body correctly sees the power of sin that is in the body and its parts. But it mistakenly assumes that the evil *is* the body and its parts, and it does not come to terms with the tendencies to sin, the sinful meanings and intentions, that possess those parts through their habituation in a world of sin.

In this respect Paul's teaching, explained above, that we are to offer the parts of our bodies *in slavery to righteousness leading to holiness* (Rom 6:19), stands in shocking opposition to the assumptions of the classical thought of his day, as well as to those of most thinking now. The same is true for his teaching that the body of the redeemed is a temple of the Holy Spirit, and that therefore *the body is not meant for sexual immorality, but for the Lord, and the Lord for the body* (1 Cor 6:13). *Do you not know*, he continues, *that your bodies are members of Christ himself?* (1 Cor 6:15).

Well, they didn't know, apparently, and could hardly think or imagine such a thing. We today do little better. Theirs was the same understanding of the body that led Paul's hearers in Athens to scoff at the idea of a resurrection of the body (Acts 17:32). 'Who wants that thing back?' you can almost hear them say. It was inconceivable to them that the body and its parts should be honoured and treasured as the habitation of God in the redeemed person. And the same is true for most people today; indeed, it is true for most professing Christians.

For normal people in normal circumstances, the body runs, drives and controls life. Contrary to the words of Jesus (Matt 6:25), for normal people life is not more than food, nor the body more than clothing. As a matter of simple fact, their time and energy is almost wholly devoted to caring for their body, how it looks, smells and feels, and to how it can be used to meet the need for admiration, sexual gratification and power over others.

As the elderly apostle John pointed out, *everything in the world – the cravings of sinful man, the lust of his eyes and the boasting of what he has and does – comes not from the Father but from the world* (1 John 2:16). This is the *sinful mind*, as Paul calls it, which is in opposition to the mind focused on and driven by the Spirit (Rom 8:4–11). And John sees exactly the same outcomes for these two human options that Paul and all of the biblical writers did: *the world and its desires pass away, but the one who does the will of God lives for ever* (1 John 2:17; cp. Is 4:6–8; Jas 1:10; 1 Pet 1:24–25).

The body betrayed

Now the body is betrayed by its own nature when it is thus made central to human life. It is created for spiritual life in the kingdom of God, and is to be honoured, indeed glorified, in that context.[3] But when taken out of that context and made the central focus of human experience and endeavour, it is betrayed – robbed of the spiritual resources meant to sustain it and proper to its functioning – and in turn it then betrays anyone who centres life around it.

Our Western societies worship youth and beauty: they focus on the body. But body hatred is the opposite side of this coin, and it shows itself in the fear, shame, disgust, and even anger, directed at fat, old (or just aging) people, at death and dying, which dominate our culture. For an outlook focused entirely on the body, the failure and death of the body is the ultimate insult. This is a crucial insight for understanding modern Western life and culture.

This misplaced focus on the body explains many intractable problems now facing our world: the sexualization of practically everything, abortion, eating disorders, racial and other discrimination, to mention a few at random. All of these are rooted in taking the body to be the person. We thus deprive ourselves of a spiritual perspective on the person, and on personhood itself, which can enable us to cherish the body and to properly understand its central role in life.

Body hatred comes from fear of the body, fear of what it is going to do to us. Not accepting God as God puts us in his place, and leaves us with nothing to trust and worship but our body and its natural powers. The frenzy over physical attractiveness that we see all around us today, and the despair over its eventual loss, in aging and death, is one of the main characteristics of the contemporary climate of life. But that only illustrates, once more, how to be obsessed with the merely natural is death indeed. But by contrast, to be spiritually minded, that is, to be focused on our nature as spiritual beings and on our place in God's eternal life and kingdom, is *life and peace* (Rom 8:6). Then the body is in its proper place.

My body is not my property

Nowhere does the modern frenzy of self-assertion and the 'me' god come more clearly into view than in the claim now often made that 'My body is my own.' This is taken to mean that I alone have the right to say what is done in and with it. Now there is an important truth here, especially in a world where there are so many ways of getting at you through your body. But it is a truth misstated and misunderstood. Safety lies in a proper solidarity with others, not in isolation and going it alone.

'No man is an island', nor any woman either. I did not produce my body; I could not care for it for many years; my body is not self-sufficient now. There will probably come a time when I cannot care for my body again. I did not determine its basic properties: there is very little about my physical body that is due to me. The body is a gift, and just as we have received care and sustenance from others, so we also should give them to others.

We are essentially social beings, and what is done with our bodies strongly affects others around us. So I do not and cannot have exclusive say over what happens in and with my body. It is not mine to do with as I want. To think it is, is irrational. Such irrationality is the response of someone fundamentally terrified about their vulnerability through their body. As a mature and competent individual, I am responsible for the care of my body, and it is the centre of all the other responsibilities I have. But that does not imply that I and I alone have the right to say what is to be done with it, or that I alone own my body. We are stewards of our bodies.

And this is all the more true for an apprentice of Jesus, whose body and whole being have been bought back from evil by God through the death of his Son. It is therefore God's to do with as he pleases, and he pleases that our bodies should be a showplace of his greatness. Christians are the last people on earth who should say, 'My body is my own, and I can do with it what I please.'

Reasonable use of the body

So, Paul urges, *offer your bodies as living sacrifices, holy and pleasing to God – this is your spiritual act of worship* (Rom 12:1–2). This total yielding of every part of our body to God, until the very tissues and muscles that make it up are inclined toward God and godliness, breaks all conformity with worldly life. It moves us into conformity with the age to come, by the *renewing of our minds* – our powers of thought and imagination and judgment are deeply rooted in our bodies.

'Don't even think about it,' we sometimes say. And the mark of the renewed mind is that it will not even think about some things. And this freedom from even the thought of evil requires that the automatic responses toward evil are no longer running the body and its parts. The bodily tendencies no longer incline us or start us moving toward evil without thinking, dragging our thoughts and feelings after them, and with them the will also.

Mind and body

The body is the main source of gratification for many today. For this reason we are reluctant to put up with discomfort. Compared with earlier societies, we have an astonishing degree of dependence on drugs of various kinds. In some cases, of course, the discomfort is due to strictly physical conditions, and prescription drugs necessarily treat physical symptoms. But often it is not, but is due to psychological wounds, fears, unsatisfied desires, shames, losses, ambitions and false images of the self. We may deny these things, but frequently the mind is at war with the body, and we silence the mind with drugs like alcohol. But drugs can disrupt our body and even take over our life through the body's automatic responses.

Frank Laubach – partly because, to be noble, he had voted for the other candidate – was denied a position as President of a college in the Philippines where he had been serving as a missionary. He lost by one vote. He became frustrated and bitter, and for two years was almost continuously ill. His biographer writes:

> He suffered from flu, appendicitis, paratyphoid, a strained leg muscle, an ulcerated eye, and shingles! In a state of bitter self-pity, he hobbled around, worked inefficiently, and wore a patch over one eye much of the time. His failure to accept the defeat was costing him his health. The fact that his desire to exercise Christian principles resulted in hurting himself increased the inner tension and conflict. These were years of despondency and aimlessness. He was fighting the battle of his soul.[4]

What we see in a case like this is spiritual unease manifesting itself in physical disorders, which in turn threaten to take over life, and could even lead to physical death. Thank God, Frank Laubach in time found the spiritual key to turning all this around and became a person radiant with the presence of Christ.[5]

Taking steps

We have examined the nature of the human body and its place in life. What are some things that can be done to place our body and its parts fully at the disposal of the redeeming power which God intends to live in them? Changes are required in other aspects of the person than the body, but these other aspects and changes can never be adequately understood or dealt with in isolation from each other. But there are things that we can do for the sake of spiritual transformation that bear precisely on the body.

Before looking at some particular steps, however, I would like to mention two books which are of great practical help with the matters here discussed. The first is a little book by Frances Ridley Havergal, *Kept For the Master's Use*. Many know and have sung her song 'Take my life, and let it be', but the fundamental spiritual attitude expressed in the words of the song is spelled out with remarkable intelligence and biblical force in her book.[6] The second book is by Margaret Magdalen, *A Spiritual Check-Up: Avoiding Mediocrity in the*

Christian Life.[7] This lovely treatment imagines each bodily part, from the feet up, as it enters the waters of baptism, and the place it has in the transformation of all our life 'in godliness. It is extremely helpful in thinking about the body and our spiritual life.

So, now, in approaching the spiritual formation of our body, what should we do? Here are a number of things:

1. *We must actually release our bodies to God.* That is what Paul means when he tells us *to offer [our] bodies as living sacrifices, holy and pleasing to God* (Rom 12:1). It needs to be a definite action, renewed as appropriate, perhaps on a yearly basis. You will not drift into this position before God, and you will not, without decisive action, stay there.

You could do it like this. Decide to give your body to God on the basis of understanding how important it is, and that scriptural teaching requires it. Satisfy yourself, therefore, that it is a good and indispensable thing to do. Then take a day in silent and solitary retreat. Quiet your soul and your body, and let them get clear of the fog of your daily problems and preoccupations. Meditatively pray through some passages of the Bible before the Lord, especially those dealing directly with the body, already cited and emphasized in this chapter.

I recommend that you then lie on the floor, face down or face up, and explicitly and formally surrender your body to God. Take time to go over the main parts of your body and do the same for each one. What you want to do is to ask God to take charge of your body and each part, to fill it with his life and use it for his purposes. Accentuate the positive, don't just think of not sinning with your body. You will find that not sinning will follow naturally from active consecration of your body to God's power and his purpose. Remember, a sacrifice is something to be taken up in God.

Give plenty of time to this ritual of sacrifice. Do not rush. When you realize it is done, give God thanks, get up, and spend some time in praise. A reading of Psalms 145 – 150 (singing, walking or dancing) would be an excellent exercise in this context. Put your body into it. Later, share what you have done with a spiritual friend or pastor, and ask them to bless it. Review your ritual of sacrifice in thought and prayer from time to time over the following weeks, and plan to renew the same ritual surrender year by year.

2. *No longer idolize your body.* That means that you no longer make it an object of ultimate concern. You have, after all, now given it up to God and he can do with it as he wishes. You have taken your hands off the controls, and the outcomes are in God's hands. You care for it only as it serves God's purposes in your life and the lives of others. You don't worry about what will happen to it – sickness, aging, death – for you have put God in charge of all that, and any issues that arise in this area you take up with him in prayer. You take good care of your body, but only within the framework of values clearly laid down by God and exemplified in Jesus Christ. You don't live in fear of your body and what it might do to you.

3. *Closely allied with the above is that you do not misuse your body.* This means primarily two things: you do not use it as a source of improper sensual gratification, and you do not use it to dominate or manipulate others. Addictions of various kinds result from seeing sensual gratification as a necessity. These are misuses of the body. Bodily pleasure is not in itself a bad thing, but when it is exalted to a necessity and we become dependent upon it, then we are slaves of our body and its feelings.

The second thing this means is that we do not use our bodies to dominate or control others. This has different implications for different people. For example, we do not present our bodies in ways that elicit sexual thoughts, feelings and actions from others. We do not try to be sexy. We can be naturally attractive without that. This might ultimately be a fatal blow to the fashion industry and to other large segments of the economy, but we have to leave them to look after themselves. Another example on this point has to do with intimidation by means of our body. There are many aspects of this, up to and including brute force. The most common forms of it are social: gossip, sarcasm, knowing looks and remarks, even jokes. Having given up our body to God, we do not then use it or its parts in these ways.

A final example, for the moment, is overwork. In our current world this is a primary misuse of the body. It is now said that work is the new drug of choice. Often this is associated with competitiveness and trying to beat others in some area of life. Sometimes this is a matter of wearing our body out in order to succeed, perhaps in circumstances that we regard as imposed upon us by others. It is still a misuse of the body, and a failure to work things out with God. God never gives us too much to do. He long ago gave us these words: *In vain you rise early and stay up late, toiling for food to eat – for he grants sleep to those he loves* (Ps 127:2).

4. *The positive counterpart of the remarks just made is that the body is to be properly honoured and cared for.* The first step in this direction follows from what has already been said. That is, the body is to be regarded as holy, because it is owned and inhabited by God.

Of course that means it will be withheld from engagement in what is wrong. *The body is not meant for sexual immorality, but for the Lord, and the Lord for the body* (1 Cor 6:13). *Do you not know,* Paul goes on, *that your bodies are members of Christ himself? Shall I then take the members of Christ and unite them with a prostitute?* (6:15). The answer is obvious, as obvious as whether or not you should kick a sleeping baby. Of course not! *Never!* is Paul's response. But that is equally true of theft, lying and violence, once you think of it. Any part of the body of Christ is too holy for that.

But because it is holy we will also properly care for it: nourish, exercise and rest it. The way to care properly for your body is shown in God's provision of the Sabbath. Now Sabbath is a profound and intricate subject, and we cannot deal adequately with it here. But no treatment of spiritual formation and the body can be complete without at least touching upon the meaning of Sabbath.

The Christian philosopher and scientist Blaise Pascal commented, 'I have discovered that all the unhappiness of men arises from one single fact, that they cannot stay quietly in their own chamber.'[8] This remark, though rather an exaggeration, contains a deep insight. The capacity simply to be, to rest, would remove most of the striving that leads to misery. This capacity comes to fulness only when it reaches our body. Peace is a condition of the body as much as the mind, and until it has enveloped our body it has not enveloped us. Peace comes to our body when it is at home in the rightness and power of God.

Sabbath fulfilled in human life is really celebration of God. Sabbath is inseparable from worship, and, indeed, genuine worship is Sabbath. The commandment to observe the Sabbath, the fourth commandment, is the fulfilment in practice of the first three. When we can joyously *do no work* it is because God is so exalted in our minds and bodies that we can trust him with our life and our world, and can take our hands off the controls.

Now for most of us Sabbath is first to be achieved in the practice of solitude and silence. This must be carefully sought, cultivated and dwelt in. When they become established in our soul and our body, they can be practised in company with others. But the body must be weaned away from its tendencies to take control, to run the world, to achieve and produce, to attain gratification. These are its habitual tendencies learned in a fallen world. Progress in the opposite direction can only be made in solitude and silence, for they take our hands off the controls as nothing else does. And that is the meaning of Sabbath.

Rest is one primary mark of the condition of Sabbath in the body, as unrest is a mark of its absence. So if we really intend to submit our bodies as living sacrifices to God our first step well might be to start getting enough sleep. Sleep is a good first use of solitude and silence. It is also a good indicator of how thoroughly we trust in God. The psalmist, who knew danger and uncertainty well, also slept well: *I lie down and sleep; I wake again, because the Lord sustains me. I will not fear the tens of thousands drawn up against me on every side* (3:5–6), he said, and *I will lie down and sleep in peace, for you alone, O Lord, make me dwell in safety* (4:8) .

Of course that does not mean that we can just sleep our way to sainthood. Sometimes people sleep because they are depressed, or are sad, or have a physical condition, or are just evading reality. Nor does it mean that really godly people do not work hard and are never exhausted. But the 'saints' who have separated their bodies to God have resources not at the disposal of ordinary people running on fumes and promises. We have to learn how to get to where they are and take our bodies into the rest of God.

If we do not rest, the body makes its presence more strongly felt, and the tendencies of its parts call out more strongly for gratification. The sensual desires and ego demands have greater power over us when we are tired. In addition, our awareness of what the body is doing and what is happening around us will be less sharp and decisive. Confusion is the enemy of spiritual orientation. Rest, properly taken, gives clarity to the mind. Weariness, by contrast, can make us seek gratification and an energizing buzz from food or drugs, or from illicit relationships or egoistic postures. Weariness pulls us away from reliance upon God and his power.

Much more could be said of the role of spiritual disciplines in the spiritual formation of the body. A full discussion of disciplines focused on the body would have to deal with how exercise and diet can contribute to easing the influence of the sin that is part of our *earthly nature*. As finite, bodily creatures we cannot ignore such things. In particular, specific disciplines go a long way in retraining particular parts of our body away from the specific tendencies to sin that are localized in them. They enable us to stop the practice and remove the tendency in question by entering special contrary practices, and thereby break the force of habit that has us in bondage. But for now we must leave further treatment of these details aside.

The body spiritually adorned

What we must be sure about, in concluding this chapter, is that God has made every provision for the body we actually have to serve us and him well for his purposes in putting us here on earth. There may be severe problems with our bodies from the human point of view. I do not mean to deny or disregard that. But, as Peter said to women of his day (and it applies equally well to men), the real power of life lies in who we are as redeemed people, and how our behaviour is caught up in that. So we should not concentrate on *outward adornment, such as braided hair and the wearing of gold jewellery and fine clothes.* This is no legalistic ban on jewellery, though such things can be wrongly used. Rather, the adornment we should look for is that of the inner self, *the unfading beauty of a gentle and quiet spirit, which is of great worth in God's sight* (1 Pet 3:3–4). This is a clear indication of where the genuine beauty, health and strength of the body come from, and of what incredible grace lies in the spiritual transformation of the body.

Matters for thought and discussion

1. Do you agree that the body lies right at the centre of the spiritual life? Why or why not?
2. How is the body wrongly positioned in life on our own?

3. In what respects are my life and identity inseparable from my body?
4. Is it possible that much of our character consists in what our body is prepared to do without being told?
5. What does Paul mean by *put to death whatever belongs to your earthly nature* (Col 3:5)? Can we do that?
6. Discuss James's view (Jas 3:1–12) of the power of the tongue to run 'on its own' and influence our whole body. How does that happen?
7. Do you agree that when we lose our temper, we lose it to our activated body, which then takes off on its own?
8. What is the source of body hatred, and how does Christ deliver us from it?
9. Is my body my property to do with as I wish?
10. What are some of the ways we can bring our body to peace and strength in God?
11. What does Sabbath mean for your body?
12. Can the body have a spiritual beauty?

*The communities of God, to which Christ has become
teacher and guide, are, in comparison with communities of
the pagan people among whom they live as strangers, like
heavenly lights in the world.*
(Origen[1])

*We know that we have passed from death to life, because we
love our brothers. Anyone who does not love remains in death.*
(1 John 3:14)

CHAPTER 9

TRANSFORMING OUR SOCIAL DIMENSION

Now we must find out what our relationships with others should be like if we are to be spiritually formed in Christlikeness.

Circles of sufficiency

Human life is fundamentally social. Just as firm footing is necessary for walking and secure movement, so being sure of others is necessary for stable, healthy life. There are many ways this can be present in individual cases, but it must be there. If it is not, we will be walking wounded.

This kind of relatedness to others is sometimes discussed in terms of 'circles of sufficiency'. Perhaps the most fundamental is that of a mother and child, closely focused on each other and the latter utterly dependent on the former. Of course numerous forms of human association can take on some degree of 'sufficiency', even exclusivity, depending on the precise nature of the relationships involved.

These circles of sufficiency are natural and essential, and are often profoundly beautiful to behold. But they in some senses illusory at the merely human level, and even the illusion itself is terrifyingly fragile. To reassure an anxious child we say, 'Everything is okay now.' But even in a limited sense it is seldom true, and perhaps it is least true in those very situations when we feel the need to say it. We are trying to exclude the reality that makes the child anxious by making our relationship sufficient.

Every human relationship presupposes a larger context or circle that supports it. The mother and child, for example, presupposes a larger family that sustains them, that makes it possible for them to be absorbed in one another as they need to be. These larger circles depend upon yet larger circles, which, while ever less intimate, are still crucial to making the inner circles possible. The togetherness of the mother and child may be drastically affected by economic conditions on the other side of the earth.

These facts make it clear that, important as they are, human 'circles of sufficiency' can never be truly sufficient: relationships change and are dependent on factors beyond our control. The only genuine circle of sufficiency is that of the Father, Son and Holy Spirit. For that is the only relationship that is truly and totally self-sufficient. Every human circle is doomed to dissolution, and it is only in the sufficiency of the Trinity that our need for sufficient, lasting relationships can be met.

The reality of rejection

Many people know a great deal about being rejected, being left out, or just not welcome, not acceptable. The parent–child relationship is perhaps the most perfect illustration of a circle of sufficiency in human life, but it is also the relationship where the deepest and most lasting wounds can be given. If children are surrounded with love in their early years, they will very likely have a 'rootedness' that enables them to withstand most of the rejection which may come to them in later life. They will have a solid basis for relationships, grounded in the love for and from their family. That love will stay with them throughout life, even long after the loved ones are dead. The person is nourished and strengthened by loving relationships.

By contrast, children not adequately loved can die from it; or, if they survive, they can find it difficult to give and receive love in human relationships for the rest of life. They will be perpetually 'left out', if only in their imagination. And in this matter imagination can have the force of reality. Thus the final words of the Old Testament speak of one who must come and *turn the hearts of the fathers to their children, and the hearts of the children to their fathers* (Mal 4:6), or else the land will be cursed.

Failures of various kinds, real or imagined, can bring rejection or detachment from parents and other significant figures. Unfaithfulness in a mate, or a divorce, failure in career advancement, unemployment, disloyalty of children, or just never making it to wherever the 'in' place may be[2] – all of these break up relationships and the 'circles of sufficiency' that we rely on. They may leave us unconnected to others at levels of our soul where lack of nourishment from deep relationships with others means spiritual starvation. On top of this, many people experience failure, either their own or that of others, as rejection by God; and this sense of worthlessness often runs too deep for conscious awareness or words.

Two basic forms of evil in relationships

So when we come to deal with spiritual formation of our social dimension, we have to start from woundedness. It is hard to imagine anyone in this world who has not been deeply injured in their relationships by others. The exact nature of the poison of sin in our social dimension is fairly easy to describe, though extremely hard to deal with. It has two forms. They are so closely related that they really are two forms of the same thing, of lovelessness, lack of proper regard and care for others. These two forms are *assault* or attack and *withdrawal* or distancing. They are so much a part of ordinary life that most people think they are just normal, and never imagine that we could live without them.

If spiritual formation in Christ is to succeed, the power of these two forms of evil in our own lives must be broken. So far as it is possible, they must be eliminated as attitudes we take toward others. They must be disarmed. And they must be eliminated in our social environment, especially in the fellowship of Christ's followers. Perhaps we must be reconciled to the fact that they cannot be entirely eliminated from our world, or even from our fellowships, until a new epoch dawns, but we can eliminate them from our own being. We can live without them.

We *assault* someone when we act against what is good for them, even with their consent. It is not only when we harm them or cause them pain against their conscious will. Hence, seduction is assault, as is participation in or compliance with institutionalized wrongdoing and evil. The more explicit and well-known forms of assault are dealt with in the last six of the Ten Commandments – murder, adultery, theft, and so on. These commandments are more fully explained by Jesus, especially in his Sermons on the Mount and on the Plain (Matt 5 – 7 and Luke 6), and by Paul in such passages as Colossians 3 – 5 and 1 Corinthians 13.

We *withdraw* from someone when we regard their well-being and goodness as matters of indifference to us, or perhaps go so far as to despise them. We don't care.

Both assault and withdrawal primarily involve our relations to those close to us, those affected by what we do and who we are in the natural course of our living. Clearly that means members of our family or household, those who live intimately with us, those with whom we work or play, and those with whom we share common goods, our community. In the modern world it is hard to draw the boundaries in terms of the community in which we live, because we live in a connected world where we depend on people thousands of miles away.

Now we always 'distance' ourselves from those we assault, and withdrawal is nearly always a way of assaulting those we withdraw from. So we should think of the distinction between assault and withdrawal as only a matter of emphasis, useful for the understanding of how lovelessness works.

Spiritual formation is social

Spiritual formation is always profoundly social. You cannot keep it to yourself. Anyone who thinks of it as a merely private matter has misunderstood it. People who say, 'It's just between me and God,' or 'What I do is my own business,' have misunderstood God as well as themselves. Strictly speaking there is nothing 'just between me and God'. For all that is between me and God affects who I am; and that, in turn, modifies my relationships with everyone around me. My relationships with others also changes me and deeply affects my relationship with God. Hence those relationships must be transformed if I am to be transformed.

Jesus gave the outcome of spiritual formation under his guidance a distinguishing feature: we become people who love one another (John 13:35). And he did not leave love unspecified. Instead, we read, *A new command I give you: Love one another. As I have loved you, so you must love one another* (13:34). The age-old command to love is transformed, made a new command, by identifying the love in question as that of Jesus for us (see also 1 John 2:7–8). Love of this supernatural kind allows us to know that *we have passed from death to life* (1 John 3:14). We simply can't love in that way unless we have a different kind of life in us. And love here is identified as that which is in Christ because it makes us ready to *lay down our lives* for others (1 John 3:16).

Failure to love others as Jesus loves us chokes off the flow of eternal life that our whole human system cries out for. The old apostle does not mince words: *Anyone who does not love remains in death* (1 John 3:14). Notice that he does not say 'anyone who hates', but simply *anyone who does not love*. The mere absence of love is deadly. It is withdrawal. Notice also that he does not say 'anyone who is not loved'. That too is death, but our purpose cannot be to get others to love us. Love comes to us from God. That must be our unshakable circle of sufficiency.

Our purpose must then be to become those who love others with Christ's *agapē*-love. That purpose, when developed, will transform the social dimension of individuals and all of our relationships with others. Love is not a feeling, or a special way of feeling,[3] but the divine way of relating to others that shapes every dimension of our being and restructures our world for good.

Love deeply rooted in human nature

Desire for the love that Jesus was talking about is deeply rooted in our basic nature. Love expresses itself in the beautiful circles of sufficiency with which we opened this chapter. Human life is all about relating to others. We are born through relations and into relation.

One of the heart-rending stories concerning Mother Teresa of Calcutta is about an 'untouchable' who had lived on the streets or wherever he could find some kind of shelter. Dying, he was brought by Mother Teresa into her community and loved and cared for. His words were: 'I have had to live my life like an animal, but now I can die like a human being.' Simply because he had been taken in by others who gave him something! Welcoming someone, providing for their needs, making a place for them, is one of the most life-enhancing things a human being can do. They are basic acts of love. Our lives were meant to be full of such acts, drawing on the abundance of God. In a small way they are fulfilment of the command of Jesus, a step on the way toward *laying down our lives* for others.[4]

Relationships affect every aspect of life. Relatedness is the basic reality of moral existence, from which we retreat only into the living death of isolation. If we make it our purpose to save our life by withdrawal, we lose it, as Jesus said. But this is not only revealed truth, it is a testable fact of life. If you want to live, give – and receive.

God is love

This is possible, and can be put into practice, because of what God is. *God is love*, to be sure. But we must not miss the essential point. The good news is not just that he loves us; that is not the whole truth. A pretty mean person can love someone else for a variety of reasons (Matt 5:46–48). But God is love and sustains his love for us from his basic reality as love.

God is in himself a sweet society of love, with a first, second and third person to complete a social matrix where not only is there love and being loved, but also shared love for another, the third person. Community is formed not by mere love and requited love, which by itself is exclusive, but by shared love for another, which is inclusive. And within the Trinity there is only linguistically a first, second and third person: the numerical order is purely a convention. There is equality within the Trinity, not because of some metaphysical argument, but because the Trinity is love.

The nature of personality is communal, and only the Trinity does justice to what personality is. Aristotle, pagan but profound, says this of human personality:

> The individual, when isolated, is not self-sufficing, and therefore he is like a part in relation to the whole. But whoever is unable to live in society, or who has no need of it because he is sufficient for himself, must be either a beast or a god.[5]

This fundamental fact about human personality is rooted in the nature of its Creator, and the writers of the Bible were well aware of it. We are told on the earliest pages of the Bible that God said, *It is not good for the man to be alone,* and so God decided, *I will make a helper suitable for him* (Gen 2:18). Centuries later, Paul pointed out that *none of us lives to himself alone and none of us dies to himself alone* (Rom 14:7). Paul knew something that Aristotle could not know, that *whether we live or die, we belong to the Lord,* and that *for this very reason, Christ died and returned to life so that he might be the Lord of both the dead and the living* (14:8–9). Human beings are really together only in God, and all other ways of 'being with' others fall short of the needs of basic human nature.

The secret of all life-giving relationships with others lies in the fact that the primary 'other' for us, whether we want it or not, is always God. John Donne wrote a beautiful exposition of Paul's words:

> All mankind is of one author and is one volume; when one man dies, one chapter is not torn out of the book, but translated into a better language; and every chapter must be so translated. God employs several translators; some pieces are translated by age, some by sickness, some by war, some by justice; but God's hand is in every translation, and his hand shall bind up all our scattered leaves again for that library where every book shall lie open to one another.[6]

One nation under God?

In America we 'pledge our allegiance' to a flag that represents 'one nation under God, indivisible, with liberty and justice for all'. But who has any idea of what this would mean for real life on the street, and how it applies to them? The biblical vision of human unity under God is one which few people today can even imagine, much less regard as realistically possible for themselves or others. Only the message and people of Jesus Christ can give it substance.

Perhaps someone with no real knowledge of Christ could imagine that kind of community for a few people, carefully selected. People of the right sort, but certainly not people in general, and especially not those lumped together by accidents of birth, history or society. Sin embedded deeply in our souls and bodies has almost totally disabled us for those relationships with others which our hearts desire and which were intended by God. These are relationships which public discourse idealizes without understanding what they are.

Larry Crabb writes:

> When two people connect, when their beings intersect as closely as two bodies during intercourse, something is poured out of one and into the other that has power to heal the soul of its deepest wounds and restore it to health. The one who receives experiences the joy of being healed. The one who gives knows the even greater joy of being used to heal. Something good is in the heart of each of God's children that is more powerful than everything bad. It's there, waiting to be released, to work its magic.

Then he adds: 'But it rarely happens.'[7]

That is sadly so. The power of life in Christ is seldom realized. But spiritual formation in Christ would mean that what Larry Crabb describes would routinely happen. That is what the image of the church as the body of Christ means, that members should nourish one another with the transcendent power that raised Christ from the dead. That is what produces 'the Church as we see her spread out through all time and space and rooted in eternity, terrible as an army with banners'.[8] The church, which anyone can look at if they will, is the outward manifestation in history and society of the invisible church which God alone sees. Of this invisible reality Dietrich Bonhoeffer says:

> The spiritual unity of the Church is a primal synthesis willed by God. It is not a relationship that has to be established, but one that is already posited (*iustitia passiva*), and remains invisible. It is not made possible by concord,

similarity or affinity between souls, nor should it be confused with unity of mood. Instead it is real just where seemingly the most intractable outward oppositions prevail, where each man leads his quite individual life, and it is perhaps absent where it seems to prevail most. It can shine more brightly in the conflict between wills than in concord.[9]

We come into this church when we put our trust in Jesus. He takes us in and forms a circle of sufficiency that is real and ultimate. We first of all 'connect' with him, and we can then begin to see how the flow of love from him comes through others to us and from us to others. This happens in imperfect communities and congregations now. But the new life can and must eventually transform our entire social dimension, so that it reflects the heavenly future in which we shall know as we are now known by God and 'where every book shall lie open to one another'.

Thoroughly understanding the wrongness

Here as in all the other dimensions of life, the progress of spiritual formation in our relations with others depends upon what we do as well as what God does for us and in us. And in order to do our part in the process of spiritual formation we must identify and understand what is wrong in our relations with others, whether that wrong is coming from us or toward us, and how it can be changed. So we return to assault and withdrawal.

Assault comes first in the development of a child, and it arises, primarily from conflicts of desire. The child wants something that another has. It does what it can to take that thing away from the other. But the other resists, and the children involved become angry with each other. They therefore try to harm each other. This is the story of Cain.

Or perhaps they experience envy, and are displeased with one another because of that. Perhaps there is a status that one enjoys and the other does not. Feelings of resentment and contempt may arise and play back and forth between them. As they grow older, theft, lying, murder, adultery and settled attitudes of covetousness fall into place. These are all forms of assault on others.

Central to them all is the will to make another suffer. As we have already noted, the last six of the Ten Commandments deal with assault, with the ways in which we injure, by aggressive action, those in social relation with us. With the exception of the sixth commandment, they are all explicitly negative – 'Thou shalt not . . .' The sixth commandment, *Honour your father and mother*, deals with a relation so intimate that the command must be positive, for to omit the positive here would amount to an injury to both parties. That is also why this is *the first commandment with promise*, as Paul says (Eph 6:2). Violation of it disrupts the human soul and makes dysfunctional people as nothing else does.

Now we can see immediately that spiritual formation in Christ will mean becoming people who do not want to, and therefore do not, assault others. Of course the overall teaching of the Bible about assault is much more profound and subtle than just these six commandments, which can be regarded as the rock-bottom essentials for right relations with others. But there are many ways of assaulting people, and these merge into our other category of wrong in relationships, withdrawal.

Here again we see the power of the tongue. A verbal assault, which can be done in very refined as well as brutal ways (we speak of a 'cutting remark' or being 'scathing'), is specifically designed to hurt its object, or to inflict loss of standing or respect before others. You will find many people who never recover from a particular verbal assault, or from non-verbal forms of harassment, or from degrading treatment they have received. Most often this happens to people when they are young, or otherwise vulnerable.

But withdrawal in a relationship, like assault, also wounds those involved. And the tongue can assault by withdrawal; you can withdraw by not speaking. So, once again, we can see that it is unwise to draw too sharp a line between assault and withdrawal: withdrawal is often intended as assault or attack. Some forms of it are not, however, and may instead be motivated by weakness, fear or uncertainty, rather than any direct will to harm. Often our own weaknesses and limitations make us withdraw without intending injury or even recognizing it as a possibility. Yet injure it does. For those without full consciousness of God's love and power, no combination of good motives and explanations can prevent or heal the wounds of withdrawal. Without God, we can at most become hardened against them and struggle on.

The social area of our lives is meant by God to be a play of constant mutual blessing. Pain and dysfunctionality result from the lack of this. Of course there are degrees in the closeness and involvement that we have with one another. This makes a difference in the precise character of the mutual blessing that we can communicate and give to one another. But every contact with others should be one of goodwill and respect, with a readiness to acknowledge, make way for or assist the other in suitable ways.

Our current coldness is not normal

Today we are not so far removed in time from a social world in which such a constantly generous response to others and from others was the ideal. I recall from my childhood that my father, as he drove along in his car, always raised his hand to the driver of an oncoming vehicle, and they nearly always reciprocated. (Just recently while driving in rural Georgia, a man acknowledged me in this way. I was mildly shocked.) Of course there were not that many oncoming vehicles then. My father also never passed anyone on the sidewalk without acknowledging them, unless he was in a crowd; and he would always tip his hat to a woman.

These, it might be thought, are small, old-fashioned things, and you would probably wreck your car if you tried to acknowledge all the drivers you meet today. If you spoke to people on the sidewalk they would think you were crazy or dangerous. No doubt the profound moral insight of our times would also point out the hypocrisy involved in such courtesies.

Admittedly, we now live in a different world. But is it a better world for that? Could the addictions and dysfunctions from which people suffer possibly be related to the fact that we are constantly in the presence of people who are withdrawn from us, who don't want to acknowledge we are there, and frankly would feel more at ease if we weren't? People who in many cases explicitly reject us and feel it only right to do so? Isn't the desperate need for approval which drives people so relentlessly today causing them to go to foolish and self-destructive lengths to be attractive or at least get attention, just the echo of a lost world of constant mutual welcome and blessing in family, neighbourhood, school and work? Being attractive and getting attention is scraping the bottom of the barrel of relationships, the fifteen minutes of fame (for which Andy Warhol is famous) that is now down to fifteen seconds.

I do not mean to suggest that anyone can overcome our desperate social situation by an individual act of will. Far from it. Whatever can be done, that isn't it. To do anything of substance about it will require grace and wisdom that is at no individual's disposal, and a long-term plan of personal and social development is required. No doubt God has one in mind.

But to make a start where we are we must recognize that this our world is not normal, but is only usual at present. We must try to see the world for what it is, and then begin to think of specific ways grace and truth can begin to change it. And above all, we who follow Jesus must understand that a couple of hours a week of carefully calibrated distance in a church setting will be of little help, and may only enforce the patterns of withdrawal that permeate our fallen world. What could we do in our fellowships that would really help make a difference?

Families

It is especially in our families and similarly close associations that we must identify the elements of assault and withdrawal that defeat love and right relations with others. By insight and practice we must break away from them and reverse them. First we must learn calm but firm non-cooperation with the poisonous elements of assault and withdrawal, then we must initiate goodwill and blessing in the midst of them. What we do in our meetings as Christians should be focused on enabling us to love one another. Those meetings can and should be centres from which a powerfully redemptive sense of community spreads.

Where to start? In the United States publicly owned vehicles, like those of the police and schools, have bumper stickers that say, 'There's no excuse for domestic violence.' It's a wonderful idea. But we need to go deeper, of course. We need to become the kind of people for whom domestic violence is unthinkable and never an option. We must be transformed in such a way that our minds and bodies simply do not have the make-up for it. This is the work of Christian spiritual formation.

We must begin in the family. Here the slogan must be 'There's no excuse for assault or withdrawal in the home.' Do you think if that slogan were put into practice it would take care of domestic violence? Of course it would. But the reverse is not true, merely avoiding domestic violence does not free the home from assault and with-drawal; it can still be a hell of cutting remarks, contempt and coldness. Such a situation can all too often be found in the homes of Christians and even of Christian leaders. Frequently they honestly seem to think that such a condition is normal, and have no knowl-edge of any other way. Their very theology may strengthen this tragically false outlook.

Marriage

Today in America close to half of all marriages break down, and the rate is not much lower for professing Christians. But the problem is not divorce, though divorce generates a set of problems all its own. The problem is that people don't know how to be married. They don't actually get married in many cases, though they go through a legal and possibly a religious ceremony. They are, sad to say, incap-able of marriage – the kind of constant, mutual giving that can make two people in conjugal relation one whole person (Eph 5:22–33). It is not their fault. Who teaches them?

To be married is to give yourself to another person in the most intimate of human relationships, to support them for good in their life and in every way possible – physically, emotionally, spiritually, and in every conceivable aspect of their being. Nothing ever given to humanity more adequately portrays what marriage is than the trad-itional service, 'The Form of Solemnization of Matrimony', in the old *Book of Common Prayer* of the Church of England.

Just consider some of its wording: anyone who wants to under-stand marriage should begin with careful study of the giving of

oneself and the receiving of another in the vows. 'I, N, take thee, N
. . . to have and to hold from this day forward, for better for worse,
for richer for poorer, in sickness and in health, to love and to cherish,
till death us do part.' The vows clearly bring out why the ideal for
marriage is one man, one woman for life. The 'mutual submission to
each other in awe of the Lord' eliminates both assault and withdrawal from this most basic of human relationships. Thereby it provides
the matrix from which, in God's plan, whole human beings can
emerge to form whole human communities.

This matrix or 'womb' is then the home of the child, and not just
while the woman is in pregnancy. Birth should be a move from one
part to a larger part of the same home. This home is as much the
man's responsibility as the woman's, for it is the man's role to make it
possible for the woman to do what she alone can do for the child.
And for her part, then, she is to help in making it possible for him to
do what he alone can do for her and the child. And they do this in
constant sacrificial submission of each to the overall good of the
other. In case there are no children involved, they still *lay down their
lives* for each other. That is what marriage involves.

The 'market' approach to marriage

Since the two world wars, it has for various reasons been increasingly
unclear how such a union of souls can be realized in practice.
Individual desire on the one hand, and market forces on the other,
have come to be the standard and rule of everything. How are we to
serve one another in intimate relationship, if individual desire is the
standard for everything, and if what we want can be acquired from
many competing providers?

The ways in which man and wife, or parents and children, would
naturally serve one another are increasingly viewed as available from
other sources; sources usually imagined to be less expensive and of
better quality.[10] This is true all the way from food, clothing and
entertainment, to sexual gratification. The perilous condition of
labourers competing with others to sell their labour is now the condition of everyone in society. Individual desire and economic
competition are accepted as principles governing everything.

What, then, does devotion to another mean when one or both parties are constantly shopping for a better deal or constantly appraising one another in the light of convenient alternatives? Withdrawal, rejection and assault will naturally become a factor in the most intimate of human relationships. This is something that Satan has consistently used to defeat God's plans for human community on earth, from Adam blaming Eve for his own sin, to Cain killing Abel, to the millions of children living on the streets and in the sewers of urban centres around the globe or starving in rural poverty. The very same principle of withdrawal and assault operates at the highest levels of cultural, social and political interaction, with constant glorification in the popular arts and media.

Children

The spiritual malformation of children is an inevitable result. Their souls, bodies and minds cannot but absorb the reality of assault and withdrawal when their parents or other adults are constantly engaged in them. And of course they are soon in the line of fire themselves. They are soon being attacked and frozen out, or their 'love' is being bought as a commodity by competing estranged parents. In such a context you can almost see the child shrivel.

Their only hope of survival is to become hardened. They withdraw. It is a defensive posture, which, incidentally, makes attack on others and on themselves easy. Hardened, lonely little souls, ready for addiction, aggression, isolation, self-destructive behaviour and violence, go out to mingle their madness with that of others like them on nightmarish street corners and clubs. They turn to their bodies for gratification and to control others, or withdraw into isolation and self-destruction.

The wonder is not that they sometimes destroy one another, but that the adults who produced them and live with them can, with apparent sincerity, ask, 'Why?' Do they really not know? Can they really not see the poison? It is another case of the blind leading the blind, and both falling into a pit (Matt 15:14).

Marching onward in life, these little people become big people and move on with their malfunctioning souls into work, citizenship and leadership. From them proceeds the next generation of wounded souls. Many of these big people try hard to rectify the situation. They sponsor solutions to the problem, such as education or embracing diversity or promoting tolerance. But these turn out to be sickeningly shallow.

It is not that these are not good in themselves. They are. But they do not come close to the root of the human problem. They are superficial. The deep root is not ignorance, not prejudice, and not intolerance. A very small percentage of human evil comes from them, everything considered. Far from being the primary sources of evil, ignorance, prejudice and intolerance draw and feed upon the deeper-lying soul habits of assault and withdrawal, without which they would have little effect.

Difference serves as an occasion of assault and withdrawal. If sources deeper than that are not effectively dealt with, education, diversity and tolerance will only yield another version of secular self-righteousness and legalism. They will further crush the already famished human soul. Instead of healing human relationships they will establish a somewhat more socially stable context within which people shrivel and die.

Minister to marriage

So, to heal the open sore of social existence there is no doubt we must start with the marriage relationship, or, more inclusively, with how men and women are together in the world. If that relationship is wrong, all who come through it will be damaged. And they will be further damaged by a surrounding world of similarly damaged people, who are trying to manage their ways of being together on the assumption that assault and withdrawal are just normal. So spiritual formation, and all our efforts as Christians to minister to people, must focus on this central relationship.

But we sometimes see families arriving at church frozen in coldness or seething in anger, sometimes even about what it took to get them there on time. And then we may have people conducting services who can hardly endure one another because of disagreements and painful incidents which have occurred between them, perhaps even in the process of deciding how the service should be done. Do we need a bumper sticker that says, 'There is no excuse for hostility and coldness among Christians'?

Obviously this is relevant to us all. But we can only begin to recover the proper social dimension of our lives under Christ by recognizing that there is no human answer to these problems, not even a religious answer. There is no human way to dissolve the habits of assault and withdrawal that characterize our individual and corporate life.

The churches must return to the transcendent power of Christ in which they stand. They must drain the assault and withdrawal, the attack and coldness, from the individual men and women who form families under their ministry. We must affirm, and make clear by teaching and example, that it takes 'three to get married' as Fulton Sheen taught years ago. The 'third' of course is God, and without him the marriage relationship is doomed to failure simply as a matter of statistics. From the basis of Christian love in the home, established and encouraged through the church, the power of God can decisively break the deadly hold of assault and withdrawal over our social relationships.

Spiritual formation of our social dimension

What will this look like in ordinary human relations? This is what must be explained and abundantly exemplified in the context of the church. Spiritual formation of our social dimension must start here, though it will apply to conjugal relationships and families. Above all it must be seen in the family relationships of those who lead and teach. Here are four major elements in the spiritual formation of our social dimension.

Receiving God's vision

The first main element in the transformed social dimension is for individuals to come to see themselves whole, as God sees them. Such a vision allows them to see beyond the wounds and limitations of their past relationships with others. God's committed love for us shows that he sees us as valuable, and this makes it possible for us to regard ourselves in that way, as blessed, no matter what has happened. *For you died,* Paul tells us, *and your life is now hidden with Christ in God. When Christ, who is your life, appears, then you also will appear with him in glory* (Col 3:3–4). We have stepped into a new life where our primary relationship is with Christ and we are assured of being with him forever.

God has a plan for each of us, and no-one can prevent this from being fulfilled if we put our hope entirely in him. Our life in him is whole and it is blessed, no matter what has or has not been done to us, no matter how shamefully our human circles of sufficiency have been violated. It is God's sufficiency that secures everything else for us. Paul says we have everything we need in God (2 Cor 3:5 and 9:8). It is the God-given vision of ourselves as complete in him that draws all the poison from our relationships with others, and enables us to go forward with sincere forgiveness and blessing toward them. Only in this way can we stand, free of the wounds of the past and free from bitterness toward those who have assaulted or forsaken us.

Defensiveness gone

The second element in transforming our social dimension is for us to abandon all defensiveness. This can occur only in a social context where Christ dwells, that is, among his special people. But it would occur naturally in the absence of attack and withdrawal.

This abandonment of defensiveness includes a willingness to be known in our most intimate relationships for who we really are. It includes abandonment of self-justification, evasiveness and deceit, as well as manipulation. That is not to say we should impose all the facts about ourselves upon those close to us, much less on others. Of course we shouldn't. But it does mean that we do not hide from reality, and we do not adopt strategies for making ourselves look good. Jesus' teaching about not performing for public approval, about letting our yes be yes and nothing more, and about not being hypocritical – having a face different from our heart – is important here (Matt 5 and 6).

Genuine love

And then all pretence would vanish from our lives. That is the third element in the spiritually transformed social dimension. Love between Christians would then be genuine. And that is the central factor in the beautiful picture of what the local gatherings of disciples into churches should be like, given by Paul in Romans 12:1–21. Each person would be carrying out their particular work in the group with a grace and power not from themselves, but from God (12:3–8), and each one would be exhibiting the following qualities (12:9–21):

1. Letting love be completely real.
2. Rejecting what is evil.
3. Clinging to what is good.
4. Being devoted to one another in love.
5. Outdoing one another in giving honour.
6. Serving the Lord with zeal.
7. Rejoicing in hope.
8. Being patient in affliction.
9. Being devoted to prayer.
10. Contributing to the needs of the saints.
11. Practising hospitality.
12. Blessing persecutors and not cursing them.
13. Being joyful with those who are joyful and being sorrowful with those in sorrow.
14. Living in harmony with each other.
15. Not being proud, but associating with people in low positions.
16. Not seeing oneself as wise.
17. Never repaying evil for evil.
18. Having due regard for what everyone takes to be right.
19. Being at peace with everyone.
20. Never taking revenge, but leaving that to God.
21. Providing for needy enemies.
22. Not being overwhelmed by evil, but overwhelming evil with good.

This is the fullest biblical description of what a spiritually transformed social dimension looks like. We should pause to contemplate it. Just think for a moment what it would be like to be part of a group in which this list was the conscious, shared intention, and where it was actually lived out, even if with imperfections. You can see, I think, how it would totally transform the marriage relation and the home and family. Its effect on the community would be incalculable, as it in fact has been wherever it has been realized throughout history.

The abandonment of all defensiveness and its many strategies could clearly be achieved in such a group. There would no longer be any need for defensiveness. In its place would be receptiveness and blessing for all, even enemies. This attitude depends on us having heard and accepted the gospel of grace. It depends on participation in the life of Jesus, and sharing in his defenceless death on the cross. It depends on his acceptance of us into his eternal life beyond the worst that could be done to him or to us. In order to live this genuine love, we must stand safe and solid in Jesus' kingdom.

Opening up

The fourth element is an opening up of our social dimension to redemption. Not having the burden of defending and securing ourselves, and acting now from the resources of our new life in God, we can devote our lives to the service of others. This is not just a matter of not attacking or withdrawing. Redemption will naturally and rightly be chiefly focused in blessing those closest to us, beginning with our family members, and moving out from there.

We cannot be the wife or husband or parent God intends except in the power of God. That holds true for life as a whole. We do not even know how to pray as we ought, Paul tells us (Rom 8:26). But that hardly means we should not pray. Of course not, for *the Spirit himself intercedes for us with groans that words cannot express* (8:26). And the Spirit of God will enter into all our social relationships if we invite him, wait on him and proceed as best we can. We have the promise of Jesus that we shall have *living water*, a limitless source of God's power, that will become *a spring of water welling up to eternal life* (John 4:14), and *streams of living water will flow from within* us to others (John 7:38; Is 58:11).

Spiritual formation in Christ obviously requires that we increasingly live in and by the direct upholding of God. This is clearly what the Bible calls for, and especially what Jesus himself lived and presented as the truth. Only with this gospel outlook on life can we begin to approach the godly reformation of the self in its social world. But with that outlook we can turn away from assault and withdrawal, and move toward blessing all whose lives we touch.

Matters for thought and discussion

1. What 'circles of sufficiency' have you experienced in your lifetime? Describe in detail some occasions when you experienced complete sufficiency in a relationship. Or an occasion when the relationship was broken.
2. Why does rejection affect us as it does? How does it affect us? Can you recall an occasion when you rejected someone and how they responded?
3. Do assault and withdrawal adequately cover the range of evils people inflict on others? Think about the role these play in ordinary life. Is it possible to disagree with or correct others without assault or withdrawal?
4. Consider the things forbidden in each of the last six of the Ten Commandments as forms of assault. What do they do to people?
5. How would loving as Jesus loved eliminate assault and withdrawal in personal relationships?
6. How does the Trinitarian nature of God cast light on what human relations should be like?
7. 'One nation under God.' How could that possibly be realized?
8. How do assault and withdrawal find their way into the lives of children?
9. Must we accept coldness between people as normal?
10. Do you agree that redemption of marriage is central to any hope for transforming our broader social situation today? Or is that just too much to expect of any man–woman relationship?
11. How can we come to see ourselves as complete in God, and how would that help heal our social dimension?
12. Could Paul's picture of the redemptive fellowship of Christ's people (Rom 12:1–21) work in your group?

Only be careful, and watch yourselves closely so that you do not forget the things your eyes have seen or let them slip from your heart as long as you live.
(Deut 4:9)

Take my yoke upon you and learn from me, for I am gentle and humble in heart, and you will find rest for your souls.
(Matt 11:29)

CHAPTER 10

TRANSFORMING THE SOUL

What is running your life at any given moment is your soul. Not external circumstances, or your thoughts, or your intentions or even your feelings, but your soul. The soul is that aspect of your being that correlates, integrates and enlivens everything going on in the various aspects of the self. It is the life-centre of the human being. It regulates whatever is occurring in each of those aspects of life, and how they interact with each other and respond to surrounding events. The soul is deep in the sense of being basic or foundational, and also in the sense that it lies almost totally beyond consciousness.[1]

In the person with a well-kept heart, the soul itself will be properly ordered under God and in harmony with reality. The outcome will be a person who is prepared for and capable of responding to the situations of life in ways that are good and right. Such a person will be in a right relationship with God. With his grace, the soul will be subject to God, and the mind will be subject to the soul. The social context and the body will then be subject to thoughts and feelings that are in agreement with truth and with God's purposes for us. Any event in life will then work for good, because our soul is functioning properly under God.

Psalm 1

That is how it is with the person described in Psalm 1. He is first characterized in terms of what he does not do, which is perhaps the most immediately obvious thing about him. He does not determine his course of action by what those without God are saying, even their latest brilliant ideas. That is, he does not live as if God does not exist, nor does he make plans purely according to human understanding. He plans on God (1:1).

Because of that he does not stand with people who live by doing wrong. If you live only according to human wisdom, you will find it necessary constantly to do what is wrong. And in that case you will become an authority on what is right and wrong, because in the end you will have to manage right and wrong. You will have to have ready explanations of why, though you do wrong things, you are still a good person, and why those who do not do as you do are fools. You will become an expert scorner, able to put everyone in their place with appropriate doses of contempt (1:1).

By contrast, the Psalm 1 person delights in the law that God has given. Note, he delights in it (1:2): he loves it, is thrilled by it, can't keep his mind off of it. He thinks it is beautiful, elegant, wise, an incredible gift of God's mercy and grace. He therefore dwells upon it day and night, turning it over and over in his mind and reciting it to himself. He does not do this only to please God but because the law pleases him. It orients his whole being.

The result is a flourishing life. The image used here is that of a tree planted by streams of water. No matter what the weather or the surface condition of the ground, its roots go down into the water source and bring up life. As a result, it bears fruit when it is supposed to, and its foliage is always bright. It prospers in what it does, and likewise with the man who is rooted in God through his law, *whatever he does prospers* (Ps 1:6; cp. Josh 1:8). We must come back to the vital relationship between the law and the soul later.

For most of us, this ideal arrangement of life under God will be only partially realized, at best. For many, it remains an impossible dream, for their soul is in chaos and their life is a mess. They are *dead in transgressions and sins,* living off incoherent dreams and illusions. Enslaved to their desires or their bodily habits, or blinded by false ideas, distorted images and misinformation, their soul cannot find its way into a life of consistent truth and harmonious pursuit of what is good. It is locked in a self-destructive struggle with itself and with all around it. Normally, unfulfilled desires and poisonous relationships are the most prominent features of such lives. As a counsellor of those in trouble, I am often stunned by the reasons people give for not doing the only things that could possibly be of help to them.

The formation of the soul – the character it has taken on through life – is seen in the thoughts, feelings, social relations, bodily behaviours and choices that the person has or makes. In most cases, people are not in harmony within themselves, much less with truth and with God. Their habitual condition is one of conflict, and they act other than how they themselves intend or regard as wise. Their good intentions are not effectively related to the other components of their person, the thoughts and feelings, the bodily habits, the social dynamics, the relationship to God's kingdom, in a way that would bring the good about. The failure of good intentions is the outcome of the underlying disconnections between thoughts, feelings and actions, permitted or enforced by the disordered soul. The aspects of the self are not coherently drawn together by the soul to form a whole life devoted to God and to what is good. Such people 'get it all together' or 'get their act together', as we say now. That language is not metaphorical, but expresses the reality of their life. Extreme cases of this are people who cannot make or maintain basic personal or social relationships. Often they have been damaged by early experiences, by severe deprivation or suffering. Their soul cannot integrate what their mind tells them about their value as people and what their experiences and feelings tell them about their worthlessness.

The soul develops: if it does not receive what it needs to grow, its further progression toward wholeness is hindered. It will never be what it might have been. Sometimes horrible events in later life have similar effects, where the soul turns in on itself and may never recover. However, we must not underestimate the powers of recovery of the soul under grace. Robert Wise observes, 'Reconnected to the Spirit of God, lost souls discover they have power and capacity beyond anything they could have dreamed. The restoration of soul is more than a recovery of connectedness. Significant strength, ability to achieve, guidance, and awareness are imparted.'[2] Truly we are *fearfully and wonderfully made* (Ps 139:14). The soul has amazing capacity for recovery when it finds its home in God and receives his grace.[3]

Modern difficulties with the soul

Now of all the aspects of the human being which must be dealt with in spiritual formation, the soul is by far the most controversial in today's world. For various reasons, the idea of the soul was rejected in psychological work – discussed dismissively under the title the 'theory of the soul' – as it tried to develop a scientific understanding of humans. It could not find a verifiable, tangible centre that organizes life into a whole. The supposed lack of a soul in humanity has become part of accepted modern thought.

The issues here certainly run deep, and should not be dismissed lightly. But they are not the kinds of issues that can be dealt with effectively here. There is a wide range of relevant material that can be read by anyone who wants to pursue questions about the soul.[4] But here it is worth simply pointing out that science does not have answers to fundamental questions of human thought and motivation, for example, and these are things which are as 'real' as chemical reactions. The reality of the soul, however we may name it, is empirically verified by our very existence.

Soul unavoidable

There has been a great wave of popular publications and media presentations on the soul in recent decades. 'Soul' has become almost as attention-getting as sex, and is widely used as a selling point. People pride themselves on having and knowing and expressing soul, and spirituality is something everyone wants. This is a natural reaction to a deeply felt need, for indeed the soul, or, more generally, the 'spiritual' side of life, simply cannot be indefinitely suppressed. Fundamental aspects of life such as art, sleep, sex, ritual, family, parenting, community, health and work all are, in part, soul functions, and they fail to be meaningful as soul diminishes. One of the reasons that modern intellectuals might have failed to locate the soul is that this really is no longer significantly present in their lives. Perhaps something like a soulless life really is possible, and not just something in fashionable works of literature.

That would explain why meaning is such a problem for people today. Meaning is fundamentally a matter of transcendence: what we do or feel or say points to something beyond itself. Meaningful experience is not that of the moment, something which leaves us indifferent and unchanged. Wordsworth's poem 'Lines Written a Few Miles Above Tintern Abbey', is essentially about this kind of meaning, and he puts it like this:

> here I stand, not only with the sense
> Of present pleasure, but with pleasing thoughts
> That in this moment there is life and food
> For future years.

Meaning nourishes the soul. It is one of the greatest human needs, one of our deepest hungers – perhaps it is the most basic human need.[5] Almost anything can be borne if life as a whole is meaningful. But in the absence of meaning, boredom or self-obsession, mere effort or willpower are what is left. Dead religion or a dead job or a dead relationship are those that have no meaning, or are merely habitual.

People who are well-off by physical, financial and social standards, find a meaningless life unbearable. But meaning can make pain and exertion, tedium and sorrow not only bearable but even exhilarating. We are in fact reaching out to a power beyond ourselves. We are nourishing our soul.

Performance, fanaticism and the broken soul

Where meaning is lacking, performance is at a premium. Performance, in art or sport for example, creates the illusion of meaning for a magical moment. Whether the performance is a success or a failure, it creates an illusion of meaning because of the effort involved and the feeling of exaltation or depression that depends on the outcome. A glance at the *Guinness Book of Records* will show the lengths people will go to to get their names into the record books, to perform; but the meaning, real or imagined, of many of the feats is difficult to determine. It must be acknowledged that concern with performance may also be found in religion: we too often play the numbers game, or regard having lively music as essential to worship. But performance is of no value unless it deals effectively with life and reality: acting will not do.

Fanaticism in art, politics, sport or religion, takes performance further. Fanaticism is the result of people with meaningless lives becoming obsessed with performance, and then trying to make a meaning out of it. Being a fan of something is generally thought to be deep and important. The commitment a fanatic expresses is essentially distorted; it is a failure to see reality whole. Fanaticism takes over thoughts, feelings, behaviour and social relations. It takes the place of reality, and gives the meaning to life that would not otherwise be there. It can be intoxicating. Life is no longer subject to ordinary tests of truth, reality and reason: all sense of proportion is lost.

In this way, a team winning a championship can lead to fans looting, burning and killing. Being in love can become an obsession. Success can lead to workaholic absorption. All of these reflect the non-functioning or breakdown of the soul, leading to people having inadequate resources to deal with the whole of life. The person with a non-functioning soul is easy prey, subject to pressure from others. Such people become 'the lonely crowd'.[6]

People who deny the soul for whatever reasons still have to live, and they need to find the resources for it.

Our strategy here

Let us try to understand the soul a little more. First, we will draw a picture or image of the soul, and second, we will look at certain things said about the soul in the Bible.

The soul is like an inner stream, which refreshes, nourishes and gives strength to every other element of our life. When that stream flows properly, we are refreshed and content in all we do, because our soul is rooted in God and his kingdom. We are in harmony with God, reality, the rest of humanity and nature at large. A child allowed to develop properly, and nurtured in all aspects of its being, gives us a good idea of what a life with a healthy soul looks like.

God is the source of life and the soul. *In his hand is the life of every creature and the breath of all mankind,* Job tells us (Job 12:10). Living things receive life from God, and human beings receive a particular gift of God in being formed by him and having his life breathed into them (Gen 2:7). God *alone is immortal* (1 Tim 6:16), God alone is self-initiating, self-directing, and self-sustaining, but he gives this power in part to us, and this derivative life flows through us as our soul. When we speak of the human soul, then, we are speaking of the deepest level of life and power in the human being.

Older translations of the Bible often refer to God's soul. God warns Judah through Jeremiah, *Be thou instructed, O Jerusalem, lest my soul depart from thee; lest I make thee desolate, a land not inhabited* (Jer 6:8, AV). But more recent versions translate this as *Take warning, O Jerusalem, or I will turn away from you and make your land desolate so no-one can live in it* (NIV). In this and other cases the words *nephesh* in the Hebrew texts and *psychē* in the Greek are used with reference to God. This is in order to indicate the depth of God's feeling to the wickedness of his people. That depth is not successfully communicated by the alternative language of the self. The true meaning is hollowed out and lost. Especially is this the case today, when that language is used in justification of selfishness ('what about *my* needs?'). The heart of the matter is that when we refer to someone's soul we are saying something about the depths of their being, something which is different from the self seen in terms of desires, wishes and preferences.

Biblical cases

Now if you take this idea of the deepest level of a life and put it alongside biblical references to the human soul, you will see that it makes great sense of what Scripture is saying. Human life has many aspects that are superficial, not the real essence of life. They are not soul. Let us consider some texts.

Consider Jesus' teaching: *What good will it be for a man if he gains the whole world, yet forfeits his soul? Or what can a man give in exchange for his soul?* (Matt 16:26). Before even considering the question of profit, one might well ask how it is possible to forfeit one's soul? What does it mean to lose your soul? Can you actually do that?

Well, it means that your life is no longer under the direction of your inner stream, but has been taken over by exteriors. The rich farmer who said to himself, to his soul, *You have plenty of good things laid up for many years. Take life easy; eat, drink and be merry* (Luke 12:19) is a case in point. He had abandoned his soul in favour of externals. He had stored up things for himself, but was not rich toward God (12:21). He is an illustration of the selfishness and self-satisfaction that cut people off from the meaning and purpose of life. He has given his very being over to those *sinful desires, which war against [the] soul* (1 Pet 2:11). A step beyond the misguided farmer are people who delight in doing evil. *The wicked man craves evil,* the proverb tells us (21:10), that is, his soul desires it and seeks it out. In his deepest depths he is committed to wrongdoing.

On the positive side, Mary sings, *My soul glorifies the Lord and my spirit rejoices in God my Saviour* (Luke 1:46). Paul wrote to the Thessalonians, *We loved you so much that we were delighted to share with you not only the gospel of God but our lives as well, because you had become so dear to us* (1 Thess 2:8): they shared their very souls with them.

The book of Psalms is, of course, the great 'soul book' of the Bible, because, more than any other, it deals with life in its depths. *O God, you are my God, earnestly I seek you; my soul thirsts for you, my body longs for you, in a dry and weary land where there is no water* (63:1). *My soul yearns, even faints, for the courts of the Lord; my heart and my flesh cry out for the living God* (84:2). *As the deer pants for streams of water, so my soul pants for you, O God. My soul thirsts for God, for the living God. When can I go and meet with God?* (42:1–2). The water image earlier noted naturally stands out in these passages because of the similarity of water to the nourishing flow of God's life from which the soul draws its strength.

These and many other passages make clear that the soul is the most basic level of life in the person. We must take care to do whatever we can to keep it in God's hands, recognizing all the while that we can only do this with his help.

Acknowledging our soul

And the very first thing that we must do is to be mindful of our soul, to acknowledge it. In spiritual formation and transformation it is necessary to take the soul seriously and deal with it intelligently. We must be sure to do this for ourselves, individually, and also in our Christian fellowships.

I suspect that this emphasis will seem strange to some. Isn't the soul something 'religious' after all? And doesn't religion deal with the soul all the time? Such questions have a historical point to them, for the soul has very much been at the centre of traditional Christianity. But in contemporary Christianity you will hear very little about the soul in groups of whatever kind, and you will find very few people seriously concerned about the state of their own soul. There is very little said from the pulpit about the soul as an essential part of our lives, and almost no serious teaching about it.

Some conservative and evangelical churches still sometimes talk about *saving* the soul, but even this is much less the case than it used to be. And once the soul is saved it is usually treated as needing no further attention. Ignoring the soul is one reason why churches have become fertile sources of recruits for cults and other religious and political groups. It is not reasonable to think that the soul is properly cared for when it is not even seriously acknowledged. So this has to change.

The care for the soul necessary for spiritual transformation is made difficult by the elusiveness of the soul and the loss of Christian terminology for understanding it. It still breaks through in the Bible and older Christian writings, and in odd places here and there in contemporary life and art. The impact of secular theories here has been detrimental. We all dimly feel and discern our own soul's condition, but we can hardly articulate or express it. Certainly we cannot express things about our soul in such a way that we can reflect on and discuss these things usefully and with precision. We have very much lost 'soul' language and often are embarrassed by it.

Now this is not a desirable situation, and certainly it is not compatible with the serious undertaking of spiritual formation. Preachers and teachers must emphatically and repeatedly acknowledge the soul as the living centre of Christian life, and they must resume their responsibility for the care of souls, long assigned to them in Christian tradition.[7] We as individuals must 'own' our souls and take responsibility before God for them, turning to our pastors and teachers for the necessary help.

On the other hand we must recognize the recent upsurge of 'soul talk' in all kinds of popular literature and in business books and seminars. 'Soul' has become profitable. That would be fine if it were joined with a proper presentation of the soul in relation to God. But unfortunately this rarely is the case. We must never forget that the indispensable first step in caring for the soul is to place it under God.

The cries of the soul

Once we clearly acknowledge the soul, we can learn to hear its cries. Jesus heard its cries from the wearied humanity he saw around him. He saw the soul's desperate need in those who struggled with the overwhelming tasks of their life. He saw the multitudes around him, and it tore his heart, *because they were harassed and helpless, like sheep without a shepherd* (Matt 9:36). And he invited such people to become his students by yoking themselves to him, that is by letting him show them how he would share with them in pulling their load. He promised people rest for their souls (Matt 11:28–30).

His own greatness of soul made gentleness and humility the natural way for him to be (Phil 2:3–11). Being in his yoke is not a matter of taking on additional labour, but a matter of learning how to use his strength and ours together to bear our load. We will find his yoke an easy one, and his burden light, because in learning from him, we have found rest to our soul. What we have learned is to rest our soul in God. Rest to our soul is rest in God. My soul is at peace only when it is with God.

Abandoning outcomes

What we most learn in his yoke is to abandon outcomes to God, accepting that we do not have in ourselves the wherewithal to make them come right. This is true even if we feel helpless; if, for example, we *suffer according to God's will*, we should commit ourselves to our *faithful Creator and continue to do good* (1 Pet 4:19). Now this is a major part of that meekness and lowliness of heart which we also learn in his yoke. And what rest comes with it!

Humility is the framework within which all virtue lives. Angela of

Foligno observes that 'Our Lord did not say: Learn of Me to despise the world and live in poverty . . . but only this: Learn of Me for I am gentle and lowly of heart.' And: 'One of the signs by which a man may know that he is in a state of grace is this – that he is never puffed up.'[8] So *clothe yourselves with humility toward one another, because,* '*God opposes the proud but gives grace to the humble*', Peter says (1 Pet 5:5). *Humble yourselves,* Peter continues, *under God's mighty hand, that he may lift you up in due time. Cast all your anxiety on him because he cares for you* (5:6–7). Humility is a great secret of rest for the soul because it does not presume to secure outcomes.

Here is a simple fact: we live in a world where, by God's decision, *the race is not to the swift or the battle to the strong, nor does food come to the wise or wealth to the brilliant or favour to the learned; but time and chance happen to them all* (Eccles 9:11). God has a plan for our life that goes far beyond anything we can work out. We simply have to rest in his life as he gives it to us. The knowledge that he is good and great enables us to leave outcomes with him. We find this knowledge in the yoke of Christ. Resting in God we can be free from all anxiety, which means deep soul rest. Whatever the circumstances, we are enabled to *be still before the Lord and wait patiently for him* (Ps 37:7). We don't fret or get angry because others seem to be doing better than we are.

No soul rest with sin

But sin, or disobedience to what we know to be right, distances us from God. That makes soul rest impossible and is very destructive to the soul. Pride is the root of all disobedience. We think we are 'big enough' to take life into our own hands and disobey, instead of humbling ourselves *under God's mighty hand.* This will certainly be driven by the thought that if we do not take things into our own hands, we will not get what we want – another blow to our pride. By contrast, our attitude should be that there is no particular reason why we should get what we want, since we are not in charge of the universe.

This no doubt lies behind Peter's warning that we should *abstain from sinful desires, which war against* [*the*] *soul* (1 Pet 2:11). How do sinful desires war against the soul? Very simply, by enticing us to pull away from God, which will deprive our soul of what it needs to function correctly in the regulation of our whole being. To allow strong desires to govern our life is to exalt our will over God's.

That is why Paul calls covetousness *idolatry* (Eph 5:5 and Col 3:5). We set ourselves up as god and we are prepared to sacrifice the well-being and possessions of others to the god we have set up. Paul also speaks of those whose God is their stomach, that is, their desires (Phil 3:19). James also assigns the origin of sin to our strong desires or lusts (1:14), and we can now see how that works.

So sin, through desire and pride, alienates our soul from the life that is in God, and leaves us in turmoil, struggling to live on our own. Those who go so far as to abandon themselves to evil, consciously choosing evil as their goal, will be totally abandoned by God. Arrogant wrongdoing is the deepest possible wound that can be inflicted on the soul. Efforts at spiritual formation in Christlikeness obviously must reverse this process of distancing the soul from God and keep it in union with him. What can help us to do that? The law of God.

'The law of the Lord is perfect, reviving the soul'

The law that God gave to the Israelites is one of the greatest gifts of grace. It is a part of the blessing which God promised would come to all the families or nations of the earth through Abraham and his descendants. There is much more to the law than rules or commandments. It provides a picture of reality: of how things are with God and his creation. The Prophets and the Gospels share with the law this vital function of enabling human beings to know God, what God is doing, and what we are to do: to know, in short, wherein true well-being lies.

Moses challenged the people, *What other nation is so great as to have their gods near them the way the Lord our God is near us whenever we pray to him? And what other nation is so great as to have such righteous decrees and laws as this body of laws I am setting before you today?* (Deut 4:7–8).

The law of the Lord is perfect, as Psalm 19:7 says, and should be gratefully received, studied, and internalized, so that we can obey it. There is nothing lacking in it for its intended purpose. It revives the soul of those who seek it and receive it. It is a spiritual power in its own right, as is the word of God generally. It is living and powerful, capable of distinguishing soul from spirit and dealing with them appropriately (Heb 4:12).

There is nothing in the Old Testament that suggests for a moment that what the law does in the human heart is a human accomplishment. Rather, all benefit is ascribed to the law itself and to its giver: this will become clear if you study Psalm 119 carefully. It simply does not work if we somehow try to use the law on our own, for in the attempt we would have thrown ourselves back into self-idolatry, utilizing the written law as a tool for managing ourselves and God.

This mistake is what led to the horrible degradation of the law at the time of Jesus and Paul, turning it from a pathway of grace into an instrument of self-righteousness and human oppression. *Woe to you experts in the law,* Jesus said, *because you have taken away the key to knowledge. You yourselves have not entered, and you have hindered those who were entering* (Luke 11:52).

'He restores my soul'

Now it is always true, from the beginning to the end of the Bible, as well as in history, that human deliverance comes from a personal relationship with God established in God's gracious love and power. But the law is an essential part of that relationship. The inadequacy of human effort taken by itself is simply assumed. Still, the law was given as an essential way for God and human beings to meet in a covenant relationship, when the sincere heart would be instructed and enabled by God to walk in his ways. God is the only restorer of souls. When those walking in personal relationship with him take his law into their heart, that law quickens and restores connection and order to the flagging soul. But that never happens without the personal presence and gracious action of God in the person involved.

Some of the greatest assurances of God's personal presence are found in the Old Testament. In the book of Isaiah, for example:

> *do not fear, for I am with you; do not be dismayed, for I am your God. I will strengthen you and help you; I will uphold you with my righteous right hand ...*

The poor and needy search for water, but there is none; their tongues are parched with thirst. But I the Lord will answer them; I, the God of Israel, will not forsake them. I will make rivers flow on barren heights, and springs within the valleys. I will turn the desert into pools of water, and the parched ground into springs . . . so that people may see and know, may consider and understand, that the hand of the Lord has done this, that the Holy One of Israel has created it. (Is 41:10–20)

Covenant and law always go hand in hand within the path of spiritual formation, for it is the path of one who walks with God.

Hatred of the law: antinomian Christianity?

And on this point we are in the greatest of dangers today. There are many who in effect do just what Jesus said not to do. They annul the law and teach others to do the same (Matt 5:19). That ends all prospects of spiritual formation.

In the Western world today we live in an antinomian culture. This culture in part derives from our religious and secular history. But it reinforces antinomian tendencies among Christians. 'Antinomian' means 'against the law'. It was a term coined to designate those who held that the moral law was not important for Christians, who live by grace. The antinomian tendency is much older than the debates of the Reformation when the word was particularly used. It is based upon the mistaken idea, strongly rejected by Paul, that since we are not justified by keeping the law but by faith in Jesus, we can have no use for the law and can simply disregard it.

If the antinomian position were true, we would be free to hate the law as our 'oppressor', or despise it, or regard it as at best a good thing that failed. These are common attitudes among professing Christians today, based, more often than not, on simple ignorance of Scripture rather than on a carefully worked out understanding. Details vary from group to group, but the essential point of antinomianism is that sinning or not sinning, obeying or not obeying the law, has nothing to do with being saved. Some groups have advocated extreme licence, others not. God's law is irrelevant to one's standing before God in either case.

During the Commonwealth in England (1649–60), antinomianism was adopted by high Calvinists who maintained that a member of the Elect, being predestined to salvation, need not keep the moral law and indeed, need not repent. Others said 'that good works hinder salvation, and that a child of God cannot sin; that the moral law is altogether abrogated as a rule of life; that no Christian believes or works any good, but that Christ only believes and works good'.[9]

Now you have only to think for a moment to see what a disaster this will be for spiritual formation and the development of character. It amounts to rejecting it entirely, except in so far as it may be done to you or for you by God, without your effort. And you have only to glance briefly at the behaviour of professing Christians currently to realize the practical outcome of holding the law, and obedience to the law, to be irrelevant to the life of faith in Christ.[10]

The basic practice of Western Christianity today is, I fear, strongly antinomian. Here is a true story from the current Christian scene. Test your theology on it. A long-time, faithful church member comes to his pastor and says, 'I'm going to divorce my wife and marry someone else.' The pastor, aghast, says, 'You can't do that! You're a devoted Christian, and so is your wife. Divorce in these circumstances is clearly wrong.' 'Yes,' the man replies, 'I know that, but I'm going to do it anyway. I just can't stand her any longer. I know it's wrong, but after it's all over I'll ask God for forgiveness and he will forgive me. He will, because I believe that Christ died for me. That's what you teach.'

Extend this to imaginary extreme cases: murdering someone who deserves it, a once-in-a-lifetime, career-making, crooked deal, and so on. How, precisely, does our version of salvation rule out a judicious use of sin? And what does growth in Christlikeness mean if one can hold such a use in reserve? Just something to think about . . .

Law and grace go together

Now everything in the Scriptures goes against spurning the law. Jesus himself identified those who love him as those who keep his commandments (John 14:23–24). John says bluntly, *sin is lawlessness* (1 John 3:4). Paul, equally bluntly, says, *avoid every kind of evil* (1 Thess 5:22). And Jesus again says, *why do you call me 'Lord, Lord,' and do not do what I say?* (Luke 6:46). Paul makes a point of explaining,

> For what the law was powerless to do in that it was weakened by the sinful nature, God did by sending his own Son in the likeness of sinful man to be a sin offering. And so he condemned sin in sinful man, in order that the righteous requirements of the law might be fully met in us, who do not live according to the sinful nature but according to the Spirit. (Rom 8:3–4)

The availability of the Spirit and grace is not meant to set the law aside, but to enable us to conform to it from an inwardly transformed personality. We walk in the spirit of the law and the letter naturally follows. You cannot separate spirit from law, though you must separate spirit and law from legalism.

The law by itself kills off any hope of righteousness through human effort, but it kindles hope in God as we walk in the law through Christ. Grace does not set law aside. On the contrary, law is itself a primary manifestation of grace. It is a primary instrument of spiritual transformation: law comes with grace into the renewed soul. There is no such thing as grace without law.

Affinity between law and soul

There is, in fact, an inner affinity between the law and the soul. That is why rebellion against the law makes the soul sick and distances it from God. That is why love of the law restores the soul. Law is good for the soul, is an indispensable instrument of instruction and a standard of judgment of good and evil. Walking in the law with God restores the soul because the law expresses the order of God's kingdom and of God's own character. That is why it restores the soul. Grace is also essential, not to thrust the law aside, but to make it a delight.

The correct order that the soul requires for its vitality and proper functioning is found in the royal law of love (Jas 2:8), abundantly spelled out in Jesus and his teaching. That law includes all that was essential in the older law, which Jesus fulfilled and enables us to fulfil through discipleship. Anyone whose aim is less than obedience to the law of God in the Spirit and power of Jesus will never have a soul at

rest in God, and will never advance significantly in spiritual transformation into Christlikeness.

In summary, then, transformation of our soul requires that we
acknowledge its reality and importance, understand scriptural teaching about it, and take it into the yoke of Jesus, learning from him
humility and the abandonment of outcomes to God. This brings rest
to the soul. Then our soul is re-empowered in goodness by receiving
the law and the Word into it in covenant fellowship with God by
grace. The law gives structure to a life of grace in the kingdom of God.

Other things may be required for soul recovery: perhaps special
acts of deliverance, or ministries of inner healing or psychological
counselling. The good news of Jesus is always presupposed when we
refer to these ministries. But the most powerful force for transformation of the soul is to walk in righteousness, upheld by grace.

Matters for thought and discussion

1. 'The soul is deep.' What do you understand that to mean? How
   does it relate to intellectual and cultural tendencies of the twentieth and twenty-first centuries? To biblical teachings?
2. Is 'Psalm 1 man' realism? For you? For others you know? What
   would it look like on the job and in the home?
3. How does 'failure of good intentions' relate to disorders of the
   soul?
4. Why is 'meaninglessness' such a problem for modern life? Is it a
   soul problem?
5. Why does fanaticism hold such attraction for the broken soul?
6. Do you find the image of the soul as an inward stream of water
   intelligible? Helpful in understanding the Psalms, etc.?
7. What are some ways in which you can acknowledge your own
   soul?
8. How does humility fit in with the 'rest of soul' Jesus promises?
9. How do *sinful desires . . . war against your soul* (1 Pet 2:11)?
10. What is antinomianism and how does it affect life and faith
    today – especially prospects for spiritual formation?
11. How is law and obedience to law an expression of grace? Does
    the idea of an affinity between law and the soul make sense?

You were once darkness, but now you are light in the Lord. Live as children of light (for the fruit of the light consists in all goodness, righteousness and truth) and find out what pleases the Lord. Have nothing to do with the fruitless deeds of darkness, but rather expose them.
(Eph 5:8–11)

The simple program of Christ for winning the whole world is to make each person he touches magnetic enough with love to draw others.
(Frank Laubach[1])

CHAPTER 11

THE CHILDREN OF LIGHT AND
THE LIGHT OF THE WORLD

The significance of human life on the earth must either be very small or very great. It is very small from the strictly natural point of view. If we represent earth's history on a twenty-four hour clock, from midnight to midnight, then, according to the evolutionary story, our remotest human ancestors appeared at 11:59pm, and the civilization of the last several thousand years is represented as the pop of a flashbulb at midnight.[2] From the scientific point of view, the earth will not support human society for any great period of time in cosmic terms, and if the future of the earth resembles its astonishing past, for a few thousand more years at most.

God's purposes for human history, as set forth in the Bible, are quite another matter. According to the biblical picture, the function of human history is to bring forth an immense community, *from every nation, tribe, people and language* (Rev 5:9; 7:9; 11:9), who will be *a kingdom of priests* under God (Rev 1:6; 5:10; Exod 19:6), and who in the future will actually govern the earth under him (Rev 5:10). They will reign with him in the eternal future (Rev 22:5).

These people as a living community will become a special dwelling place for God. It will be one that allows his magnificence to be known and gratefully accepted by all of creation through all ages

(Eph 2:7; 3:10; Phil 2:9–11). Those who have taken on the character of Christ, *children of light* in Paul's language, will, in eternity, be empowered by God to do what they want, as free creative agents. And what they want will always harmonize perfectly with God's own purposes.

Spiritual formation in Christlikeness during our life here on earth is a constant movement toward this eternal appointment which God ordained for each of us in our creation – the inheritance, *the kingdom prepared for [us] since the creation of the world* (Matt 25:34; Luke 19:17). This movement forward is now carried on through our apprenticeship to Jesus Christ. It is a process of character transformation toward complete trustworthiness before God.

'Children of light'

Now let us compose a picture of the *children of light*, drawing on how they have changed in the various essential aspects of their being. To call them *children of light* is, in biblical terminology, to say that they have the basic nature of light.

Now these people are not perfect and do not yet live in a perfect world. But they are unusual. The difference is not a pose they strike, or things they do or don't do, though their behaviour is very different and distinctive. Where the children of light differ is primarily and most importantly on the 'inside' of their life. It lies in what they are in their depths.

Thought life. Perhaps the first thing we notice when we get to know their inner life is what they think about, or what is on their mind. They think about God. He is never out of their mind. They love to dwell upon God and upon his greatness and loveliness, as brought to light in Jesus Christ. They adore him in nature, in history, in his Son and in his saints. One could even say they are 'God-intoxicated' (Acts 2:13; Eph 5:18), though no-one has a stronger sense of reality and practicality than they do. Their mind is filled with biblical ideas of God's nature, actions, and his plans for the world. They do not dwell upon evil. It is not a big thing in their thoughts. They are sure of its defeat, but they still deal with it appropriately in specific situations.

Because their mind is centred upon God, all other good things are also welcome there: *whatever is true, whatever is noble, whatever is right, whatever is pure, whatever is lovely, whatever is admirable – if anything is excellent or praiseworthy* – they think about such things (Phil 4:8). They are positive, realistically so, because they understand the nature of God.

Feelings. And then perhaps we notice – and small wonder given what has already been observed – that the emotional life of these *children of light* is characterized by love. That is how they invest their emotions. They love lots of good things and they love people. They love their life and who they are. They are thankful for their life, even though it may contain many difficulties, even persecution (Matt 5:10–12). They receive all of it as God's gift, or at least as his allowance, and they know his goodness and greatness will outlast any trouble they might have, and that they will live with him forever. And so joy and peace are with them even in the hardest of times, even when they suffer unjustly. Because of what they have learned about God they are confident and hopeful and do not indulge thoughts of rejection, failure and hopelessness.

Will. Looking a little deeper we find that these *children of light* are devoted to doing what is good and right. Their will is habitually attuned to it, just as their mind and emotions are habitually homing in on God. They are attentive to rightness, to kindness, to helpfulness; and they find out about what people need, and try to do what is right and good in appropriate ways.

These are people who do not think first of themselves and what they want, and they really care very little about getting their own way. Paul wrote, *Do nothing out of selfish ambition or vain conceit, but in humility consider others better than yourselves. Each of you should look not only to your own interests, but also to the interests of others* (Phil 2:3–4), and these are easy and good instructions to them. They are abandoned to God's will and do not struggle and deliberate as to whether they will do what they know to be wrong. They do not hesitate to do what they know to be right. It is the obvious thing to do.

Body. That, of course, involves their bodies. Their body has been trained to do good. It is constantly prepared to do what is right and good without thinking. And that also means that it does not automatically move into what is wrong, even contrary to their resolves and intentions before they can think. It is no longer true of them that *the spirit is willing but the body is weak* (Matt 26:41). They know by experience that these words of Jesus are not a description of the inevitable condition of humans, but the diagnosis of a condition to be corrected. The Spirit has substantially taken over their body and its parts.

Consequently, we do not see them always being trapped by what their tongue, facial expressions, eyes, hands, and so on have already done before they can think. For their body and its parts are consecrated to serve God and are habituated to being his holy instruments. These people instinctively avoid the paths of temptation. There is a freshness about them, a kind of quiet strength, and a transparency. They are rested and playful in a bodily strength that is from God. He who raised up Christ Jesus from the dead has given life to their bodies through his Spirit who dwells in them.

Social relations. In their relationships with others they are completely transparent. Because they walk in goodness they have no use for deceit, and they achieve real contact or fellowship with others, especially other apprentices of Jesus. John wrote, *If we walk in the light, as he is in the light, we have fellowship with one another, and the blood of Jesus, his Son, purifies us from all sin*; and later, *whoever loves his brother lives in the light, and there is nothing in him to make him stumble* (1 John 1:7 and 2:10). These people do not conceal their thoughts and feelings, though they do not impose them upon everyone. Because of their confidence in God they do not try to manipulate and manage others. Needless to say, in their social contexts they do not go on the attack, intending to use or to hurt others.

Moreover, they are non-condemning, while at the same time they will not participate in evil. They pay evil only the attention absolutely required in any social setting, and, beyond that, patient and joyful non-participation is the rule. They know how really to 'be there' without sharing in evil, as was true of Jesus himself. Of course others may disapprove of their 'being there', and there are some places and situations where it is better not to 'be there' at all. But they do not reject or distance themselves from the people who may be involved in such situations. They know how to 'love the sinner and hate the sin', gracefully and effectively.

Soul. Finally, as you come to know these people, you see that all of the above is not just at the surface. It is deep, and, in a certain sense, it is effortless. It flows. That is, the things we have been describing are not things the *children of light* are constantly trying hard to do, gritting their teeth. Rather, these are features of life that well up out of souls which are at home in God.

This is the outcome of spiritual formation in Christlikeness. Again, it doesn't mean perfection, but it means that we have people whose soul is whole; people who have integrity because they have internalized the law of God. Through the gospel and the Spirit they have a restored soul. Every aspect of the person functions as God intended it to.

The scriptural high points

Now let us return to some of the New Testament descriptions of what the apprentices of Jesus are to be like. We are now in a position to understand them in a new and, I believe, very encouraging way. Usually, I think, these bright passages may inspire longing, but a longing that is tinged with hopelessness and guilt. Now we are in a position to change all that.

The passages I have in mind are very well known. Of course Matthew 5 – 7 heads the list, but properly understood it goes no further than familiar passages in Paul's letters, or in those by Peter, James and John. And there are similar passages in the Old Testament. (We might cite in this connection Rom 12:1–21; 1 Cor 13; 2 Cor 3:12 – 7:1; Gal 5:22 – 6:10; Eph 4:20 – 6:20; Phil 2:3–16 and 4:4–9; Col 3:1 – 4:6; 1 Pet 2:1 – 3:16; 2 Pet 1:2–10; 1 John 4:7–21.) Perhaps Micah 6:8 could serve well as an Old Testament point of reference. Deuteronomy 10:12–21 would also serve. I urge the reader to plan a full day in silent retreat to read and reread these passages meditatively.

The contrasting picture of darkness

These passages portraying the *children of light* are given additional force by contrasting passages on the *fruitless works of darkness* (Eph

5:11). In Galatians 5 Paul describes *the acts of the sinful nature*, when natural human impulses and abilities are allowed to be the rule of life. *The acts of the sinful nature are obvious: sexual immorality, impurity and debauchery; idolatry and witchcraft; hatred, discord, jealousy, fits of rage, selfish ambition, dissensions, factions and envy; drunkenness, orgies, and the like* (Gal 5:19–21).

Another of Paul's dark passages is 2 Timothy 3:2–5. Speaking of the last days, when evil on earth will have had time to 'ripen', he says that *people will be lovers of themselves, lovers of money, boastful, proud, abusive, disobedient to their parents, ungrateful, unholy, without love, unforgiving, slanderous, without self-control, brutal, not lovers of the good, treacherous, rash, conceited, lovers of pleasure rather than lovers of God.* They will be religious in lifestyle, but will deny all that is genuine in it: *having a form of godliness but denying its power.*

Now we know from Jesus' teachings that all of these defiling things come out of a sick and rebellious heart (Mark 7:21–23). The trouble lies hidden in the heart. Conversely, whatever is good also comes out of the heart. *No good tree bears bad fruit, nor does a bad tree bear good fruit*, says Jesus, and *the good man brings good things out of the good stored up in his heart, and the evil man brings evil things out of the evil stored up in his heart* (Luke 6:43 and 45).

Each dimension of the human self must change

So there is no mystery about all of this. When people live in evil it is because of what is wrong inside. Similarly, the way to a life fruitful with goodness is the transformation of every dimension of the inner or spiritual side of the self. You cannot bypass any of those aspects if the life is to be transformed. Each one must of necessity be a source either of weakness or of strength. The renovation of the heart simply requires that each inner dimension of the human self be rectified and established in righteousness by effectively and thoroughly receiving *the grace of God that brings salvation*:

> *The grace of God that brings salvation . . . teaches us to say 'No' to ungodliness and worldly passions, and to live self-controlled, upright and godly lives in this present age, while we wait for the blessed hope – the glorious appearing of our*

*great God and Saviour, Jesus Christ, who gave himself for us to redeem us from
all wickedness and to purify for himself a people that are his very own, eager to do
what is good.* (Titus 2:12–14)

So we now understand what lies behind the glowing passages such
as Matthew 5 or 1 Corinthians 13 or Colossians 3 or 1 John 4. It
is the process of inner transformation which we here call spiritual
formation.

Spiritual growth laid out by Peter

This is set out more clearly in some passages than others, one of the
clearest being 2 Peter 1:3–11. Here, he starts from the bedrock of
God's *divine power* which *has given us everything we need for life and
godliness* – stop now and think about how much *everything* leaves
out. The he goes on to point to the *great and precious promises* of God
that make it possible for us to *participate in the divine nature and
escape the corruption in the world caused by evil desires* (1:3–4).

And how is this escape to come about? By putting forth our very
best *efforts* – *applying all diligence*, a good translation says – making
*every effort to add to your faith goodness; and to goodness, knowledge;
and to knowledge, self-control; and to self-control, perseverance; and to
perseverance, godliness; and to godliness, brotherly kindness; and to
brotherly kindness, love* (1:5–7).

Starting from faith, Peter says, we train ourselves to do what is
good and right. Obviously this is something we are *to do*, something
which will not be done for us.

And then we add on knowledge or understanding to goodness.
That is, we learn why the good and right we do is good and right. We
operate from insight, not merely from instinct. And then we add on
self-control. That is, we learn our own limits and tendencies and
learn not be thrown off course by any turn of events.

And then we add on perseverance. This is the capacity to stay the
course, to carry on for the long haul, regardless of how we feel. And
then we add on godliness. Perhaps we can best think of this as depth
and thoroughness in relying on God's grace. God is our inexhaust-
ible resource of goodness.

And then we add on that kindness and gentleness of care which we see among devoted siblings and true friends. We extend family feeling and action to include people in our wider community. Just think of what that would mean to this wounded world. But it is possible to do this superhuman thing only through the goodness and strength of godliness.

And then we add on *agapē* love. This is the kind of love that characterizes God himself. It goes far beyond brotherly love and into the very heart of God. We are not just to love as family, but as God loves us (John 13:34). *Agapē* love is always presented, in the biblical descriptions of the *children of light*, as the ultimate move which completes all the other gains in spiritual progress (see Rom 5:5; 1 Cor 13; Gal 5:14; Eph 4:15–16; Col 3:14; 1 John 4:16; etc.).

Peter concludes this great progression by telling us *if you do these things, you will never fall, and you will receive a rich welcome into the eternal kingdom of our Lord and Saviour Jesus Christ* (1:10–11).

A common misunderstanding

Now the mistake most commonly made by people today, as they approach these glowing passages about the *children of light* is simply this. They do not understand the presupposition of inner transformation into Christlikeness that underlies all the passages. They assume that we are supposed to do all the glowing things mentioned in such passages without loving God with all our heart, soul, mind and strength. In fact they think we must do them while our heart, soul, mind and strength are still strongly inclined against God. And of course their despair is totally justified. What they imagine would be completely impossible.

To the person who is not inwardly transformed in each essential dimension, evil and sin still look good. This is what Peter in the above passage calls *the corruption in the world caused by evil desires* (2 Pet 1:4). To such people the law is hateful because it denies them what they have their hearts set on; and everything must then be done to evade the law so that they can do what they want to. The force of their whole being is set against Christlikeness, even if they suffer from a bad conscience that tells them they are in the wrong.

As Jesus trains them and *cleanses them for himself,* however, that begins to reverse. The law begins to appeal as a beautiful gift of God, as precious truth about what is really good and right. It becomes, in the language of the psalmist, *sweeter than honey, than honey from the comb* (Ps 19:10 – fresh honey tastes good!). At that point sin looks stupid and ridiculous, as well as repulsive, which it really is. Resistance to sin is then based upon that new and realistic vision of what it is, not on fear of punishment. The illusion that sin is really a good thing arbitrarily prohibited by God is dispelled, and we see with gratitude that his prohibitions are among his greatest kindnesses.

Understanding sanctification

And now we can begin to speak of sanctification as a condition of the soul established in righteousness. It is the condition of the soul in the mature *children of light.* What are we to make of it? Especially, is it to be taken as a goal for every apprentice of Jesus? Is sanctification sensible or is it magical?

Sanctification used to be much better understood than it is now, and we turn to some older authors. In his *Systematic Theology,* A. H. Strong quotes the famous New Testament scholar Godet:

> The work of Jesus in the world is twofold. It is a work accomplished for us, destined to effect reconciliation between God and man; it is a work accomplished in us, with the object of effecting our sanctification. By the one a right relation is established between God and us; by the other, the fruit of the reestablished order is secured. By the former, the condemned sinner is received into the state of grace; by the latter the pardoned sinner is associated with the life of God . . . How many express themselves as if, when forgiveness with the peace which it procures has been once obtained, all is finished and the work of salvation is complete! They seem to have no suspicion that salvation consists in the health of the soul, and that the health of the soul consists in holiness. Forgiveness is not the reestablishment of health; it is the crisis of convalescence. If God thinks fit to declare the sinner righteous, it is in order that he may by that means restore him to holiness.[3]

Strong goes on to quote a striking illustration from another (now unknown) author:

> The steamship whose machinery is broken may be brought into port and made fast to the dock. She is safe, but not sound. Repairs may last a long time. Christ designs to make us both safe and sound. Justification gives the first – safety; sanctification gives the second – soundness.

And, finally, A. A. Hodge on the inseparability of accepting forgiveness and accepting sanctification: 'Any man who thinks he is a Christian, and that he has accepted Christ for justification, when he did not at the same time accept him for sanctification, is miserably deluded in that very experience' (p. 869).

Strong himself then adds these vital comments:

> Not culture, but crucifixion, is what the Holy Spirit prescribes for the natural man . . . Sanctification is not a matter of course, which will go on whatever we do, or do not do. It requires a direct superintendence and surgery on the one hand, and, on the other hand a practical hatred of evil on our part that cooperates with the husbandry of God . . . The Holy Spirit enables the Christian, through increasing faith, more fully and consciously to appropriate Christ, and thus progressively to make conquest of the remaining sinfulness of his nature. These comments fill out the meaning of his own definition of sanctification as 'that continuous operation of the Holy Spirit, by which the holy disposition imparted in regeneration is maintained and strengthened'. (pp. 869–870)

A contemporary interpretation

An excellent contemporary writer, Wayne Grudem, opens his discussion of sanctification by describing it as

> a part of the application of redemption that is a progressive work that continues throughout our earthly lives. It is also a work in which *God and man cooperate*, each playing distinct roles. This part of the application of redemption is called sanctification: *Sanctification is a progressive work of God and man that makes us more and more free from sin and like Christ in our actual lives.*[4]

It may be that only one clarification would be useful here, in respect of my own understanding of sanctification. Although it is certainly true that the work or process of sanctifying the apprentice begins immediately in the regenerated heart, the 'safe' but still 'unsound' person (to use language quoted above) is not in a condition of settled, pervasive righteousness which is appropriately named sanctification.

Sanctification in this life will always be a matter of degree, to be sure, but there is a point in spiritual growth before which the term 'sanctification' simply does not apply. We do not apply the word 'hot' to water until it has reached a certain temperature, even if it is in the process of being heated.

Summary on sanctification

Sanctification is a consciously chosen and sustained relationship of interaction between the Lord and his apprentices, in which the apprentices are able routinely to do what they know to be right before God because all aspects of their person have been substantially transformed. Sanctification applies primarily to the moral and religious life, but extends to the practical life as well.

Sanctification is not an experience, though experiences of various kinds may be involved in it. It is not a status, though a status is maintained by means of it. It is not an outward form, and has no essential connection with outward forms. It does, however, become a 'track record' and a system of habits. It comes about through the process of spiritual formation, through which the heart of the individual, and the whole inner life, takes on the character of Jesus.

Some marks of the 'children of light'

Several characteristics mark those who have become established in their whole being as *children of light*. One is that whenever they are found to be in the wrong, they will never defend it, neither to themselves or to others, much less to God. They are thankful to be found out, and they fulfil the proverb, *rebuke a wise man and he will love you*

(Prov 9:8). Indeed, when falsely accused of being in the wrong, they will not defend themselves, but will say only as much as is required to prevent misunderstanding of the good and to assist those who truly desire to know the facts of the case. Thus the meaning of being justified by grace alone has penetrated to the core of their being and they rest there.

Another of their characteristics is that they do not feel they are missing out on something good by not sinning. They are not disappointed, do not feel deprived. They *do not fret because of evil men* and are not *envious of those who do wrong* (Ps 37:1). They know that better is *the little that the righteous have than the wealth of many wicked* (37:16). They do not regard sin as something good, but as rubbish – which is exactly what everyone knows after engaging in it. Why stick your head, your soul or your body into *that*?

Another characteristic is that the *children of light* are mainly governed by the pull of the good. Their energy is not invested in not doing what is wrong, but in doing what is good. For example, they are not struggling with commands not to covet, but rejoicing that others have the good things they do. Desires they might have for what is forbidden by God are regarded as ridiculous, not as something to be seriously thought about. Good is the only thing worth considering.

Finally, here, life in the path of rightness becomes easy and joyous. That is a characteristic of *children of light* who are well on their way. Walter Marshall, a Puritan contemporary of Richard Baxter, says, 'I acknowledge that the work of God is easy and pleasant to those whom God rightly furnisheth with endowments for it.' He also writes truly, 'Those who assert it to be easy to men, in their common condition, show their imprudence in contradicting the general experience of Heathens and Christians', but 'the wisdom of God hath ever furnished people with a good persuasion of a sufficient strength, that they might be enabled both to will and do their duty'.[5]

Virtuous and happy

The good news of Jesus Christ is that such a life is available to all. A depressed and hopeless man came to John Wesley to enquire what message he had for the multitudes of hearers he regularly addressed, morning and evening. Wesley replied:

> You ask, what I would do with them: I would make them virtuous and happy, easy in themselves and useful to others. Whither would I lead them? To heaven; to God the Judge, the lover of all, and to Jesus the Mediator of the new covenant. What religion do I preach? The religion of love; the law of kindness brought to light by the Gospel. What is this good for? To make all who receive it enjoy God and themselves: to make them like God; lovers of all; contented in their lives; and crying out at their death, in calm assurance, 'O grave, where is thy victory! Thanks be unto God, who giveth me the victory, through my Lord Jesus Christ.'[6]

No talk here of 'the crushing burden of piety', as it has been called, or of religion as a 'life sentence' instead of a life. Our walk with Christ, well learned, is a burden only as wings are to a bird or the engines are to an aeroplane. The mature *children of light* are like their master. They know God and his word, they think straight, and they live in the truth, because every essential dimension of their being has been transformed to serve God: heart, soul, mind and strength.

The Amplified Bible gives a version of Ephesians 5:15–17 that gets this just right:

> Look carefully then how you walk! Live purposefully and worthily and accurately, not as the unwise and witless, but as wise (sensible, intelligent people),
>
> Making the very most of the time [buying up each opportunity], because the days are evil.
>
> Therefore do not be vague and thoughtless and foolish, but understanding and firmly grasping what the will of the Lord is.

'The light of the world'

Jesus stood out as *the light of the world* (John 8:12; 9:5). What did that mean? *In him was life, and that life was the light of men*, the apostle wrote, a light of such power that the darkness in the world could not extinguish it (John 1:4–5). Light here means both energy and knowledge. From Christ there uniquely came into the world the energy and knowledge by which human beings could be delivered from evil and enabled to live life as it ought to be lived.

This is why we said earlier that when Jesus sent out his apprentices to make apprentices of all ethnic groups on earth, what he had in mind was worldwide moral revolution. We can only imagine what that would mean if we think of the population of the earth being transformed into *children of light* – if ordinary human beings in their ordinary positions in life were empowered by him to be *the light of the world*. It would no more be possible to hide them than it is possible to hide a city on a hill (Matt 5:14–16).

Darkness declared to be light

Now modern humanity, say since the late nineteenth century, has lived in a rage of moral self-righteousness. Its intellectual leaders have expressed an attitude of superiority and condemnation toward the morality of the culture that is supposedly Christian. Its greatest prophets and thinkers have weighed Jesus in the moral balances and found him wanting. They have found ways of dismissing him, and have found those who profess to be his followers wanting. Fearsome 'Christian' types – the Enforcer, the Holier-Than-Thou, The Propagandist, the Happy-Clappy, the Obsequious Self-Promoter, the Cowardly Faithful, the Heartlessly Successful, and so on and on – are relentlessly hammered in the media as proving the moral bankruptcy of the way of Christ, though in fact these are human types, found in all cultures. Modern humanity has officially, in its governing institutions, forsaken the light of the world, Jesus himself.

If there is to be an accurate history written of the nineteenth and twentieth centuries, it will have to give prominence to the fact that the highest ethical teaching the world has ever been given was rejected by the intellectual and political leaders of humanity, in favour of teachings that opened the way to forms of human behaviour more wicked than any the world had seen to that point. It is true to say that this was partly due to the failure of Christians to stand as the manifest *children of light*. But even today those who are concerned about contemporary culture do not seem to realize fully what has happened. They do not realize that the attacks on what we might call traditional Christian morality, or just traditional values, is a moral attack: an attack from the point of view of supposed moral superiority.

People in Hollywood, who are sometimes criticized as purveying immorality, do not in general see themselves that way. Rather, they regard themselves as pushing a better way of life, if not a better morality. Traditional Christian practice is held up as morally inferior to the values sponsored by Hollywood, and as having been intellectually discredited. Of course the same is true of the Islamic critique of the West. And in pop culture, lyrics from the Beatles onwards undermine the moral stances of 'the establishment'. No doubt there is much there to criticize justly. But the final result is that darkness is now said to be light, and now the vilest and most brutal 'music' is delivered with an assurance of moral superiority and a self-righteousness so palpable that most people, I think, cannot recognize it for what it is. And that is now true of most art forms.

In any case, moral assuredness and self-righteousness in the practice of what in the past would have been regarded as blatant evil is now a feature of our world. 'Sex and violence' in the media is but one symptom of this overwhelming fact, and very far from being the central issue. The central issue is the replacement of Jesus Christ as the light of the world by people like Nietzsche and John Lennon, or Freud or Mao.

Now is the time to *be* 'children of light'

This is where we are now in the world. We are beyond the point where mere talk can make an impression. Demonstration is required. We must live what we profess. The test is reality. If the bewildering array of spiritualities and ideologies that throng our times really can do what apprenticeship to Christ can do, what more is there to say?

There is no effectual response to our current situation except for the *children of light* to be who and what they were called to be by Christ. Mere reason cannot respond effectively, because it is now under the same influences as are the arts and public life generally, namely the rejection of Christ and Christianity. Only when those who really do know that Jesus Christ is *the light of the world* take their stand with him and fulfil their calling from him to be *children of light*, will there be any realistic hope of stemming the tide of evil and showing the way out of that tide for those who really want out.

The call of Christ today is the same as it was when he left us here. That call is to be his apprentices, alive in the power of God, learning to do all he said to do, leading others into apprenticeship to him, and teaching them how to do everything he said.

If we follow that call today, then, as in past times, the most important thing happening in our communities will be what is happening in our churches. And now that we know what it takes to become mature *children of light*, how can we be excused for not taking that open path and leading others into it? We will then, once again, see among us the presence of God. As Moses asked the Lord long ago: *What else will distinguish me and your people from all the other people on the face of the earth?* (Exod 33:16).

Spiritual formation in the local church

This must be the focus of the local church. We must take the path of maturity and lead others into it. Local groups of disciples will usually have people at all stages of the apprenticeship. Churches can be compared to hospitals, with people at various stages of recovery and progress toward health. Some will be undergoing radical surgery or other strong treatment. Some will be in ICU. Others will be taking their first wobbly steps after a lengthy time bedridden. And others will be showing the flush of health and steady strength as they get ready to resume their ordinary life. And there would be old warriors with many battle scars and many victories, with the steady gleam of hope for *a better country* (Heb 11:16) in their eyes. Parallels to these stages should be found in every church.

What these congregations look like is spelled out in more detail in Ephesians 4:17 – 6:24. It would be worth the reader's time at this point to step aside and review this passage. It makes clear that those described are the ones in whom spiritual formation in Christlikeness has done and is doing its steady, ongoing work. They are the emerging and the mature *children of light*, and they *shine like stars* in a darkened world, *blameless and pure, children of God without fault in a crooked and depraved generation* (Phil 2:15).

God's plan for spiritual formation

Matthew 28:18–20 is God's plan for the growth and prospering of congregations as well as of the church at large. It is his plan for spiritual formation in the local congregation, and has three stages:

1. Making disciples, that is, apprentices, of Jesus. The New Testament does not recognize a category of Christians who are not apprentices of Jesus Christ, though it clearly does recognize 'baby' apprentices who are still predominantly preoccupied with and dependent upon natural human abilities.
2. Immersing the apprentices at all levels of growth in God. This is the major component in the prospering of the congregation: the healing and teaching God among them.[7]
3. Transforming disciples inwardly, so that doing what Christ did and commanded is not the focus but is the natural outcome. This is the main function of the local congregation, so far as human effort is concerned.

Stage one

We begin with the making of apprentices of Jesus, because it is presupposed in everything that follows. We must be clear on several points.

Most fundamental, of course, is to be clear on what an apprentice of Jesus is. Apprentices are those who have trusted Jesus with their whole life. Because they have done so they want to learn everything he has to teach them about life in the kingdom of God. They are yearning to be like Jesus. That is, they are learning to live as he would live in their circumstances.

Two different, though inseparable, aspects of discipleship need to be discerned. One is the specifically religious aspect. Here we are learning to understand and do the things which Jesus gave us in specific commandments and teachings. We are studying his words and deeds in the Gospels. This learning is primarily developed through the teaching ministry of the church. Here, for example, we will be learning what it means to trust ourselves wholly to Christ, and to love our enemies and pray for those who persecute us and so on. We are learning how to do these things in real life. We learn in the church, but we take what we learn into all our activities, at home and work, and increasingly practise there the things that Jesus taught.

The second aspect of discipleship is what we call our secular, non-church life. How we run a business, how we live with parents, how we raise a family. How we get along with neighbours, participate in government, get an education, engage in the cultural life of society. These too are matters in which we are to be constantly learning how Jesus would live in our circumstances. In these matters of ordinary human existence, Jesus is our teacher: 'He walks with me and he talks with me,' as the old hymn says.

All that is required to begin

Now when we first become disciples, we simply believe that Jesus is the one who really is in charge of everything, and that he is good and trustworthy. We don't want to be left out of what he is doing, for we sense that his work is all that really matters and that our life is nothing without it. We find forgiveness for our sins and start to take his yoke upon us and learn from him (Matt 11:29). The idea that these can be separated is, as A. W. Tozer pointed out years ago, a modern heresy. It is choking the life out of the contemporary Western church.[8]

When setting out as his apprentices, we will encounter all the harmful things that are in us: false thoughts and feelings, self-will, bodily inclinations to evil, ungodly social relationships and patterns, and soul wounds. Our Saviour and Teacher will help us remove these through his own presence and through the ministry of his people. All will be bathed in the Holy Spirit. Spiritual formation in Christlikeness is a process through which all the dimensions of our life are transformed as they increasingly take on the character of our Teacher.

We must recognize, sadly, that churches which are not based on discipleship have assumed that someone can be a Christian and not be a disciple in the New Testament sense. This is a flawed view of what it is to have faith in Christ. Most professing Christians today have 'prayed to receive Christ' because they felt a need and wanted him to help them deal with it. But the thing that needs fixing now is rarely the real problem. We should of course be sympathetic with people who are lonely and guilt-ridden, but these are not their problem.

Their problem is that they have rejected God, for whatever reason, and have chosen to live life on their own. They have not surrendered their will to him. They want to do what they think is best. And they are lost because of that, in the sense explained in an earlier chapter. They do not know what their real needs are, and do not think of themselves as rebels and outlaws who must radically change because they are not acceptable to God. They do not think they need the grace of God for radical transformation of who they are: they just need a little help. They are good people. Or so it seems to them.[9]

Now becoming a disciple of Jesus cannot be negotiated on this basis. It is rather a matter of giving up your life. Jesus made this starkly clear in Luke 14 and elsewhere. Without that giving up it is impossible to be his disciple, because you will still think you are in charge and just in need of a little help from Jesus for your project of a successful life. But our idea of a successful life is precisely our problem.

Clearly, then, the first stage of Jesus' plan for spiritual formation in local congregations, as outlined in Matthew 28:18–20, has to do with the vision and intention sections in our V-I-M pattern of spiritual growth. If spiritual formation is to be the central focus of the local congregation, the group must be possessed by the vision of apprenticeship of Jesus as the central reality of salvation. And they must have formed a clear intention of being disciples and making disciples as the central purpose of their group.

Disciples are us

To achieve this, the leadership of the local congregation, the ministers and elders, must recognize that the primary candidates for

discipleship are the people who are already there. And they must recognize that the first step in leading the people who are there to
become apprentices of Jesus is for the ministers and elders to be
apprentices of Jesus.

It is an error to make outreach a primary goal of the local congregation, and especially so when those who are already there have
not become clear-headed and devoted apprentices of Jesus.
Outreach is one essential task of Christ's people, and there will
always be those especially gifted in evangelism. But the most successful work of outreach will be what turns people into lights in the
darkened world.

A simple goal for the leaders of churches would be to bring every
adherent to understand clearly what it means to be a disciple of
Jesus and to be solidly committed to discipleship. This goal will
have to be approached very gently and lovingly and patiently with
existing groups, where the people involved have not understood this
to be a part of their membership commitment. We don't need to be
picky over the means; we don't need to invent techniques. It just
needs to be done, and pastoral care must constantly help the people
along.

We are not talking about purifying the church, by getting rid of
all the *weeds* (Matt 13). Even *weeds* are to be loved and served and
called to apprenticeship to Jesus. Even those who falsely professes to
be Christian can be led to participate fully in spiritual transformation. They need to be led into apprenticeship of Jesus. But the Lord
is the only purifier of groups, and he has his own schedule for it. Our
task is to be fruitful and to cultivate others to be so.

Who we are in our inmost depths is the most basic issue. Ray
Stedman wrote some years ago:

> God's first concern is not what the church does, it is what the church *is*.
> Being must always precede doing, for what we do will be according to what
> we are. To understand the moral character of God's people is a primary
> essential in understanding the nature of the church. As Christians we are to
> be a moral example to the world, reflecting the character of Jesus Christ.[10]

In our present context, to be sure, serious work will have to be
done, and there may be failures on the way.

Stage two

But now let us turn to the last two stages in Jesus' pattern for spiritual formation in the local congregation. These concern the M in our V-I-M. They concern means. The second stage has to do with immersing apprentices in the presence of God in the group. The presence of God is the only sure mark of the true church. Spiritual transformation will only take place in the presence of God. God's intention is to be present among his people and heal them, teach them and provide for them.

In Leviticus 26:11–12 God says, *I will put my dwelling place among you, and I will not abhor you. I will walk among you and be your God, and you will be my people.* In Exodus 29:44–46 he says, *They will know that I am the Lord their God, who brought them out of Egypt so that I might dwell among them. I am the Lord their God.* Deuteronomy 7:21 says, *the Lord your God, who is among you, is a great and awesome God.* The psalmist cries out, *it is good to be near God. I have made the Sovereign Lord my refuge* (73:28). Jesus promised his presence to his disciples: *where two or three come together in my name, there am I with them* (Matt 18:20). And Paul describes how the outsider coming into the church *will be convinced by all that he is a sinner and will be judged by all, and the secrets of his heart will be laid bare. So he will fall down and worship God, exclaiming, 'God is really among you!'* (1 Cor 14:24–25).

So what should we expect of a local congregation of disciples of Jesus? We should expect it to be a place where divine life and power is manifestly present to glorify God and meet the needs of repentant human beings. This would imply an atmosphere of honesty, openness, acceptance of all, supernatural caring, with utter confidence in Jesus.

The element of performance should be absent in the church, as should the constant worry over 'how the service went'. God is the primary agent in the gathering, and the truth is that only he knows how the service went; and it cannot be judged by reading the responses of the congregation. The sufficiency of Christ is the basis of our efforts in worship and service. Those who minister should, with time and experience, expect to receive profundity of insight, sweetness and strength of character, and abundance of power to carry out their role. Ministers do not need tricks and techniques, but need only speak Christ's word from Christ's character, standing within the manifest presence of God. It is a matter of character, not momentary inspiration.

The congregation, too, needs to eliminate performance. We are not coming to be entertained; we are not checking the performance of the leaders. We are coming to encounter God. We expect to find Christ in others and that is all we are looking for. We don't worship worship or a fine service or impeccable teaching or fine-looking people. Far too often we approach worship prepared to major on minors. Why look at some aspect of performance when you could look at Jesus?

Stage three

The third stage in God's plan for the growth of the church is arranging for the inner transformation of disciples. This is what Jesus described as teaching the disciples to do all he commanded. But doing what he commanded is not the focus of our activities at this point. Rather, it is the natural outcome. The focus is on inner transformation of the five essential aspects of human personality which we have been studying. Implementation of the means for this inner transformation is the third stage of the divine plan, and it should be the local congregation's constant preoccupation.

We must respect the mind, and not try to bypass it. Our beliefs and feelings cannot be changed by choice. It is a mistake to think that people can choose to believe and feel differently. We cannot just choose to have different beliefs and feelings. But we do have some liberty to take in different ideas and information and to think about things in different ways. We can choose to take in the Word of God, and, when we do that, beliefs and feelings will be steadily pulled in a godly direction. The will must be moved by insight.

My father was a two-pack-a-day smoker until he was in his seventies. Then one day in the Veterans' Hospital he saw a man smoking with the aid of a special machine that enabled him to smoke even though his lips had been eaten away by cancer caused by smoking. My father saw the foolishness of smoking, and he believed it. He

never smoked another cigarette. That is what belief does. Belief is
when your whole being is set to act as if something is so. And that is
how the commands of Jesus finally come to us as we grow. We see
them as reality.

We must seek to know truth and teach others. Respecting the priority of the mind in spiritual formation means that we seek to
understand the truth of the Bible and to help others understand it.
We work in depth. We can choose to turn our minds toward these
truths. Belief will come as God's gift within the hidden depths of our
life, and it will grow under the nurturing of the Spirit. That is what is
going on in a local congregation which is following God's plan for
spiritual formation.

But sometimes the way to this is blocked, even among people who
have genuinely become apprentices of Jesus and have the best of
intentions. They are not capable of receiving truth. Their body, soul,
feelings, thoughts, and their social atmosphere, are in such turmoil,
or so badly inclined, that their mind cannot be reached just by periods of teaching. They cannot be significantly helped by regular
church services. They may need ministries of deliverance. Or they
may need to be taken out of their ordinary routine and given lengthy
periods of time in retreat, under careful direction. We must be Spirit-
led, Bible-informed, intelligent, experimental and persistent.
Intensive training away from ordinary life is exactly what Jesus did in
the spiritual formation of the selected few who were to be his disciples. He gave them almost three years of special training away from
their ordinary life. Only after that were they given power from on
high and let loose to start the church.

Two steps of confidence

Having this goal of teaching people to do what Jesus said, local congregations will be drawn onward if they explicitly do two things.
These are actually very simple things, but they are also great acts of
confidence in Jesus.

First, congregations need to expect apprentices to learn to do the
various things that Jesus taught us to do. At present, there is no such
expectation. We know, in general, that people respond well to high

but credible expectations. There is no hope for real progress without expectations, realistic instruction and recognition of progress.

Start with simple things like being genuinely kind to hostile people, or returning blessing for cursing. Often we have plenty of opportunity to practise and refine these in our own families. Develop understanding of such situations, listen to testimonies of successes and failures, and give further teaching and practical suggestions. Keep going. Disciples might be invited to keep a journal of which things they have learned.

Second, announce that you teach people to do the things that Jesus said to do. Put it out in front of your building on a sign, state it on your web page. Publicize and run training programmes designed to develop specific points of the character of Christ as given in the New Testament. Put the whole weight of the staff and the congregation behind this. Who you and your congregation will have to be, and what you will have to do to back this up and carry it out, will make utterly real God's plan for the spiritual transformation of human life on earth.

In bringing this chapter to a close, we want to emphasize once again that all of the other details of church activities will matter little, one way or the other, as long as everything is organized around God's plan for spiritual formation. So far as they do matter, these details will sort themselves out and fall into place when we have our eyes on what really counts before God. And if everything is not organized around that plan, what difference does it really make if we regard some ways of 'doing church' as more successful than others? Biblical and historical Christianity has brought forth *children of light* to be, with Jesus himself, *the light of the world*, only when it has steadily drawn people into his kingdom and taught them to live increasingly in the character and power of God.

No special talents, personal skills, educational programmes, money or possessions are required to bring this about. We do not have to purify and enforce some legalistic system. Just ordinary people who are his apprentices, gathering in the name of Jesus and immersed in his presence, and taking steps of inward transformation as we put on the character of Christ. That is all that is required.

Let that be our aim, and the triumph of God in our lives and our times is assured. The renovation of the heart, putting on the character of Christ, is the key. It will provide for human life all the blessing that money, talent, education and good fortune in this world cannot begin to supply. And it will be a foretaste of the full presence of God.

Matters for thought and discussion

1. Have you known people who fit the picture of the *children of light* drawn in this chapter? Some who were close? Some moving in that direction?
2. Do you take the scriptural descriptions of the *children of light* to be accurate portrayals of what earlier apprentices of Jesus actually became?
3. How do you understand the central thesis of this book, that spiritual transformation actually happens as each essential aspect of the self is transformed into Christlikeness under the direction of a regenerate will interacting with grace from God? Do you agree or disagree with this claim?
4. Can people in our churches today put into action the plan for spiritual growth outlined by Peter (2 Pet 1:3–11)? Why or why not?
5. How would you go about adding self-control to knowledge (or any of Peter's other 'add tos')?
6. What do you think of the view of sanctification presented in this chapter? Is it biblically and psychologically accurate?
7. Is the list of characteristics of the *children of light* given here adequate? What would you add or take away from it?
8. Is the emphasis placed here on the ease of the sanctified life appropriate? Or must we say that the holier you are the harder life gets?
9. How do you see the relationship between the modern rejection of Jesus as authoritative teacher of the world and the present state of the popular arts (music, films, literature)?
10. What is Christ's plan for spiritual formation in the local congregation and worldwide?
11. Describe a disciple, and how one becomes a disciple.
12. How do misunderstandings of what faith in Christ is disconnect it from spiritual transformation?

13. Could it really be true that outreach should not be a primary goal of church life? What should be primary goals? See the Ray Stedman quotation.

14. Could we really eliminate performance from our church gatherings? What would our meetings be like if we did?

15. How does the priority of the mind in spiritual formation affect the means employed to advance spiritual formation in the local congregation?

16. What things could your local congregation do beyond regular church services to advance spiritual transformation in its members?

17. Could we really publicly announce that we teach people how actually to do the things Jesus said for us to do? What would have to change around the church if we were to do that?

18. Should spiritual formation be the main focus of Christian life?

POSTLUDE

Now it is time to look back and to look forward: back to what we have studied in this book, and forward to the life which lies ahead of us, where we will become the people we will be for eternity.

In this book I have tried to present the path of spiritual formation, the authentic formation of the human person, as seen in the people of Jesus Christ through the ages. I have tried to ignore the many vessels of spiritual formation that litter historical and contemporary history and concentrate on the treasure, Jesus Christ himself, living with increasing fullness in every essential aspect of the personality of individuals devoted to him as Saviour and Teacher.

Renovation of the heart in Christlikeness is not something that concerns the heart alone. The heart cannot be renovated if the other aspects of the person remain in the grip of evil. Will-power, even inspired will-power, is not the key to personal transformation. Rather, the will and character only progress in effectual well-being and well-doing as the other aspects of the person come into line with the intention of a will brought to newness of life by the Word and the Spirit.

The path of renovation of the heart is therefore one in which the revitalized will takes grace-provided measures to change the content of the thought life, the dominant feelings, what the body is ready to do, social relationships, and the deep currents of the soul. These all are to be progressively transformed toward the character they have in Jesus Christ. This is what we call 'putting on the character of Christ'. And as it happens, the individual or group more and more effectively act for the good things they intend, and their will deepens its devotion to good and the God of good.

This is the great race of life, run before the *great cloud of witnesses*. As the writer to the Hebrews says:

> *You have come to Mount Zion, to the heavenly Jerusalem, to the city of the living God. You have come to thousands upon thousands of angels in joyful assembly, to the church of the firstborn, whose names are written in heaven. You have come to God, the judge of all men, to the spirits of righteous men made perfect, to Jesus the mediator of a new covenant, and to the sprinkled blood that speaks a better word than the blood of Abel.* (Heb 12:1 and 22–24)

To run this race well, to hear at the end, *Well done, my good servant! . . . Because you have been trustworthy in a very small matter, take charge of ten cities* (Luke 19:17), is to become the kind of person whom God will welcome to participate with him in his future reign (Rev 22:5). *You have been faithful with a few things; I will put you in charge of many things. Come and share your master's happiness!* (Matt 25:21). Our Lord loves to create and sustain everything that is good. That is to be our joy and happiness as well.

To run the race well, to be faithful in small things, is our part. And as we look at the road ahead, we must deal with details. That is, we must take the particular things that slow us down, and the sins which entangle us, and put them aside in a sensible, methodical way (Heb 12:1). We remove their roots from our minds and feelings. We are neither hysterical nor hopeless about them. We find out what needs to be done and how to do it, and then we act. We know God will help us with every problem as we take appropriate steps.

So our running is also with patience. We take the long view of the race that is set before us. We don't try to accomplish everything at once, and we don't force things. If we don't immediately succeed in removing a weight or a sin, we just keep running steadily and patiently, while we find out how it can be removed in God's way.

All the while, we keep looking up at our Teacher, who we know gave us faith to run in the first place and will bring us safely to the end (Heb 12:2). We concentrate on him. We are constantly learning from him, and he shows us how to let the weights and sins drop off so we can run better.

As we run we sense divine assistance making our steps lighter. We realize truth more strongly, see things more clearly. We find greater joy in those running with us, our companions in Christ, and those who went before and are coming after. His yoke is easy, we find, and his burden is light. As our outer being fades, our inner being is renewed on a daily basis (2 Cor 4:16). And no matter what the difficulty, we sing as we run, 'deliverance will come!'

But, as we look forward, now is the time for specific planning. Individually we must ask ourselves what the particular things are we need to do in order to bring about the triumph of Christ's life in the various aspects of our being. Are there areas where my will is not abandoned to God's will, or where old segments of fallen character remain unchallenged? Do some of my thoughts, images or patterns of thinking show more of my kingdom or the kingdom of evil than they do God's kingdom? For example, as they relate to money or my social life? Is my body still my master in some area? Am I its servant rather than it mine?

And if I have some role in leadership among Christ's people, am I doing all that I reasonably can to aid and direct their progress in transformation into Christlikeness? Is that progress the true aim of our life together, and are there ways in which our activities might better support that aim? Is the teaching appropriate to the condition of the people, and is my example one that gives clear assurance and direction? Can everyone see my progress (1 Tim 4:15)?

Whatever the situation is, now is the time to make the changes and undertake the initiatives that are indicated by this book. Spiritual formation in Christlikeness is the sure outcome of well-directed activities that are under the personal supervision of Christ and are sustained by all of the means of his grace. This aching world is waiting for the people explicitly identified with Christ to be, through and through, the people he intends them to be. Whether it realizes it or not, there is no other hope on earth.

Strangely, perhaps, it is only spiritual formation in Christ that makes us at home on earth. We are pilgrims and we look for a better city (Heb 11:16), but we are content for that to be in the future. Christ brings us to the place where we are able to walk beside our neighbours, whoever they may be. We are not above them. We are beside them: their servant, living with them through the events we all encounter.

We are not called to judge them, but to serve them as best we can by the light we have, humbly and patiently, with the strength we have and the strength God supplies. If it is true that our ways will at some point part for eternity, we will love them none the less for it. And the best gift we can give them is always the character and power of Christ in us. Beyond that we look to God for the renovation of their heart as well. We know that, whatever happens, he is over all.

NOTES

Notes to chapter 1

General note

My thanks, as always, to the many persons who have helped me along the way. To my family, above all, and especially to Bill Heatley, who read the entire manuscript and gave many insights and suggestions, and to John S. Willard, who typed a lot of it and who also made numerous penetrating comments. James Bryan Smith suggested helpful revisions for the earlier chapters.

[1] See, for example, Pierre Hadot, *Philosophy as a Way of Life: Spiritual Exercises from Socrates to Foucault*, edited by Arnold I. Davidson and translated by Michael Chase (Cambridge, MA: Blackwell, 1995), and Martha C. Nussbaum, *The Therapy of Desire: Theory and Practice in Hellenistic Ethics* (Princeton, NJ: Princeton University Press, 1994). There is, of course, an ocean of literature from Eastern thought on the formation of the human spirit.

[2] The former statement has a long scholarly background at this point, but is mainly associated with the thought of Paul Tillich: see pp. 3 and 9 of Paul Bjorklund, *What is Spirituality* (Plymouth, MN: Hazelden Foundation, 1983). The second statement is by Leo Booth, *When God Becomes a Drug* (Los Angeles: Tarcher Inc., 1991), p. 20. What is at work here is the relentless drive of human beings to be 'spiritual' without God. We have a gnawing need for spiritual sustenance that even explicit atheism will not protect us from. This manifests itself at a popular level through the popular

magazines and the kinds of topics dealt with by people like Oprah and Shirley Maclaine. But it runs much deeper than this.

[3] Paul Shore, 'The Time Has Come to Study the Face of Evil', *The Humanist*, November/December 1995, pp. 37–38. Paul Shore is a professor of education and American studies at Saint Louis University. There are some indications that the inability of the academic world to deal with evil may be changing. Recent publications such as Iris Chang's *The Rape of Nanking* (New York: Penguin Putnam Inc., 1997), and, especially, Jonathan Glover, *Humanity: A Moral History of the Twentieth Century* (London: Jonathan Cape, 1999), suggest a greater realism about evil. But we are still far removed from any realistic and widely understood notion of evil that would begin to allow us to deal with it in ourselves and in our world.

[4] *Christianity Today*, 10 July 2000, p. 72. It is one of the greatest ironies of human history that the founding insights and practices of the most successful 'recovery' programme ever known – insights and practices almost 100% borrowed from bright spots in Christianity, if not outright gifts of God – are not routinely taught and practised by the churches. What possible justification or explanation could there be for this?

[5] Edith Schaeffer, *Affliction* (Old Tappan, NJ: Fleming H. Revell Co., 1978), p. 212.

[6] John Calvin, *Institutes of the Christian Religion* (Grand Rapids, MI: Wm. B. Eerdmans Publishing Co.), vol. 2, p. 7.

[7] Calvin, vol. 2, p. 9.

[8] Dietrich Bonhoeffer, *The Communion of Saints* (New York: Harper & Row, 1963), p. 71.

Notes to chapter 2

[1] In the midst of much misunderstanding of Jesus, the historian Will Durant correctly grasped the role of Jesus as world revolutionary:

> He is not concerned to attack existing economic or political institutions . . . The revolution he sought was a far deeper one, without which reforms could only be superficial and transitory. If he could cleanse the human heart of

selfish desire, cruelty, and lust, utopia would come of itself, and all those institutions that rise out of human greed and violence, and the consequent need for law, would disappear. Since this would be the profoundest of all revolutions, beside which all others would be mere *coups d'état* of class ousting class and exploiting in its turn, Christ was in this spiritual sense the greatest revolutionist in history.

Will Durant, *Caesar and Christ* (New York: Simon & Schuster, 1944), p. 566.

[2]This is from an article 'We Grow in an Atmosphere of Love' excerpted from chapter 10 of Warren Wiersbe's book *Being a Child of God.* I am unable to supply the precise bibliographic details.

[3]The figure is given from *Newsweek*, 16 April 2001, p. 49.

[4]See my *The Divine Conspiracy* (San Francisco: HarperSanFrancisco, 1998), ch. 7.

[5]R. Daniel Reeves and Thomas Tumblin, 'Council on Ecclesiology: Preparation and Summaries', for Councils 2 and 3 at Beeson Divinity School (Birmingham, AL) and Westminister Theological Seminary (Escondido, CA). Unpublished notes.

[6]For further discussion see chapters 6 and 7 of my *The Spirit of the Disciplines* (San Francisco: Harper & Row, 1988).

[7]*An Augustine Synthesis,* edited by Erich Przywara (Gloucester, MA: Peter Smith, 1970), p. 89.

Notes to chapter 3

[1]On this and on points immediately following concerning the body and its role in life and in the spiritual life, see my *The Spirit of the Disciplines* (San Francisco: Harper & Row, 1988), chs. 5–7.

[2]On this point nothing more helpful has been written than Bonhoeffer's excellent study of the texture of the church, *The Communion of Saints: A Dogmatic Inquiry into the Sociology of the Church* (New York: Harper & Row, 1963), especially ch. 2.

[3]Quoted from Aylmer Maude, *Tolstoy and his Problems* (New York: Grant Richards, 1901), p. 64.

[4]An overly cynical but painfully instructive parody of the hymn 'Onward Christian Soldiers' reads:

> Like a mighty tortoise
> Moves the Church of God.
> Brothers we are treading
> Where we've always trod.

We may be, but for sure, God is not.

Notes to chapter 4

[1]For a study of the deep roots of Calvin's spirituality in the Christian past, see Lucien Joseph Richard, *The Spirituality of John Calvin* (Atlanta: John Knox Press, 1974).

[2]John Calvin, *Institutes of the Christian Religion* (Grand Rapids, MI: Wm. B. Eerdmans Publishing Co., 1975), vol. 2, p. 7.

[3]See Calvin's *Institutes*, vol. 2, ch. 7.

[4]*The Imitation of Christ* (many editions), Part 3, ch. 25.

[5]*The Works of John Wesley*, 3rd ed. (Peabody, MA: Hendrickson Publishers Inc., 1986), vol. 8, p. 344.

[6]Erich Fromm, *The Art of Loving* (New York: Harper, 1974), pp. 18–19.

[7]See B. McCall Barbour, 'If It Die ...', Deeper Life Series 3 (Edinburgh: B. McCall Barbour, n.d.), p. 24. For many other testimonies see the remainder of this little booklet and the others in the same series.

[8]For further discussion of the roots and centrality of anger in life apart from God, see chapter 5 of my *The Divine Conspiracy* (San Francisco: HarperSanFrancisco, 1998).

[9]For development of this understanding see chapters 1 and 2 of *The Divine Conspiracy*.

[10]In his 'On the Improvement of the Understanding' the Jewish philosopher Spinoza (1632–77) wrote of his decision 'to inquire whether there might be some real good having power to communicate itself, which would affect the mind singly, to the exclusion of all else: whether, in fact, there might be anything of which the discovery and attainment would enable me to enjoy continuous, supreme, and unending happiness'. This is the universal human desideratum, for all who have not despaired.

Notes to chapter 5

[1]Tozer, *The Knowledge of the Holy* (New York: Harper & Brothers, 1961), p. 10. See also his *Worship: The Missing Jewel* (Harrisburg, PA: Christian Publications Inc., 1992).

[2]Henri J. M. Nouwen, *Life of the Beloved* (New York: Crossroad, 1992), p. 21.

[3]Roland H. Bainton, *Here I Stand: A Life of Martin Luther* (New York: The New American Library, 1955), p. 144.

[4]See further J. P. Moreland, *Love Your God with All Your Mind* (Colorado Springs, CO: NavPress, 1997), and James W. Sire, *Habits of the Mind: Intellectual Life as a Christian Calling* (Downers Grove, IL: InterVarsity Press, 2000).

[5]Pages iii–iv of the 1996 edition (Morgan, PA: Soli Deo Gloria Publications). First published 1724.

[6]Thomas Watson, *All Things for Good* (Carlisle, PA: The Banner of Truth Trust, 1986), p. 74. First published 1663.

[7]One of the best places to begin in understanding the spiritual disciplines, what they are and how they work, is Richard Foster's *Celebration of Discipline: The Path to Spiritual Growth* (San Francisco: HarperSanFrancisco, 1998).

[8]See, for example, Richard Foster's *Streams of Living Water* (San Francisco: HarperSanFrancisco, 1998) and James Gilchrist Lawson's *Deeper Experiences of Famous Christians* (Uhrichsville, OH: Barbour Publishing Inc., 2000).

Notes to chapter 6

[1]Leo Tolstoy, *A Confession, etc.*, translated by Aylmer Maude (London: Oxford University Press, 1958), p. 17.

[2]Thomas Hibbs has a masterly study of what is really presented in such so-called 'sitcoms'. See his *Shows About Nothing: Nihilism in Popular Culture from The Exorcist to Seinfeld* (Dallas, TX: Spence Publishing Company, 1999).

[3]Robert Reich, who served as Secretary of Labor under the Clinton administration, has written a very useful analysis of 'The Age of the Terrific Deal', in *The Future of Success* (New York: Alfred A. Knopf,

2001). See the excellent summary on pp. 221–223. His suggestions as to what might be done to help are, I think, profoundly misguided. For a very different and deeper approach to essentially the same problems, see F. H. Bradley's *Ethical Studies* or John Ruskin's *Unto This Last*, both in numerous editions.

[4]Jeff Imbach, *The River Within* (Colorado Springs, CO: NavPress, 1998), is a very helpful book for clearing up the importance of feeling to human life and spirituality.

[5]Baruch Spinoza, *Ethics*, book 3, 'Of Human Bondage', and Somerset Maugham's novel *Of Human Bondage*, the title of which is taken from Spinoza. Both books have appeared in numerous editions.

[6]Amy Carmichael, *Gold Cord* (Ft Washington, PA: Christian Literature Crusade, 1996), p. 141.

[7]For a full treatment of this subject see my *The Divine Conspiracy* (San Francisco: HarperSanFrancisco, 1998), chs. 5–7.

Notes to chapter 7

[1]William James, *The Principles of Psychology* (London: Macmillan, 1918), vol. 2, pp. 578–579.

[2]Kant is still the best expositor of this point. See his *Foundations of the Metaphysics of Morals*, 2nd section, many editions.

[3]See Walter Kaufmann, ed., *Existentialism from Dostoevski to Sartre* (New York: Meridian Books, 1968).

[4]Quoted from Frederick Buechner, *Speak What We Feel* (San Francisco: HarperSanFrancisco, 2001), p. 40.

[5]See Jonathan Glover, *Humanity: A Moral History of the Twentieth Century* (London: Jonathan Cape, 1999), and Philip Hallie, *Tales of Good and Evil, Help and Harm* (New York: HarperCollins, 1997), for the shocking realities of twentieth-century history.

[6]Edith Schaeffer, *Affliction* (Old Tappan, NJ: Fleming H. Revell Co., 1978), pp. 126–127.

[7]Andrew Murray, *Absolute Surrender* (Chicago: Moody Press, n.d.), p. 124.

[8]From Margaret Magdalen, *A Spiritual Check-Up: Avoiding Mediocrity in the Christian Life* (Guildford: Highland, 1990), p. 101.

⁹The picture of the life crushed by a 'master passion' in Plato's *Republic*, books 8 and 9, teaches us a great lesson in moral and spiritual psychology.

Notes to chapter 8

¹Disagreements about the nature of the body abound in the fields of health care and medicine today. For an older but very illuminating treatment of the body, see Walter B. Cannon, *The Wisdom of the Body* (New York: Norton, 1932), as well as, more recently, Paul Brand and Philip Yancey, *Fearfully and Wonderfully Made* (London: Marshall Pickering, 1993).

²For further discussion on these matters, see chapter 7, 'St. Paul's Psychology of Redemption', in *The Spirit of the Disciplines* (San Francisco: HarperSanFrancisco, 1988).

³On the spiritual nature and calling of the body, see chapters 4–6 of my *The Spirit of the Disciplines*.

⁴Karen R. Norton, *Frank C. Laubach: One Burning Heart* (Syracuse, NY: Laubach Literacy International, 1990), p. 11.

⁵For the remarkable story of Laubach's recovery and further spiritual growth, see the rest of Norton's biography (n. 4), and the writings of Laubach himself in *Frank C. Laubach: Man of Prayer* (Syracuse, NY: Laubach Literacy International, 1990).

⁶Frances Ridley Havergal, *Kept for the Master's Use* (London: James Nisbet & Co., 1897).

⁷Margaret Magdalen, *A Spiritual Check-Up* (Guildford: Highland Books, 1990).

⁸Blaise Pascal, *Pensées*, section 135, 'Diversion'. This appears in Richard H. Popkin, ed., *Pascal: Selections* (New York: Macmillan Publishing Co., 1989), p. 214.

Notes to chapter 9

¹Origen, *Against Celsus*, III, 29, quoted from John Hardon, *The Catholic Catechism* (Garden City, NJ: Doubleday, 1975), p. 215.

²C. S. Lewis's discussion of the attraction of 'the inner ring' as 'one of

the great permanent mainsprings of human action' is at p. 61 of C. S. Lewis, *The Weight of Glory* (Grand Rapids, MI: Wm. B. Eerdmans Publishing Co., 1973).

[3]The finest exposition of the biblical and moral concept of love I know of is in Charles Finney, *Lectures on Systematic Theology*, lectures 12–15. In particular Finney clearly shows that love is not a feeling.

In Western culture there are two broadly different ways of thinking about love. Hardly anyone today rejects love as something of ultimate value. But for most people, to love someone now means being prepared to approve of their desires and decisions, and helping them fulfil them. 'If you love me you'll do what I want' is the cry here. On the biblical view, to love someone means wanting what is good for them, and being prepared to help them toward that, even if it means disapproving of their desires and decisions and attempting, as appropriate, to prevent their fulfilment.

A serious problem is created today by the identification of the good and the desired. If there is no point of reference for good other than desire, then the confusion of these two things naturally follows. And there is then no way to distinguish the desired from the desirable. Christians have ample resources for distinguishing these things in the Bible.

[4]A surprising re-emergence on the contemporary scene of the primacy of 'the other' in human obligation is in the work of the Jewish thinker Emmanuel Levinas. See, for example, the papers in *The Levinas Reader*, edited by Sean Hand (Oxford: Blackwell, 1997), and especially the paper 'Substitution', pp. 88–119.

[5]Aristotle, *Politics*, I, 2.

[6]John Donne, Meditation 17, many editions.

[7]Larry Crabb, *Connecting* (Nashville: Word Publishing, 1997), p. xi.

[8]C. S. Lewis, *The Screwtape Letters*, Letter 2.

[9]Dietrich Bonhoeffer, *The Communion of Saints* (New York: Harper & Row, 1963), p. 137.

[10]Robert Reich, *The Future of Success* (New York: Alfred A. Knopf, 2001). This book is actually a profound study in spiritual formation in the broad human sense explained earlier: that is, Reich does not seem to realize the deeper moral roots and consequences of the approach to life he is evaluating, and even less so the spiritual significance.

Notes to chapter 10

[1]Most approaches, from depth psychology to deep structures of myth and language, take for granted that there is something 'deep' in the soul. Some popular writers never really give any other idea of the soul than that it is 'deep'.

[2]Robert L. Wise, *Quest For the Soul* (Nashville: Thomas Nelson Publishers, 1996), p. 88.

[3]One of the most realistic and instructive testimonies of the soul's response to grace in tragedy is Gerald L. Sittser, *A Grace Disguised: How the Soul Grows Through Loss* (Grand Rapids, MI: Zondervan Publishing House, 1995). The final pages, 178–181, say pretty much all that needs to be said on this point.

[4]A good starting point for study of biblical terms and teaching on the soul might be sections 70 and 71 of Gustave F. Oehler, *Theology of the Old Testament* (Grand Rapids, MI: Zondervan Publishing House, n.d.). A. B. Davidson, *The Theology of the Old Testament* (Edinburgh: T. & T. Clark, 1955), chapter 6, is very helpful. Franz Delitzsch, *A System of Biblical Psychology*, 2nd English ed. (Edinburgh: T. & T. Clark, 1869), is a classic in the field. A. H. Strong, *Systematic Theology* (Valley Forge, PA: Judson Press, 1993), pp. 483–497, is useful on the 'Essential elements of human nature', as is chapter 23 of Wayne Grudem, *Systematic Theology* (Grand Rapids, MI: Zondervan Publishing House, 1994).

For a more philosophical approach, St Thomas Aquinas, *Summa Theologica* (many editions), the 'Treatise on Man', Part 1, Questions 75–89, is indispensable. I also recommend F. R. Tennant, *Philosophical Theology* (Cambridge: Cambridge University Press, 1956), vol. 1, 'The Soul and Its Faculties'; S. L. Frank, *Man's Soul: An Introductory Essay in Philosophical Psychology* (Athens, OH: Ohio University Press, 1993); and Richard Swinburne, *The Evolution of the Soul*, rev. ed. (Oxford: Oxford University Press, 1997). Finally, I recommend Kees Waaijman, 'The Soul as Spiritual Core Concept: A Scriptural Viewpoint', in *Studies in Spirituality*, June 1996, pp. 5–19; and the entire first part of *Journal of Psychology and Theology* 6 (1998), which is on the soul and ably grapples with most of the contemporary issues.

[5]Viktor Frankl has tried to make meaning and soul fundamental

concepts in the field of clinical psychology. See *Man's Search for Meaning*, 3rd ed. (New York: Simon & Schuster, 1948), and *The Doctor and the Soul*, 2nd ed. (New York: Bantam Books, 1969). Other psychologists, such as Carl Jung, have also tried to take these concepts seriously, often with astounding results, especially in so-called 'transpersonal psychology'.

[6]This language and conceptualization, from the sociologist David Riesman, *The Lonely Crowd* (New Haven, CT: Yale University Press, 1961), is vital for understanding the spiritual life of contemporary Christians and others.

[7]On this great tradition, see John T. McNeill, *A History of the Cure of Souls* (New York: Harper & Brothers Publishers, 1951). This is a thorough and careful study of what we have forfeited by our neglect of the soul today.

[8]Ann Stafford, 'Angela of Foligno', in *Spirituality Through the Centuries, Ascetics and Mystics of the Western Church*, edited by James Walsh (New York: P. J. Kennedy & Sons, n.d.), p. 191.

[9]From the excellent article 'Antinomians', in *Cyclopaedia of Biblical, Theological and Ecclesiastical Literature*, edited by John M'Clintock and James Strong (New York: Harper & Brothers, Publishers, 1895), vol. 1, pp. 264–266.

[10]Much of the anti-government sentiment in the United States today is thinly veiled hatred of law and exaltation of self-will. This easily slips over into 'righteous wrongdoing'.

Notes to chapter 11

[1]Frank Laubach, *Man of Prayer* (Syracuse, NY: Laubach Literacy International, 1990), p. 154.

[2]William K. Hartmann and Ron Miller, *The History of Earth* (New York: Workman Publishing, 1991), p. 195.

[3]A. H. Strong, *Systematic Theology* (Valley Forge, PA: Judson Press, 1907, repr. 1993), p. 869.

[4]Wayne Grudem, *Systematic Theology: An Introduction to Biblical Doctrine* (Grand Rapids, MI: Zondervan Publishing House, 1994), p. 746. See the remainder of Grudem's helpful discussion in the following pages.

[5]Walter Marshall, *The Gospel Mystery of Sanctification* (Grand Rapids, MI: Zondervan Publishing House, 1954, first published 1692), pp. 25–26.

[6]John Wesley, *Selections from the Writings of the Rev. John Wesley* (New York: Eaton & Mains, 1901), p. 138. This quotation is taken from Wesley's tract 'An Earnest Appeal to Men of Reason and Religion', published in many editions.

[7]If anyone believes that the last part of Matt 28:19 is only a command to get willing people wet while saying the words 'I baptize you in the name of the Father and the Son and the Holy Spirit,' we can only ask them to ponder the matter. The name, in the biblical world, is never just words but involves the thing named. The ritual should be a special moment of entry into the reality, and that was certainly how it was understood in biblical times. The presence of God was tangible and dangerous. People died when taking the Lord's Supper with the wrong attitude (1 Cor 11:30), or when misleading others in the fellowship (Acts 5:1–12).

[8]A. W. Tozer, *I Call It Heresy* (Harrisburg, PA: Christian Publications, 1974), p. 5.

[9]As these words were written the American public was treated once again to a government leader involved in disgraceful affairs. He was asked in an interview, after stonewalling on what he had done, if he was a moral person. He replied, 'I am a moral person.' Pretty clearly he believed it.

[10]Ray C. Stedman, *Body Life: The Church Comes Alive* (Glendale, CA: Regal Books, 1972), p. 13.